MEN OF A CERTAIN AGE

MEN OF A CERTAIN AGE

My Encounters with Rock Royalty

KATE MOSSMAN

NINE
EIGHT
BOOKS

NINE
EIGHT
BOOKS

NEB 034

First published in the UK in 2025 by Nine Eight Books
An imprint of Bonnier Books UK
5th Floor, HYLO, 103–105 Bunhill Row,
London, EC1Y 8LZ

Hardback ISBN: 978-1-7887-0564-6
eBook ISBN: 978-1-7887-0565-3

Cover design by Will Speed
Typeset by IDSUK (Data Connection) Ltd
Printed and bound in Great Britain by Clays Ltd, Elcograf S.p.A

3 5 7 9 10 8 6 4 2

Text copyright © Kate Mossman, 2025

Nine Eight Books is an imprint of Bonnier Books UK
www.bonnierbooks.co.uk

FSC
www.fsc.org

MIX
Paper | Supporting
responsible forestry
FSC® C018072

For Michael and Joanie

CONTENTS

PROLOGUE

Around the time I started putting this book together, the founder of *Rolling Stone* magazine, Jann Wenner, published a collection of his interviews with exclusively old, exclusively male rock stars. Wenner later explained that only this subspecies of musician seemed to possess the eloquence and articulacy necessary to qualify as his anointed 'rock philosophers'. He was, unsurprisingly, expunged from history soon after. I make no such claim for the subjects of this book, and blame only the pull of my unconscious for the existence of this volume. The older male rock star isn't just my specialist subject – it is my obsession. Fifteen years of my journalism reveal an alarming overconcern with the powerful archetype. Will I too be cancelled? It is a risk I must take.

The clues were there all along: a seven-year infatuation with the drummer from Queen in childhood; a lone, 5,000-mile journey to see Glen Campbell in his dotage; musical love affairs, in my thirties, with Bruce Hornsby and Jeff Beck. It was time to investigate the magical appeal of this nearly extinct species, the boys in grey flannel shorts who watched Yuri Gagarin float into space, and built their first guitars. Old rockers have always been considerably more interesting to me in later life than when they were young, particularly if their careers are on the slide. Why is it that when I am in the presence of a musical Man of a Certain Age, I feel something inside me ignite? What is this strange connection – to feel so excited, yet so at ease? Why do they get under my skin, and how do I get under theirs? How is it that in the presence of a wrinkly rock star twice my age, I sometimes feel like I'm meeting . . . *me*?

There are nineteen encounters with the elders of rock in this book, some produced when I was reviews editor at the music magazine *The Word*, and others during my time as features editor of the *New Statesman*, the august politics and culture title for which, at times, my specialist subject was an odd fit. I would creep in on bank holidays when the office was empty and chip away at a six-page feature on a Florida prog band no one in the UK had ever heard of; the next morning I'd be editing a diary by Jeremy Bowen in Lebanon. Over time they persuaded me to cover artists, writers and politicians and, in branching out, I was able to look upon my first love with more distance. What started as a meditation on that unique cultural figure, the rock star in his later years, ended up as a personal memoir.

1
MEET YOUR HEROES: IT'LL HELP YOU GET OVER THEM

Brian May and Roger Taylor

I am of a generation that had no name: we slipped down the crack between the spotty cheek of Gen X and the well-moisturised buttock of the millennials. We are the last generation that will wow our grandchildren by explaining that we came of age completely without technology. We wrote letters through secondary school; we replaced these with email when we got to university and wrote 15,000-word screeds to one another, which we still keep in files in our Hotmail accounts. Some of us ended up internet dating, but I have far more friends who settled down with their first or second love. We are neurotic, and depressive, but we didn't know it until recently.

The thing we do share with those who came after is that when it comes to music, we and our parents have no generation gap. The great songwriters of the '60s soundtracked our childhoods in their best ofs and their unfashionable '80s incarnations. In my house, 'The Frog Song' was given as much time as *Sgt. Pepper*. Pop stars rose up like venerated family elders. Music was a communal activity; we were the cassette generation, and many families couldn't afford to fly. We took long car-ferry trips to France for our holidays, listening to Joni Mitchell's *Blue* in the Volvo.

The most alienating part of the traditional teenager narrative, to me, is that which claims that, at a formative age, we want to listen to stuff our parents hate. This idea informs every music documentary ever made, and every pop origin story: it is the only explanation for the power that music holds in the life of the young. I do think this was true of the generations before mine. I have asked my own parents. But it was different when we came along. Our parents were the grooving boomers. It was felt, in your heart, and with your music, that you were always striving to catch up with them. It is entirely possible that we failed to achieve the necessary rebellion against our parents because of the death-less power of their record collection. We are the forerunners of those infants today, dressed in Joy Division babygrows, who live at home forever.

My family moved from north London to rural Norfolk at the end of the '80s, around the time that Peter Mayle published *A Year in Provence* and many people were swapping their city houses for old barns in the middle of nowhere. My parents were both self-employed. My mother owned a vintage clothing shop called Arsenic and Old Lace, which she transferred from London to a small Norfolk town, renaming it Past Caring. My father was a journalist and went on to establish the world's leading magazine about potatoes: *Potato Review*. We left London in a snowdrift in February 1988 and drove our own removal van. My older brother and I weren't put in school until the summer term, so we ran wild for a few months in our new farmhouse, riding a crazy moped round and round our garden. If you look at our village, Guestwick, on Wikipedia today it says simply, 'Guestwick lies far from any high roads'. There were no other children and no school, just a post office built into an abandoned railway carriage. At our small primary in a neighbouring village – just fifty-three pupils – I was champion of a game called crab football, where players scuttled about, chest to the sky, on hands and feet, slamming a sponge ball into the wall.

The strange possessiveness over music, in the lives of the young, is complex and rooted in a sense of the emerging self. Even without a generation gap, you will still try to find your own. By 1991, things had changed for me: I was attending a girls' private secondary school twenty miles away in Norwich, on one of those assisted places that Tony Blair would go on to abolish. High on exam results, and low on the kind of jollity that generally surrounds girls' schools in the popular imagination – school musicals, tuck shops, hockey – Norwich High School was a dour place. I was a tall, rather fat child with a single, thin plait that I did on Tuesdays and slept in the rest of the week. I had pale skin which was darker around my eyes – other girls often confused it for make-up – and my individuality was marked out only by non-regulation, cherry-red Dr Martens shoes.

I was very academic, and so tired out by my 6 a.m. start for school, for seven years, that I never once did my homework at home. I completed it all in the library at lunchtime. After-school activities were out of the question, as there was only one bus home at 4 p.m., and for some reason my brother and I never learned to drive. My mood was downbeat, but to be fair, so was everyone's. Even when they tried to be fun, my school got it wrong. At some point in the mid-'90s – and this really dates it – the school held a 'charity slave auction', in which teachers put themselves up for enslavement, based on pupils' donations. My class bought our French teacher and made her empty a bin on her knees; I still recall her crawling around with an old apple core in her mouth. She left shortly afterwards. It is a terrible memory and my friends and I still talk about it, retroactively trying to establish who in our class came up with the idea and its execution, and aware that, because we can't remember, we were all equally involved.

I came of age in the '90s, and I must say I have a bit of a problem with the '90s, because I hate them. My biggest problem with the decade was something I discovered I shared with the musician Liz Phair, a '90s icon and writer of the cult record *Exile in Guyville*, when I interviewed her thirty years later. When she spoke of it, the room span, and I felt the full force of the past: *'90s irony*.

No one lucky enough to have come of age in a different decade can truly understand '90s irony, and just how caustic it was. It is a taste, a smell, that cannot be picked up in historical revision of the decade and has been largely erased from social history – an entire way of living that might be summed up in the face of Mark Lamarr. In the '90s, the levels of irony in conversation among the young were exhausting. This was not communication; it was an exchange of taut, self-vetted opinion predicated on the understanding that one was not to express genuine enthusiasm about anything, even if one clearly loved it. In music – in Jarvis Cocker's pursed lips or Damon Albarn's feeling-free delivery – I felt a collective pressure to be joyless, which in retrospect seems so at odds with the flash, brash tone of the dominant musical culture. To create anything requires energy and joy, yet they all seemed so arch, so sneering, so *over it*. Perhaps it was *fin de siècle* ennui: after all, the second-hand nature of the music was lost on no one.

While in pop culture, particularly in the work of the Young British Artists, the ironic pose was all part of the art. It was quite another thing to live in this dead-eyed way as an adolescent, to be unable to express pleasure just at the point your own heart and mind were trying to unfold. The irony of the '90s was a cultural straightjacket for me; a kind of spiritual death when I was trying to come alive. It drove me inside myself at a tender age, and – without really knowing it at the time – my heart burned for something else: for middle-aged musicians from the '80s in jackets and jeans, and for the open-hearted, non-cynical pop times that had come before.

I have written and broadcast much about my childhood obsession with Queen, which began in early December 1991, when I had just turned eleven, after Freddie Mercury died, and ended when I went to university in October 1999. A BBC documentary was made about it – before Queen's revival but at the start of a cultural interest in fandom – possibly because it was clear to the producer, Mark Cooper, that the obsession veered into deeper (one could say darker) territory than many teenage obsessions, and therefore provided an unsettling, comic extreme against which viewers could measure their own experience.

My own independent musical life began one night when I heard Queen's posthumous single 'These are the Days of Our Lives', sitting in front of *Top of the Pops*. I felt something within myself ignite when I looked up to see Freddie Mercury's cheeky, emaciated face in monochrome. While it was clearly the start of something for me – the start of the person I am now – it is entirely probable that the energy was driven by the sense of having just missed the boat, just missed the person. This is an energy, full of strange longing, that has driven my whole life.

A modern audience will struggle to understand how unpopular Queen were in the '90s. Through the continued power of the music press, who hated them, and a barely disguised homophobic distaste, they were written out of music history. In my scrapbook, I had a cutting from a broadsheet list of rock star earnings in 1992. It put Brian May at £1 million per annum and Roger Taylor at a very modest £500,000 (John Deacon, a good investor, got a cool £2 million and Freddie was down for £0 because he was dead). The Ben Elton musical *We Will Rock You* was the start of a gigantic change in their fortunes and, after the appalling 2018 biopic *Bohemian Rhapsody*, Queen were making £40 million a year. But when I was a child, no one spoke of the band. I met them in 2011, for the piece which follows, and they were not yet at the peak of their revival, still slightly bemused by the change in fortune and suspicious of the sudden critical praise.

In the '90s, Queen were so unfashionable that I ran my obsession with some shame around even my closest friends. God forbid I would have played them a song, or showed them one of my many VHS tapes. This secrecy produced a kind of intensity that makes me rather uncomfortable now.

The greatest intensity surrounded my parents. I was, from the moment I pulled the newspaper out of the bin and discovered exactly who Freddie Mercury was, desperate for my parents, particularly my father, to applaud the band. I was not confident enough to say this overtly, or with brightness and jollity. Instead, I mounted a seven-year campaign of almost constant saturation in my home. Every car journey from 1991 to 1998 was soundtracked by Queen. Stop and think about that for a moment: *every car journey from 1991 to 1998*. As I played my tapes, my heart would race. I'd cough over bits where Freddie sounded out of tune in live recordings. The first tape I bought was *Greatest Hits*, which opened me up to the full, baroque nature of their musical output. I was embarrassed by the use of 'sex machine' in 'Don't Stop Me Now', so when it came to that song – on a trip to the dentist with my dad, I believe – I pretended to be asleep in the passenger seat.

It was a fraught and stressful obsession. On the BBC documentary, I am pictured reading extracts of the seven journals I filled with writing about Roger Taylor: how distraught I was when he shaved his beard off. The stranger side of that – there was no space to explore it in the programme – was that I was distraught that he shaved his beard off because it revealed more of his ageing jowls and he looked less attractive *to my parents*. A child of fourteen, I looked at the middle-aged man, the object of all my most heated desires, and wanted my parents to see the beauty too.

By the time I was an adult – certainly by the time I was a journalist and sent to interview Brian May and Roger Taylor by Mark Ellen, in my first job at *The Word* – Queen felt more like old flames around whom were clustered the shadow, the memory, of all sorts of stronger feelings: shame, neurosis and love. Always meet your heroes, I say: it'll help you get over them.

When I look back on my behaviour as a teenager, I think of the social opportunities it never occurred to me to take, so satisfied was I by the love I felt for Queen's drummer. I watched friends get boyfriends and knew that they 'had nothing on me'. I see a heart that could not unfold, that could not own what it wanted and loved, so powerful was the culture around me, and so desperate was I for parental approval. The campaign worked – my parents hold the band in deep affection – but it was a full-time job. Maybe if I'd loved more openly and unashamedly, I'd have moved through it all a bit quicker, and not lost my entire adolescence to Queen.

'Bismillah! We will not let you go!'
Queen: *The Word*, 2011

The A39 bends into Wadebridge, north Cornwall, past the Esso garage and the Rotary Club. Sitting in the back seat, I open my notebook and begin the quiz. I am fourteen years old.

'Question One: who wrote the song 'Death on Two Legs', from the album *A Night at the Opera*?'

I can tell by the angle of my mother's head in the passenger seat that she is pretending to be asleep. My father's eyes in the rear-view mirror are obscured behind flip-up sunglasses, his mouth set defiantly. 'Let me try,' whispers my older brother Joe, taking the notebook. 'Name four of Freddie Mercury's five cats . . .'

We're driving round Cornwall with a checklist of venues Queen played on their 1973 tour, looking for the Wadebridge Young Farmers' Club. We've already been to Hayle Rugby Club, the Camborne School of Mines and what's left of the Penzance Winter Gardens. The local concerts were organised by Queen's drummer, who grew up in Truro and still has a house nearby. It's no accident that the Mossman family holiday takes place in Cornwall every year, the magical world of Merlin and the Arthurian legends, Daphne du Maurier, pixies and Roger Taylor.

Queen held sway over the family for a decade. If you'd walked into our house in the mid-'90s, you'd have seen all the paraphernalia of a typical teenage music obsession – fanzines, scrapbooks, coloured vinyl, exotic bootlegs from Camden, a vast collection of memorabilia that covered the entire spare room – and a little bit more besides. On the mantelpiece sat a beer glass Roger Taylor had drunk from during a solo gig (I slept in the shirt I'd worn to that show). Next to the glass was a Quality Street jar in which my brother and I saved two-pence pieces – we'd found out that the drummer chartered his luxury yacht, and we were determined to hire it (we raised £89 over three years). We were drawn towards anyone who'd been in Queen's orbit, travelling down to Rayners Lane to see Cozy Powell, watching Magnum at a heavy-metal pub in Thorpe.

We were self-sufficient children. Our home was five miles from the nearest village in the north Norfolk countryside; with no public transport and no other kids living nearby, we had little to distract us, and our formative years were punctuated with obsessions. We were majorly into Catherine Cookson, for instance. We had a Joe Orton phase. We had every single James Bond film on video and a huge library of true-crime stories. My brother became an expert in cameras, then home-made rockets, then fishing reels. We listened to all the music our parents played – *Graceland*, *West Side Story*, Joni Mitchell's *The Hissing Of Summer Lawns* – but we didn't yet have our own.

It was early December 1991, I'd just turned eleven and had no interest whatsoever in the charts. Pop music felt like growing up – it was vaguely embarrassing, to be honest, a bit like body hair. But as I sat in front of *Top of the Pops* that night, pretending not to be watching, it wasn't 2Unlimited or Lisa Stansfield that caught my attention, or Simply Red with 'For Your Babies'. It was a black-and-white video of a painfully thin man with big teeth wearing a patchwork waistcoat and singing a song called 'These are the Days of Our Lives'. The thick cake make-up, the bird-like nose – Mercury looked like Joel Grey out of *Cabaret*. His frailty was at odds with his movement – he kept throwing his arms out in little bursts of energy, as though constrained by his own body. And he was grinning. What struck me about the video was its extraordinary lightness of touch. Here was an extremely sad song, yet the band communicated with little nods and smiles, as though they were having some private joke. I felt my skin prickle.

I recognised Mercury from the front page of the local paper a few days earlier and retrieved it from the bin. I didn't know what AIDS was (but I knew all about 'gay' because of our Joe Orton phase). A Freudian analyst might have sensed the two great mysteries of life – sex and death – colliding for an eleven-year-old in the figure of Queen's frontman. Whatever, I went into overdrive, collecting newspaper cuttings, charity leaflets, red ribbons; tapes and videos followed, many from a local car-boot sale.

I struggled with Queen's image. My cheeks burned at the presence of Mercury's leather-clad crotch and onstage dry-humping, but for every overblown sexual gesture, there was a softer side – Brian May in his high-waisted jeans and too-short jacket, Roger Taylor acting up for the cameras, John Deacon with his bifro, looking painfully uncomfortable. This band was a really, *really* strange mixture. They were outrageous, yet they were straight; they were famously arrogant, but they spoke with soft, kind voices. The music was full of energy but often strangely unemotional, and I simply couldn't believe – as I worked my way through twenty years of hard rock, Byronesque storytelling, funk, disco, vaudeville, flamenco, pop and various alarming lapses of taste – that it all came out of the same four people.

My main concern – as I walk down Holland Park Avenue to meet one half of the modern-day Queen in my grown-up, professional capacity – is a practical one. I think I'm going to black out. The blood is pounding so hard in my ears that the sound of my feet on the pavement seems fifty yards away. Waiting for Brian May in the back room of a small Italian restaurant, I discover that reading the menu in great detail slows the heartbeat. He is a vegetarian, so I won't eat any meat. And someone once told me, I remind myself, that he is 'almost religiously kind'. He's been informed that I was once a fan/nutcase/stalker and, strangely enough, this persuaded him to do the interview. Getting access to Queen is not easy.

Brian arrives silently in the doorway. He is six foot three including hair, and he's let it grow grey, like Tom Jones, which suits him. He's dressed in a white shirt and waistcoat decorated with badges – a leopard-skin AIDS ribbon, and a fox pin for his animal-rights charity, Save Me. Waistcoats were always big with Queen; as a young fan, I often wore a very similar outfit to the one Brian is wearing today, and this is peculiarly comforting. He seats himself opposite me, his legs so long they reach right under my chair so I place my feet on either side of his.

Encounters with May these days tend to begin with his extracurricular activities – astrophysics, photography and animals – rather than the forbidding musical legacy of which he is joint custodian. You get the feeling that's the stuff he'd rather talk about.

'I've been very lucky that I could complete all the circles,' he tells me. 'Queen opened the doors for me, and I've been able to revisit everything else at quite a high level since. I've been incredibly lucky. You couldn't write it better if you were writing a plan for your life.'

He seems to mean it, though he's a cautious speaker, his neutral delivery full of long pauses. He takes pains to answer every possible angle to my questions. I ask him what could have made a child devote the best years of her youth to a band that was defunct when she discovered them?

'It's very hard to see us from the outside,' he says, 'but for *us* – and I know most people probably won't believe this, but I can honestly tell you, God strike me dead – being famous was not uppermost in the mind. In the songs, I think you will find things that speak to normal people. Freddie was particularly good at that. Without being at all sentimental – because he never was – he managed to tap into people's psyches, and standing on stage he represented so much what could be achieved if you believed in yourself. Even though we were outrageous, there is a bit of tongue-in-cheek there. People sensed that. We would have been a bit coy of the word "entertainer" at the time, but essentially that's what we were doing.'

Queen's colourful, exaggerated identity appealed to me. In the summer of 1992, children in my class were scribbling 'Kurt Cobain' on their rough books and forcing the bus driver to play their wobbly tapes of *Nevermind*. Grunge seemed the perfect soundtrack for the hard kids sat at the back affecting listlessness; down the front with my homework on my lap, I was drawn to the Queen circus where people seemed to be enjoying themselves – even if *I* wasn't.

'There's something about a group which is a whole world,' May says, 'and it opens up to people. *These people seem to be having a good time, so I will be a part of this*. That is a huge thing.'

But my brother and I weren't 'part' of it, were we? We missed the boat – or, rather, took a running jump and landed on the slippery deck of HMS *Queen* as she sank steadily through the '90s, because the band was finished. No one was playing their records and the music press didn't appear to like them. The lack of critical interest was catnip to our obsession. When Kurt Cobain revealed in his suicide note that he'd never been able to enjoy his audience the way Freddie Mercury had done, it was the first positive review I'd read that decade. I cut it out and stuck it in my scrapbook.

I choose a clumsy moment to ask Brian May why the press hated Queen, just as he is trying to swallow a piece of goat's cheese, but I'd forgotten how much it used to bother them. 'I'm not sure, to be honest with you,' he says, wincing a bit. 'Why

don't you ask *them* what their problem was?' I have asked them,
I tell him, and I still can't figure it out.

At the start of his career, Mercury dealt out the quips and
put-downs ('We're dripping with money, darling' . . . 'I won't
be a rock star, I will be a legend') to seal the regal nature of the
brand he'd created. This was quickly returned with press contempt – most famously, that *NME* headline from 1977, 'Is This
Man A Prat?'. In later years, their egos bruised, the band kept
the critical world at arm's length and communicated through
one or two journalists who were personal friends. For the few
others who got through, Queen weren't generally what you'd
call a 'good-value' interview; Mercury could be hilarious, but
often he chose not to be.

At press conferences, he'd sit in the middle in silence, chewing
his lips and glaring mischievously while May and Taylor tried
to keep the balloon in the air. Personally, it made me warm to
them all enormously: they were awkward-looking, cliquey and
a law unto themselves – surely the sign of a *real* band. Their
lyrics were often deliberately, comically pompous ('We served
a purpose, like a bloody circus' from 'Was it All Worth it'), as
though the whole thing was one great send-up. But pastiche and
parody weren't as fashionable as they are now, and the themes
of their songs didn't tally with everyone's ideas of rock 'n' roll –
champions, vision, magic, miracle; abstract transglobal signifiers of
celebration and togetherness.

When I was fourteen, I read an old issue of *Rolling Stone* which
compared the jackbooted security guards on Queen's South
American tour with the quasi-Nazi hold that the band appeared
to have over their audience. 'I get the feeling that if Freddie

Mercury told the crowd to shave their heads, they'd do it', said the writer. But wasn't he missing the point? Queen had a Japanese song, 'Teo Torriate (Let Us Cling Together)' for their Tokyo audience; a Spanish song 'Las Palabras De Amor (The Words of Love)' for South America; when they played Budapest, Mercury sang Hungarian folk songs from notes written in biro on his hand. This didn't strike me as some great supremacist rock machine marching on the heads of the oppressed. Queen: the band that the people liked and the press hated? I probe May on the matter.

'I'm trying not to give you the easy answer,' he says. 'We have recently been involved in this 40th anniversary film – this is going to seem like I'm not answering your question, but I am – and we went back and interviewed some of these journalists. And it was interesting to watch them in front of the camera still trying to justify the position they had then, as though they had 'the answer' somehow, as though they knew what was right and wrong.'

Is he surprised at the Queen revival? When I was growing up, you hardly ever heard the music. Now it's used on every TV advert.

'I do remember a time when I thought, "We have a great catalogue of songs. Isn't it strange that nobody ever uses them?" And then suddenly there was an avalanche of interest. But of course, it doesn't happen by accident – you have choices to make. If someone comes to you and says, "We want to use 'We Will Rock You' as part of an advert for jelly beans, and we're changing the words to "We will, we will CHOMP you"', you have a decision to make. On the one hand, you think, "This is crass. This'll demean my art" or you can say, "It's a bit of fun, it will make us some money and it will keep the music alive."

'I think the people who handled the Beatles' estate made a sad mistake. Young people – my daughter's generation – don't go around singing Beatles songs and they're slightly disconnected from the music somehow. We say yes to most things. The only time we say no is if it's abusive in some way. I wouldn't want my music to be used to advertise . . . meat, for example.'

So if Wall's wanted to use 'Fat-Bottomed Girls' on a sausage ad, you'd not let them?

'I would strongly object.'

We're pushing the last of our salad around our plates and I'm wondering if it's rude to get a pudding, when May leans forward and says rather softly, 'I had my obsessions too, you know. The first hero of mine I ever met was Rory Gallagher. I was nineteen or so and we used to go and see him at the Marquee every week. One night we hid in the toilets while everyone was filing out and collared him. He was so kind to us, such a gentleman. I thought that night, "If I ever get famous, I hope I am as nice to people as he is".'

Brian May gives me a hug when it's over. 'Was it what you imagined it would be?' he says, cautiously. 'It wasn't disappointing?'

At first, I didn't pay much attention to Roger Taylor – he always seemed to be flashing his teeth or flicking his sunglasses – but by the age of fifteen, he had become the throbbing centre of my world. He had a social conscience, which I liked in a man, and he'd do strange, idealistic things, like donate cash to Manchester United in a bid to hold off the planned Murdoch takeover. He wrote a few genuinely decent songs, including, as I later discovered, that first one that pulled me in, 'These are the Days of Our Lives'.

Taylor was also the most 'available' member of the band, with a prolific, if chart-dodging, solo career. Between 1988 and 1998, he completed five solo projects. He was clearly making no money from them, but took himself out on the circuit anyway, playing tiny venues like the Waterfront in Norwich. Surprisingly, there were literally *packs* of teenagers in the front row of these gigs, most of them screaming girls of eighteen or so. Taylor had always been good-looking – I once made a lino-cut of his face – but looking back, I wonder whether those girls had also been touched by the story of a band they'd 'only just missed', and inspired by the idea of wistful, independent discovery.

'I want him to know, even just for a matter of seconds, that I actually exist,' I wrote in my diary at fifteen. It's an odd experience reading over those journals now (there are seven of them) and recognising certain aspects of oneself but at the same time nothing at all. I wrote three or four letters to Taylor himself, care of the Queen Fan Club – awkward, carefully wrought things which fell somewhere between Jane Austen and dull, academic analysis of his music (*inexplicably*, he never replied). The Cornwall holidays brought us geographically closer and, by sixteen, I was deeply worried that *I might actually bump into him some day*. How on earth would that be? I made a flowchart to prove to myself that 'it's shite however you choose to view it'.

Eleven a.m., Saturday 25 June 2011. Roger Taylor's house in Cornwall. As a mooning teenager, I stood outside these big green gates thinking I'd give my liver to be on the other side of them. And now the gates are opening. I pass the indoor swimming pool with a vague sense of children's limbs happily splashing about within (the three members of Queen have fourteen kids between them) and the row of wellies lined up at the front door. Standing in Taylor's front room, I study the Japanese lacquered piano (the Far East was always big with Queen) and the strange, spherical ship's clock on the coffee table, its numbers magnified by a thick glass face. I hear the familiar 'Rod Stewart after twenty Bensons gone posh' voice in the corridor . . .

I'd love to say that I fall on the carpet in a swoon when Roger Taylor enters the room, but that's not the way it happens. The fact is, if you *really* loved your pop star (and I really *did* love Taylor – whereas I just *liked* Brian May), you'll have used a hell of a lot of intellectual energy building an astonishingly accurate picture of them. Years later, it puts you on an equal footing somehow; I certainly know him better than he knows me. He's got the casual rock-star-at-home look (jeans, white shirt and goatee), his hair is wet (I like to think he's just got up) and he has just the demeanour I pictured (relaxed, unflappable but faintly serious). He too has been fully apprised of my previous Queen obsession. It's taken me four months to pin him down for this interview. A whole season has elapsed since I met Brian May.

A hand shoots out: 'So lovely to meet you at last!' (We've met before but he doesn't know that. My brother and I followed him into the Plaza Cinema in Truro in 1998 and sat through the whole of *Godzilla* – a terrible film – just to be near him. We got an autograph afterwards.)

Do you ever have that thing, I find myself saying when we're seated, where you go into a shop and there's a Queen song playing, and even though you know all the music like the back of your hand, you actually can't place which song is it? It's almost too familiar?

'I have that,' he says. 'It takes me a few seconds. I have a flash of "God, which one is that?" Absolutely – it's almost like you know it too well, and there's so much of it.'

I tell him Brian May's theory on Queen and advertising – that the Beatles should have allowed their music to be used on TV.

'I think he's right. I think it was naive of them. It's great to be part of the wallpaper of life – there's no shame in it. It's like bands who refuse to go on iTunes. Don't stand in front of the train, you're not going to stop it. If the music is in the air around people, it will get to them. What more could you want? There's a whole generation of very young kids that love Queen now.'

Why is that?

'Because they relate to something in Freddie. He really didn't care, did he? He gave every molecule of himself.'

'My brother and I followed you around the country in the 1990s and went to your solo gigs. We saw you play the Waterfront in Norwich.'

'Oh, God, *did you*?'

'And Truro City Hall.'

'Felt more like a Sunday-school dance.'

'Why did you do those tours?'

'I just wanted to work,' he says. 'I felt I had a bit to say. I wanted to keep functioning. It was a very difficult thing, being out the front – it's hard to know what to do with your hands. If you grasp the mic, it looks like you're holding on for dear life and you're also covering up your face. It's such a clear sign of nerves.'

Did you notice all the teenage girls in the front row?

'I did, actually,' he laughs, and stokes the fire. 'I mean, you never know what you're going to get and I'll take whatever turns up, but the shows we did with Paul Rodgers, we had some quite shockingly old people there. But you know, whoever wants to come along . . .'

I ask him about Queen's relationship with the press. 'We stopped talking to them in the late '70s because it was counterproductive, like banging your head against a wall. We decided, we don't need to be targets any more, we're already successful, the people like us and that'll do me – and maybe you'll all catch up one day.'

The print media, he says, 'wasn't working as a promotional tool', so they turned to TV and radio. I've lost count of the number of people who've told me the recent acclaimed documentary on the BBC changed their minds about Queen, as though it was some independent exercise in historical revision. In fact, it was produced by super-fan and comedian Rhys Thomas (who appeared on *Celebrity Mastermind* with Queen as his specialist subject) working closely with the band and featured very few talking heads and some rare footage from the Brian May archives. It wasn't drastically different from all the other documentaries Queen have made, but suddenly people were ready to watch it.

'I find it very cheering, the way tastes have changed towards us,' Taylor says. 'People are much more broadminded than they ever were before. I find it hilarious that one of the most antici-pated acts at Glastonbury is the Wombles. People in this country have a great sense of humour and they're much less po-faced than they were in the past. Glastonbury took itself so seriously, it was so politically correct, and then Dame Shirl comes out on Sunday afternoon and that's actually what the people want. There is room for everything. It's only a bloody record!'

Queen's final two albums, *The Miracle* and *Innuendo*, were the twin peaks of their achievement. Knowing Mercury was ill, the band decided to share all writing credits, and split all royalties, for the first time in their career. Then they turned into a kind of Fort Knox, decamping to a quiet studio in Switzerland, away from the growing paparazzi interest in his health, and recorded as much as they could against the clock.

In those albums you can hear both the tremendous urgency and the strange, cocoon-like warmth of their final months together. *The Miracle* was tough and sinewy, largely recorded live; *Innuendo* was a dark space-flight into the unknown, full of grim passion and dazzling theatrics. When I listen to these songs now, I still feel like someone's putting a bicycle pump between my ribs and blasting me with air.

The band were in their early forties when it ended. 'I put my energies into organising that concert,' Taylor tells me, meaning the Freddie Mercury tribute at Wembley. 'Deciding what we would play, and persuading people to take part. It came off okay in the end, I think.'

John Deacon is still in touch by email, apparently, involved in the business side of things, but hasn't been seen with the band since the late '90s. Nowadays, the Queen machine presents them with more paperwork than they have ever had before. 'I didn't expect to be actively engaged with it after all this time,' Taylor says, picking at the knee of his jeans. 'It's such a self-propelling organisation. It has a life of its own, it won't die. You come to the realisation that that's what you are, this is what you do, that's my job. When he suddenly went, there was a huge outpouring of emotion from some quarters, and a re-examination of our material. We've basically been exploiting that ever since.'

He and May talk in such an odd way, a kind of detached business language – a result of their caution, presumably, and years reiterating the collective concerns of the group and the 'brand'. Personal enquiries are met with genuine surprise. When I ask May when he was *happiest* with Queen, he blinks and says, 'You have hard questions!' When I ask Taylor how he felt when his musical career was ended in its prime, he goes, 'I suppose you're right, I was quite young . . .' Oddly enough, their fondest memories from the entire twenty-year life of the band are those final weeks, tucked away working on the last album. 'We became very enclosed,' says Taylor, 'very focused, and we were in our own little world.'

Our time is up. 'I've got to go and unveil a statue,' Taylor says, standing. Of himself? 'God, no. It's a drummer, though – a weird expressionist thing. I thought it would be a laugh. It's about eighteen feet high . . .'

With the first band you love as a child, you experience something that adult life will never allow – a prolonged period absorbing one music to the exclusion of all others, the highs and lows, the moments of genius and the terrible errors of judgement. Records, videos and biographies merge until the voices of the band become as familiar as your own. I don't play much Queen at all these days, but it's all still there, especially the humour of it, in an image of Freddie on stage in his tiny, tiny shorts, a column of steam riding from his head.

What I've taken away is the joy of recognising, and indulging, the start of these full-on musical love affairs whenever they decide to seize you. What happened on hearing that first Queen track, 'These are the Days of Our Lives', nearly twenty years ago, has happened half a dozen times since, with songs by other artists – the gut recognition, familiarity and excitement rolled into one, the twang of your heartstring and the fierce desire to find out more. It's the musical equivalent of eyes meeting across a crowded room. 'Wichita Lineman' by Glen Campbell, 'Jesus Was a Crossmaker' by Judee Sill – it will keep on happening, and the best thing is you never know when it's going to strike next.

I take myself down to Lemon Street in Truro, a ley line positively fizzing with Queen energy for anyone in the know. Here is Truro City Hall, where they played their first-ever gig in 1970 (these days it's hosting the tribute band Queen On Fire). On the brow of the hill is Truro School, where Taylor was a pupil, and behind us is the cinema where my brother and I stalked him. In the centre of the town square, next to Marks & Spencer, a black tarpaulin is stretched over a strangely shaped, angular structure, with a growing crowd around it.

As I stand here under a grey sky with the seagulls circling, along with half the county – skaters, hippies, people in Queen T-shirts and the lord mayor of Truro – waiting for the arrival of Roger Taylor, it occurs to me that not so much has changed in the last – dear God – fifteen years of my life.

Fifty drummers appear from nowhere, dressed like Morris dancers and beating up a storm. In true English folk tradition, someone in the middle of the throng is holding a horse's skull on a stick and snapping its jaws. Taylor stands on a scaffold, next to a man from the Eden Project. The latter makes a speech about how drumming is appropriate to Cornwall, 'battered as it is by the sea and storms', adding that Roger Taylor is the perfect person to unveil this piece of art, 'a local boy who went out into the world and marched to his own beat'.

Taylor steps down, pulls the tarpaulin back slowly and reveals . . . a naked man, cast in tin, poised atop a model of the world and beating a drum. Someone in the crowd wolf-whistles. The Queen drummer is supplied with a long stick, which he uses to beat the statue's tin drum solemnly, three times. The crowd cheers.

Afterword

I stopped listening to Queen in the autumn of 1999 when I went to university. I'd like to say I no longer needed them when I was surrounded by the fizz and bang of student life and self-discovery, but it wasn't that: it was meeting Roger Taylor, at the Truro Plaza the previous summer, which changed things. Even though I was effectively a stalker, even though I visibly frightened him when I lumbered forward in the dark for an autograph, I was symbolically breaking into his world and – who knows – even confirming my own existence in some way. The separation between a fan and the object of their obsession feels as demeaning as it does exquisite. Obsession is lonely, driven by the not-having, and though I could never have Taylor as I wanted, I do remember something easing up in my heart, in my body, once we'd met, as though I could hold my head higher and look to the sky a little more.

By the time I met Queen for *The Word*, I had years of distance from the raw, painful times of yearning and I was a professional hack, yet the tone of this piece is unlike my others: oddly tender and involved. I felt like a child again with Brian May. I couldn't believe they let me into Roger Taylor's Cornwall home, the site of my old stalking – they never even asked how I knew which house it was. In my description of Taylor, there is barely disguised eroticism – his wet hair, and my weird inference that he'd just got up – which I wasn't aware of at the time. I interviewed him for the *Guardian* years later, in another of his big houses, and it's the only interview I've ever done where I finished my questions twenty-five minutes early and stared at the clock in panic. One reason for this is that Taylor, still so hard-wired against journalists, delivers his answers in neat, twenty-word sentences and interviews are unusually short. The other reason is that I rushed my questions, transported into a place of urgency and tension that may or may not have been outwardly obvious, because on some level, I will always love him, and there will always be something getting in the way.

2
THE MUSICAL PILGRIMAGE:
WHO WOULD TRAVEL 5,000 MILES
FOR A GIG?

Glen Campbell

For ten years, from the age of twenty-seven, around the time I began my career as a journalist, I spent all my money on America. My father would get cross. 'If you didn't go to America all the time, you'd have enough money for a deposit on a flat by now,' he'd say. I spent about three grand a year on America, which was all I spent on anything, because my salary was always very low. Between 2007, when I first travelled to see Glen Campbell, and 2018, when I went to interview Sting for the *New Statesman*, I went to America thirty-eight times – alone. I have been to forty-two states. It stopped because I had a family of my own, and I often wonder where that person is now, because she certainly isn't gone.

I would make the decision sitting on my parents' sofa over the Christmas holidays, by opening Google Maps. I'd travel in June – before the school holidays, but when the weather was already hot. Being a non-driver, I would do everything by Greyhound, and as a woman travelling alone, I would check the safety of stations using Google Street View, because some were just a layby on the road – not a place for a three-hour layover in the middle of the night. I chose the stations with cafés. Greyhound cafés sold hard-boiled eggs: my ideal snack would be one of these and a Slim Jim, a piece of processed jerky formed into a cuboid, set alongside a cuboid bar of 'American cheese'.

I'd plot my route ensuring that the stretches covered the right time of day and that connections occurred in daylight: if you were passing between, say, Denver and Montrose in Colorado, you'd be a fool to do it at night because you'd miss all the mountains. I would click the little 'man' icon on Google Maps to show you the route on foot between Greyhound station and hotel, and print it out in advance in the office, stapling the journey together in order. Often these dotted-line routes took you along the edge of motorways with no hard shoulder, where I would swear and cry with fright, and get honked by passing drivers, but that was all part of the experience for me.

It was – still is – absolutely giddying to me that, after your initial flight to the continent, you could get across it for as little as seventy dollars. As soon as I reached Manhattan, I would yearn to get out of it, west, into the vast expanse. It made me crazy to think of all the land over to the left, or below, unexplored, when exploring was so easy and so cheap. I once travelled from Manhattan to Baton Rouge in November, just so I could feel the climate difference. The warmth vibrated up from the tarmac as my booted foot stepped off the bus. I stayed in a casino built on a paddle steamer stuck on the side of the Mississippi and went back to New York the next day.

What everyone says about the people you find on Greyhounds is true: that they are ones with the stories to tell. Put another way, they are Americans who have no cars, in a country where everyone has a car; many I spoke to had had them repossessed. There were young mums fleeing bad men, migrant workers who seemed impossibly young with four kids seven states away, gay teenagers leaving small towns and, perhaps the most fascinating people of all, poor American people just following the weather, upping and leaving Gary, Indiana, for Alabama because they were fed up with the winter.

What Americans get wrong about the Greyhound is that it is dodgy. I never, in thirty-eight trips, had to share a seat. No one talks to you. There is an unwritten code that once the bus starts moving, the chat stops. The lights are dimmed. Heads bob towards windows. You become aware of the difference between you on your meditative holiday and the girl with the hood pulled up who is travelling thirty hours to some distant relative because her father has kicked her out. The bus pulls out onto the freeway, leaving everyone in a state of complete solitude and liberty, no matter what they are going through.

When you're on the move, something funny happens to your thoughts. They roll with the wheels, skimming the surface. They bump up against big things, or painful things, and then retreat again, moving back and forth over them like waves on a rock. I would think about how I was single – always single! – and couldn't seem to find anyone I wanted to stay with. But it never hurt me the way it did back home. Was I simply removed from real life, or was I finally embodying my true state, alone and travelling, and unable to pretend I was upset about it?

It is not an exaggeration to say that I went to America to listen to music. Long after it was necessary to have one, I took a Discman, and seven CDs removed from their jewel cases and housed in a bright pink metallic box. I could not be eclectic – NO NEW BANDS. I remember a trip to Mexico that was ruined by the strange experience of Warren Zevon, who raised no warm and cosy feelings in me: hazardously small interconnecting planes soundtracked by the 'musical' air con unit from 'Desperados Under the Eaves'. No: it had to be something which felt like home. I timed the return trip from Benson, Arizona, to Phoenix exactly right so I could listen to 'Take it Easy' by The Eagles on repeat as the sun set. The air con broke on that bus.

But mostly I would listen to Glen.

This long American chapter in my life – and my career as a journalist – began with Glen Campbell. Working in my first job at a children's charity in London, I experienced a musical falling in love. I'd loved 'Wichita Lineman' at university – it came on a compilation called *Music to Watch Girls By*, which was often played in halls – but I'd left Glen alone for years. Then somehow – I think my mum ordered it for me – I got my hands on a DVD of a concert in Sioux Falls, South Dakota, which Glen had performed at sixty-four, long before he was rehabilitated as one of the granite-hewn faces of country music.

With the South Dakota Symphony behind him, and a shiny boot on the kind of Ottoman rug that signals *a certain class of gig*, it was Glen's bliss that had me. He was puffed on to the stage by the swell of the orchestra like a dandelion seed. His mouth opened in a little 'o' – it always perfectly fitted his bagpipes – and the voice floated out. 'It was like breathing,' his keyboard player said. 'It was like a bird flying, it was easy for him.' He laughed soundlessly with eyes shut, making a little aeroplane with his hand. In the middle of 'Wichita Lineman', he followed the movements of his guitar solo – raindrops, tumbling out – with the line of his neck, in little nods of ecstasy.

Glen would stop and do Donald Duck impressions between songs or tell jokes with the wrong punchline (his Alzheimer's was already kicking in). This was shortly before his alcohol relapse, when he drove drunk, was apprehended, kneed a policeman in the balls, ran off down the freeway and ended up in jail for ten days, where he apparently gave a gig à la Johnny Cash. The contrast between the man and the musician was fascinating to me. His cover versions – always covers, he wrote no songs – were so light and effortless compared to their originals. His refined accent, his crossed T's, obscured his Arkansas drawl when he sang, yet his manner when the music stopped was so impossibly unserious, you had the sense of a person overtaken by music when the song began.

I have loved Glen in a way I have never loved any other musician. I didn't fancy him. If he were still alive and lucid, I'm not even sure I'd want to interview him. But if I hear his voice, I feel instantly calm. In 2006, he announced a couple of small shows in California with Jimmy Webb, the man who wrote all his best songs. It would be Frank Sinatra and Sammy Cahn as far as I was concerned. I called up months in advance on the office landline, with the seating plan in front of me, and booked A15, the middle of the front row. The single booked seat sat there for a long time in an expanse of empty ones – I would check in on it from the office computer – while I saved money for the flight in a large Quality Street jar. I was twenty-six.

At this time, Glen Campbell's daughter Debbie, one of eight children and born when he was seventeen, regularly performed with him and often appeared on the Glen Campbell message board where I spent a lot of my time. I'd befriended a middle-aged man from Wales called Mike, who sent me bootleg DVDs of Glen at his mid-'70s peak. When Glen had his late life renaissance, his band of thirty years (including Debbie) were fired, and his message board was merged into a corporate website announcing news and merch. But, back then, Debbie was a presence. She worked part-time as an air stewardess for Delta Air Lines. I told her I was coming to see her father on my own from the UK and asked if I could be introduced to him: she said, 'I'll see what I can do.'

I once met, at a music industry dinner, a man my own age who, at the age of fourteen, had gone to LA alone on his father's credit card to crash the funeral of Biggie Smalls. The security guards took pity on him and he got in. I felt an immediate affinity with this man, who was by then a banker and married to the daughter of a Rolling Stone. Biggie must have felt like part of his body, for him to go to such lengths. At fourteen, of course he would be let in. At twenty-six, and a girl, of course I was allowed on to Glen's stage in Malibu, after Debbie had pulled a few strings. We had youth on our side. Obsessive older people don't get the same breaks.

What was that trip to California, psychologically? I was in LA without a car and knew no one: I'd walk for two or three hours along freeways with no hard shoulder to find the venues Glen was playing in, up the winding approaches to Pepperdine University in the Santa Monica Mountains. I got sick from a taco stand and on one of my long bus journeys through town, had to jump off and vomit on Skid Row. I enjoyed the alienation. As a road-walker, or a bus rider, you're immediately one of the castaways yourself, and I *loved* that feeling – loved the danger of some of the situations I put myself in, waiting alone at 1 a.m. on a deserted station platform as a car crawled by. I loved touching down in the States, separated from anyone who cared about me by time zones and by the sheer mystery of my itinerary. As I took my first Greyhound out into the middle of the country, or down to the south, I felt like a leaf being blown across the continent: no one could reach me if they wanted to.

There is nothing quite like the longing that you can feel for a musician. On my American pilgrimages, that longing was vividly enhanced by my position as an alien, a tramp, picking my way to plush venues through rows of SUVs in car parks that were dead by 10.30 p.m. I felt a certain shame at my situation, and the shame seemed to add another level of aliveness. On finding, after a Glen Campbell gig in Pasadena, that there was no bus back to my hostel in downtown LA, I was forced to hitch a ride in one of those big, comfortable cars. The bearded driver and his wife had energy bars and leather seats, and they drove me high up into the hills at Pepperdine University to show me the monument to Todd 'Let's Roll' Beamer, the man who had tackled the terrorists on United Airlines Flight 93. American hospitality is strong, but it is boundaried. There was fascination, particularly from older men, at my travels: this one, I think his name was Jim, wrote to me for a while, formal and friendly, sending me DVDs of Glen Campbell. Ayer's childhood was posh,

At the end of his first gig in Pasadena, I stood at the edge of the stage while Jimmy Webb did a solo number, and Glen Campbell glided out to meet me. 'Dad, Kate has come all the way from London,' his daughter said. 'How bad is that?!' I shouted in exhilaration and shame, as Glen extended his papery hand.

Shame has never left me in my work; the more you love the person you're writing about, and the further you travelled to track them down, the more keenly you feel it. You will forever be on the outside, as a journalist, and it's a pain you have to get used to. The 2007 Glen Campbell pilgrimage started my career, when a friend of mine told me that if I was going to do a trip like that on my own, to see someone no one cared about (at that point), I had to write about it.

I sat in cafés in Santa Monica and did so – a piece called 'That Campbell and Webb Sound', a weird noughties reference to the *Peep Show* comedians. Then, when I returned to the UK, I went into Borders, the giant bookstore/café close to my home on Chapel Market in Angel, Islington, and opened the music magazines, taking down the email addresses of editors. The piece was run in full by Sean McGhee in the folk and roots magazine *Rock N Reel*, for a fee of £150. It was also the first piece I ever sent to Mark Ellen at *The Word*.

3
JOURNALISM IS A DIRTY BUSINESS
Kevin Ayers

In August 2008, I was very young. Not empirically – I was actually twenty-seven – but in certain matters of the mind and heart. I was overwhelmed by my first job, at *The Word*, where I was the only woman, and the men were much older than me. *The Word* was launched in 2003 by David Hepworth and Mark Ellen, and its tagline for many years was 'Intelligent Life on Planet Rock'. The magazine eschewed the idea of cool, while being funnier and more literary than other music magazines, and my 'middle-aged man's taste' in music was regarded with amusement. It was largely why I'd got the job, I think.

Though it was the right fit for me cosmically at that point in my life – it was where I'd been destined to land, when Jude Rogers vacated the role of reviews editor in a tiny staff of five – I also laboured under that 'rightness' for many months. I was totally bound up in the place emotionally, a small girl sitting on the knee of Father Rock. By complete fluke, I lived just two minutes and seven seconds away from the office by foot. If I was unwell, Mark Ellen would come and shout up to the balcony to see if I needed anything. I was frequently in there at weekends – God knows why, no one else was – calling up the security man, Irish Gerry, to raise the heavy metal awnings to let me into the place and to my desk to get . . . what? Review copies? Forgotten sleeping tablets? On a Saturday afternoon, the hot sun beat into the small chaotic room, activating the smell of old cakes still left out on piles of back issues and CD cases. We cut the cakes using a pencil slotted through the hole in a CD, like a kind of pizza slice.

I would stand in the silence of the empty hub and, in some dim corner of my unconscious, wonder who I was without these men, and who I would be. Consciously, I just felt lost until the working week began again. But when it did, I wasn't able to concentrate; I spent my time engaging in epic word play, extreme hyperbole ('This is the *best record ever made*' is what we said of anything we put on the CD player) and phrases that seemed to get funnier every time you used them. This energy created *The Word*'s famous headlines and captions, but mainly the jokes were for us alone, as evidenced by my leaving cover (a tradition for anyone in publishing) awarded when the magazine folded in 2012. It featured fifty of the things I used to say, none of which would make any sense to an outside ear: 'Fifty pooonds' in a Scottish accent (a reference to the consistently low 'callout' fees from the BBC); 'hot items' (a reference to my appalling diet, where I justified deeply unhealthy food as long as it was small); and a reference to my first major feature in August 2008: 'Grooo, Kevin Ayers'.

One day, an offer had come in to interview the lead singer of Soft Machine, who had for many years been living in the south of France. The message came from a man called Tim who was acting as his manager and looking after his back catalogue. He had attached some recent pictures of Kevin, in his battered fishing hat, sitting on a sun-blasted riverbank somewhere, fishing rod in hand.

Kevin was a legend among men of a certain age: wistful, absurdist, a massive 'crumpeteer' and less cerebral than his jazzer bandmates. He had the feel of Syd Barrett, the one who got away. He was now, by all accounts, a great roue, living in a rock star's playground, ready to tell tales of the night Robert Wyatt fell out of the window. Who better to interview him than a girl who had never heard of him?

Exile on Mean Street

Kevin Ayers: *The Word*, 2008

There are poppy fields above the city of Carcassonne in southwestern France, and quiet houses with windows so tightly shuttered they appear to be in a permanent state of repose. The higher you get up the mountain, the closer the air becomes; there's a place where the road forks into two – a little scrap of fenced-off land in the middle planted with fruit trees and a hammock strung up in the shade. It is here, on an afternoon like this, that if you're lucky, you might catch a glimpse of Kevin Ayers.

Ayers has been living in voluntary exile in France for longer than he can remember; something about England never sat right with him. Forty years ago, when Soft Machine released their first album and toured the world with Jimi Hendrix, Ayers – lead vocalist and bass player, then twenty-four – gave up and fled to Ibiza. There, he later said, he 'lived on nothing – fruit from the trees and the fish that I caught every day'. His first solo album, *Joy of a Toy*, was a piece of psychedelic whimsy with songs such as 'Eleanor's Cake (Which Ate Her)' and 'The Lady Rachel', while the demos for his first single 'Singing a Song in the Morning' originally featured Syd Barrett – although by the time it came to the final cut, the ex-Floyd frontman was too far into his mental meltdown to remember the chords. The Whole World, a band featuring a young Mike Oldfield on bass, was assembled for a second LP, *Shooting at the Moon*, and Ayers was back in the limelight, hailed as a new David Bowie. He cancelled the promotional tour after a few dates, though, and aborted the group just as it was taking off.

The industry chased him, and the solo records kept coming through the '70s, with songs about bananas and girls in white dresses, eight-minute prog experiments and spoken-word tracks. Ayers slept with countless women – from Lady Aspinall to Nico, from the wife of John Cale to the girlfriend of Lou Reed. He lived with Brian Eno in Maida Vale, and it was at one of Ayers' famous house parties in July 1973 that Robert Wyatt, drunk and caught with the wrong girl, fell out of an upstairs window and was permanently paralysed from the waist down. Later in the decade, Ayers would once more head off in search of the sun, setting up home in Provence, Majorca and Minorca. By the close of the '70s, he had gone to ground completely.

In 2007, he released a new album, *The Unfairground*, which reunited him with many from the old scene, including Wyatt, whom he claimed he hadn't seen for thirty years. It seemed to spell a new lease of life, but a major tour of Europe and America, planned for that summer, had been abruptly cancelled. Approaching the strange little pen in the mountains now – the hammock rounded with some human form and the tip of a fisherman's hat just visible through the trees – I'm not quite sure what I'm going to find.

Kevin Ayers is perching rather uncomfortably on the edge of the hammock. He rises to meet me – 6-foot tall, dressed in a tattered velvet jacket and white trainers – and winces. He broke four ribs a few months back and has a fresh cut on the palm of his right hand from a fall he took earlier in the day. He removes his hat and scratches his messy blond hair, then covers up again self-consciously when he realises his face is exposed in the sun. I can't be sure, but I suspect that the ribs – broken in a barroom brawl – are an excuse to keep popping the tablets he carries around in a blue plastic carrier bag; 'my vitamin bag', as he calls it. Unsteady on his feet and mortally embarrassed to be seen or spoken to, Kevin Ayers is in several strange kinds of pain.

'Did you see the nunnery down in the village?' he asks, fumbling a tiny roll-up. He sounds like a BBC broadcaster from the '50s, his accent almost colonially refined, rich and sibilant, every T delicately crossed. 'It's very strange,' he goes on. 'There are about 5,000 nuns in there, but you never see any of them coming out.' We're in surreal territory, and he's brightening up. 'I think they are fed into some kind of giant sausage machine,' he says, 'or made into dog food perhaps.'

By the time we get into his car, he's drunk at least two bottles of wine and is winding down for a sedative-soaked siesta. For some reason, I'm optimistic about making it down the mountainside in one piece. At worst, we'll end up with a couple of broken ribs, I tell myself, and besides, Kevin Ayers is probably still too much of a gentleman to crash me.

Ayers' childhood was posh, lonely and miserable. His father was Rowan Ayers, the BBC broadcaster and creator of *The Open Door* and co-creator of *The Old Grey Whistle Test*, and when his parents' marriage ended, he was farmed out to live with his grandmother. His mother, 'a cold woman with a fierce Catholic guilt complex and a desire for self-improvement', set up home in Malaysia with a new husband, an army officer, and when they eventually sent for him, he made the journey alone at the age of six – a three-day trek to the Far East with a stopover at Bangkok. 'I was the only white boy among eighty pupils at school, and I spoke no Malaysian. Then they put me in a Catholic boarding school full of homosexual priests who were always trying to get into my pants because I was blond and looked like an angel.'

Back in England, Ayers was sent to 'any school that would have me'. Some expelled him, and some he escaped; the names and locations are of no interest to him now, but one of them was the Simon Langton Grammar School in Canterbury, where he met future Soft Machine members Robert Wyatt and Mike Ratledge, whose friendship represented 'the first experience of intimacy, the first family I ever had'. He tried to live with his father in Chelsea, but it backfired and he ended up on the streets 'conning', which is basically taking money for sexual favours and then trying to run away.

A car passes us by a hair's breadth and the French driver jabs a finger sideways to signal 'Get over the other side of the freaking road'. Kevin Ayers checks whether I've got my seatbelt on. We stop at his house for emergency supplies and he comes back to the car with seven bottles of wine.

'(Si Si) Je Suis un Rock Star', the Bill Wyman hit from the '80s, conjures images of a mini-chateau, a trout farm and a recording studio, PRS cheques and a comfortable life of food, drink and real estate. The Ayers residence is a tall, shuttered place at the end of a narrow street, built into the side of a gorge. The garden is on three levels with lichen-covered balustrades descending steeply and all sorts of greenery jostling together. It's redolent of an old cemetery and there's a strange, tropical ozone smell, rich in neglect. Overripe peaches spill from paper bags on the kitchen table and bits of buddleia blossom, faded and brown, have blown in on to the floor. There's a small CD system on the dresser, half a dozen albums piled on top of it. One is by the Gaelic singer Julie Fowlis ('yes, someone gave me that') and the others are by Kevin Ayers – *The Unfairground*, *Whatevershebringswesing*, *Shooting at the Moon* among them, all covered in dust. It looks as though they have been put there by someone else, to remind him who he is.

Throughout the '80s, Kevin Ayers was a heroin addict. He once received an entire portable studio as a gift from Mike Oldfield, and sold it to support his habit. His musical partner, Ollie Halsall of Patto, another 'next big thing' from the early '70s, was his drug buddy – until he died of an overdose in 1992. His death weaned Ayers off the stuff, but there is something about this house, dishevelled and unfurnished, that speaks of those former times. The bedrooms, and there are many, don't contain any bookshelves, or clothes, or clutter. He shows me his bed – green plush velvet – but each of the others appears to have been slept in too, the sure sign of an insomniac.

He takes me to a room painted red, with the beginnings of a gold leaf design on one part of the wall. 'This is the room with the woman's touch,' he says. He's referring to an American barmaid half his age who'd lived there on and off until about five years ago. The house misses her. If there is one thing Kevin Ayers can talk about freely – needs to talk about – it's love. 'I can't write songs unless I am in love,' he states. 'And I have always been that way. If I am not in love, nothing is meaningful to me. I have no energy.'

At the top of the house, there is something that could once have been a nursery, 'where I put children if I have them'. He has several, in fact, all grown up now, and he's in regular contact with Galen, his daughter by Richard Branson's ex-wife Kirsten, a deal with Virgin Records in the '70s having proved fruitful in more ways than one. There is an old typewriter that no longer works up here, too, and a four-track tape-recorder that, over the course of three years, he used to put down songs for *The Unfairground*. There are no musical instruments and few other signs of his professional activity. I ask him how he writes his music now and feel instantly as though I've embarrassed him.

Out in the garden, a pint of neat Pernod in his hand, Kevin Ayers changes places with me so the sun is on my face and his is in the shade. I am bemused at his lack of physical confidence – he did a few small gigs in France two years ago and insisted that the venues were set in near-darkness. If he compared himself to other men in their mid-sixties, he'd feel a lot better. But that's missing the point, really, because somewhere down the line, on the shores of Ibiza or Morocco forty years ago, Kevin Ayers' mind seems to have been frozen in time.

There is something unshakable about his attitude – his romanticism, his sedateness, the curious self-indulgence despite the impoverished circumstances – that sets him apart from those caricatures of the '60s bent on some kind of nostalgia trip. 'I have always denied that there was a Canterbury scene,' he says matter-of-factly when I ask him about the early days. 'There were no more than half-a-dozen people doing what we were doing – in a cathedral city that had its quota of real wankers. People would hit on me because I had a posh accent. Mike Ratledge got a first in philosophy at Oxford and Robert Wyatt came from a literary background. That was the thing that drew us together, really.

'The thing about Soft Machine and me,' he goes on slowly, 'was that I never considered another profession. My only other desire was to do as little as possible. Honestly, I just assume that whatever is going to happen to me is going to happen. There it goes: someone is there, someone isn't there. This girl is here. This food is here. I think the clever people are the ones who do as little as possible.'

In a strange kind of way, Kevin Ayers is living bang in the present – his present. If he were feeding off the memory of his early career, he would be doing more to keep it alive. In fact, as I learn later, when he saw the dates for his planned tour in the summer of 2008 – in Europe and the US – he broke down and hospitalised himself with alcohol and painkillers. It was 1969 when he first cancelled a tour. This is not a man who is 'past it', but a man who has not changed a bit.

The village is bedding down for the night and late in the evening, on the street outside his house, Kevin Ayers emerges carrying, to my surprise, an acoustic guitar. It's the first voluntary sign of his musical life that he has given me. No one dares look at him or make a fuss, anxious not to put him off, and sitting in a doorway, Ayers starts to play an old blues song. His voice rings out loud, confident and unmistakable on the cobbled street, lagging lazily just behind the beat. One by one, people creep up on the street to listen. A couple of old French people open their shutters and look down. He finishes. 'Play "May I"?!' someone calls, wanting to hear a Kevin Ayers' composition. 'How about "Lady Rachel"?' They just don't get it. 'I can't do those songs,' he says quietly, with a waver of frustration. 'Because I don't know the words and the chords.'

Afterword

When Ayers opened the door to show me a little red room with one of many unmade beds, he told me he'd make it up for me with new sheets later. I didn't put that in the piece: at the end of many days – I have no idea how long the trip was but it felt like a week – and after the denouement I describe, with him trying and failing to play his own songs on the cobbled village street, he indicated that I would be coming back to his and sleeping with him. I remained outside his house, and his manager stepped inside for a minute. After a brief silence, I heard the crash of a few pots and pans in the kitchen and the manager shouting, 'It's not 1967, Kevin!' Ayers was from a better age, when rock stars and journalists hooked up on sheepskin rugs and wrote features together in blissful, claret-fuelled symbiosis.

His set-up in Carcasonne was very strange. His manager was married to a beautiful woman from a posh family who dropped in cheeky references to arms dealing as our booze-fuelled afternoons turned into booze-fuelled nights. One evening, with the white wine working its cruel flicker on her, she looked at me and said, 'What are you anyway, *fourteen*?' I laughed along, but it hurt, because the youth she saw felt like nothing but powerlessness to me.

The Ayers' experience was the first time I felt both the responsibility of being a journalist and the awful realisation that if you're going to do your job properly, you have to tell the truth about what you find, rather than what your editor was expecting. I couldn't believe how vulnerable and unwell I had found him to be, and how isolated he was in his set-up. And I couldn't believe how quickly I found him to be activated into a confessional mode by the fact that I was young and a girl.

I knew he was telling me things because of what I looked like, and how I came across. I don't mean he was doing this as a kind of exchange – it's sad that the story sounds a bit MeToo so many years later: simply that on some level, Ayers detected a certain innocence and returned it with trust. Yet all the time I knew that I had to paint a picture of him as he was. I didn't like that feeling at all. Before I left for the airport, I wrote him a note and dropped it through the letter box. I cried all the way home on the plane.

Years later, I spoke to Ayers' daughter Galen, whose mother, Kristen Tomassi, he had seduced after a wife-swapping party with her then husband, Richard Branson. Galen had become Ayers' closest confidante and had been left to deal with the ginormous tangle of his estate, music and unpaid tax bills. She became his caretaker in his later years. She told me, 'I knew that if I looked away, he would go, "Hey, I'm going to die then!" And he did.' I told her I had found him strangely upsetting and she said, 'Well, then we are the same.' I found her empathy so touching, coming from a favoured child who referred to her father as a 'best friend, brother, son, father, god'.

Galen had spent years untangling the enmeshed relationship of the father and daughter, that glowing dynamic both romantic and safe, and trying, against the strength of the personality he left behind, to 'individuate', as she put it. 'Every other week, he'd convince some young girl to clean his house for no money,' she said. In some other dimension, that was me, wiping down the top of the telly in Carcassonne, shifting the mouldy fruit and the Kevin Ayers' CDs.

4
ON NO ACCOUNT MENTION TERENCE TRENT D'ARBY

Terence Trent D'Arby

Young musicians, in my experience, rarely have much to say about their music. That's why, these days, they often prefer to talk about anxiety and mental health. Give me a rocker in their later years, who has some perspective on how they coped with fame. None can say why they wanted it in the first place. Some talk in anecdotes, and others have no interest in dwelling on the past. A few are able to describe how they feel about a career on the slide, but most aren't able to accept that their career *might* be on the slide, which is far better copy. Broadly speaking, they fall into two categories: those who are able to see who and what they were, with reflection and distance – and Terence Trent D'Arby.

Occasionally, a story sits in plain sight and you're the first one to touch it. For years, I'd received emails about the latest release from Sananda Maitreya, who makes albums every year – vast, complex, concepty things about Greek mythology, produced by him, and featuring him on every instrument, even woodwind. Always, around two-thirds through the written press release, the publicist, sweating under the pressure of the impossible task of selling this arcane concept, would have caved in and said something about the fact that this man *had once performed under the name Terence Trent D'Arby* before a complete change of identity was prompted by a dream.

When I spoke to the PR dealing with Sananda's latest project – and was told that yes, an interview would be possible, but under no circumstances should I mention the words Terence Trent D'Arby – I felt sick with adrenaline because I knew, long before I made the trip, met him or had written a single word, that I had a huge viral hit on my hands. This has only happened a couple of times with me, and it is a peculiarly maddening feeling, because essentially the piece is already there – the concept is watertight – but it is still in the clouds because you haven't written it yet. You know exactly how it will smell and feel, and what it will be. But you still have to do it. What if you are hit by a bus? Or contract a brain disease in the days between the interview and filing date? Where will the piece go then?

I can never rest until such pieces are done, and thankfully, there have not been that many of them. I have to take sleeping pills at night; I become distant and spooky, my vision set at forty feet ahead, my shoulders hunched, my speech brusque and my nails in tatters. I still remember the taste of the Burger King I had on my hotel room bed in Milan after I'd met the former Terence Trent D'Arby, my anguished stomach relaxing to the sweet mayonnaise. I stayed there staring at the wall for a long time and looking at the Dictaphone, afraid it was going to spontaneously combust.

Usually, when someone has turned their back on their fame and former life, you don't still find them walking around looking like a rock star ready to deck a crowd of paparazzi. And usually, if someone has asked you not to mention their former self, their eyes don't flash with something like excitement when you do. As the hours wore on, through Margaret Thatcher's conspiracy to have him killed in the '80s to the underhand deeds of his nemesis Lenny Kravitz, Maitreya's whispered speech became mesmerising. After three hours, I said I was done, and he said, 'I'm happy to go on if you like.' On the one hand, he was on another plane, his eyes puffy with herb and medication; on the other, he was an ex-journalist who knew exactly how the rock press worked; he undertood that his story was a perfect cautionary tale of rock 'n' roll hubris, supplying me with one-liners and pull quotes in a series of block capital emails after our meeting.

Maitreya is married to a beautiful ex-model called Francesca, with whom he has two sons. She wanted to have a drink afterwards: you sensed her life was pretty tough. She had had a fixation with Terence Trent D'Arby as a fan when she was a teenager: she was, in essence, a walking example of what life would be like if you really got together with your rock star crush. We kept in touch after that; she tried to set me up with a few of her friends. When the piece came out, the PR got into trouble – and was cross with me – but journalist Terence was happy that people were talking about him again. When it was syndicated by Italian *Vogue*, they were thrilled. I still get occasional messages from Francesca, always passing on notes from Terence with love and kisses.

'I was killed when I was twenty-seven: the curious afterlife of Terence Trent D'Arby'

New Statesman, 2015

Imagine this. You're twenty-five and your debut album of perfectly polished soul-rock-pop-funk sells one million copies in the first three days of release. It delivers three top-ten hits, winning you numerous platinum gongs and a Grammy Award, and parachutes you right into the arena of the '80s megastars you idolise. You drive the music press into a frenzy: they say you combine the voice of Sam Cooke and the moves of James Brown with the louche beauty of Jimi Hendrix. You are mentored by Springsteen, Leonard Cohen and Pete Townshend; you spend hours on the phone with Prince and sing on Brian Wilson albums. You even meet your hero Muhammad Ali, whose attitude you've ingested, saying: 'Tell people long enough and loud enough you're the greatest and eventually they'll believe you.' In case anyone is in any doubt about just how important you are, you draw a parallel between your destiny and that of Martin Luther King.

Early one morning, at the end of one of your six-hour, joss-stick-infused overnight interviews, a journalist asks you what happens if your follow-up album isn't as successful as your first. For once, you are lost for words. 'That's like asking me what I would do if my dick fell off . . .'

The man who slips into the hotel lobby in Milan looks like a fashion district local – one scarf over his dreadlocks, another curled round his neck – but there's an inward energy about him, like one of those fragile celebrities who doesn't want to be noticed but cannot help it: it's all there in the cut of the trousers and size of the blue-bottle shgades.

I've been given instructions for my meeting with Sananda Maitreya. 1. Please don't mention the name 'Terence Trent D'Arby', as it is painful for him. 2. Please don't make any comparisons with Prince regarding his name change, which occurred in 1995 after a series of dreams. 3. Please don't ask him things like, 'What songs do you think would make a good single from your new album, *The Rise of the Zugebrian Time Lords?*'

The hotel is next to Milan's cathedral, the Duomo, where Maitreya proposed to his Italian wife, the architect and former television presenter Francesca Francone, some years ago during a Catholic Mass. We go to the sixth floor and find that nothing is quite right up there: the room is too hot; he orders a whisky and Coke and can't find a bottle opener; we find one and it doesn't work. Finally, he takes a long, reassuring slug and declares, 'I feel like I'm going on a date when I've been married twenty-five years. I don't know how to do this any more.'

He says softly: 'One thing about Italians is you can't let them in your head. They're inquisitive. The English and Germans are a dog tribe; the Italians are cats. They're very helpful, but it's in their own rhythm, their own way, and it can drive you crazy.'

It's an odd start to an interview, but even as a young man Terence Trent D'Arby liked to discourse on a broad range of subjects. An American who rejected his homeland, D'Arby was living in Britain through what he refers to today as 'the Thatcher Revolution'. He was a strange, exotic bird, dropped down in the streets of London, cruising around on a motorbike in the video for his hit song 'Sign Your Name' and appearing frequently on the Channel 4 show *The Tube* (he had a year-long affair with its host, Paula Yates). Today, his accent is New York, but back then it was English; the apostrophe he adopted was a mark of his rapid self-elevation. He was all things to all people, and once began a *Q* magazine interview deconstructing the defeat of Neil Kinnock in the 1987 election.

'Oh my God, I can't believe you thought I was a socialist,' he says now. 'I was nothing more than an opportunist. Any socialist tendencies I may have had were cured when I got my first tax bill. All artists are socialists until they see another artist with a bigger house than theirs.'

D'Arby had cut his teeth in a German funk band while stationed in Frankfurt with Elvis Presley's old regiment, and like that other army boy, Hendrix, he came to fame in a London that wanted his music more than the country he came from. The producer Martyn Ware – a founder member of Heaven 17 and the Human League – worked with him on his debut LP, *Introducing the Hardline According to Terence Trent D'Arby*, which also included the hit songs 'Wishing Well' and 'If You Let Me Stay'. He describes D'Arby as 'a box of fireworks going off in every direction. I have never met anyone so driven'. Ware would arrive at the studio in the morning and find D'Arby already sitting there in the dark, analysing live recordings of Sam Cooke. 'It was like he was studying at university to be a classic soul singer.'

Out in the world, his preternatural confidence was magnetic. 'He was *the* world's most beautiful man,' Ware says. 'I used to walk around Soho with him and women would literally stop and stare – he looked like a god because he's got that boxer's body, and he was a bit androgynous, too. Even the men fancied him.' (D'Arby once said he had sex more often than he washed his hair.)

To the music press, he posed a dilemma. As a pop star he was so perfect, Charles Shaar Murray wrote in 1988, he was 'like something invented by three rock critics on the phone'. They called him two things: a genius, and a wanker. To make things more confusing, the very same people calling him a genius were the people calling him a wanker. Worse still, D'Arby worshipped these people. While living in Germany, he had devoured the *NME* and *Melody Maker*. 'I had an intellectual crush on Nick Kent, Charles Shaar Murray and Julie,' he says today – 'Julie Burchill. But she is so reactionary now.' He knew that British rock hacks thought American artists were boring to interview so he set out to be different.

* * *

Terence Trent D'Arby's follow-up album, 1989's *Neither Fish Nor Flesh*, was not the triumph he had predicted. It was an experimental psych-soul project featuring tribal drums, surf-rock guitar and cosmic libretto: 'To an outside world, I *will* not be defined!' Early in its inception, D'Arby's old team received a Dear John letter saying that he felt like this was his moment: he wanted to produce, master and engineer the project himself. He is credited as playing, among other things, kazoo, saxophone, sitar and timpani on the record. He invited Martyn Ware to hear the album when it was finished (in another darkened studio session, which D'Arby himself did not attend). 'And although I thought it was very brave,' Ware tells me, 'I just couldn't hear the singles.'

The album stiffed – spectacularly, for its time – selling just 300,000 copies (the debut sold more than nine million). It brought about a downfall straight out of a Greek tragedy. In music lore, its creator disappeared from the face of the earth on 23 October 1989, the moment the record was released. The truth is slightly different: he soldiered on valiantly for a few years, did a naked cover shoot for *Q* in 1993 and his third album, *Symphony Or Damn*, produced four top-twenty singles in the UK, among them 'Delicate' and 'Let Her Down Easy'. But all this is irrelevant, because no one believes that Terence Trent D'Arby died in 1989 more than Terence Trent D'Arby himself.

'It felt like I was going to join the 27 Club,' he says quietly, referring to the rock 'n' roll heaven inhabited by Jim Morrison, Janis Joplin, Kurt Cobain and all the others who died at that unfortunate age. 'And psychologically I did, because that is exactly the age I was when I was killed.'

His speech has an automatic quality and there is very little eye contact. You don't interact with him. You lob questions over the top of what he's saying and hope that he might catch them.

'The bottom line is, we're all pretty much sleepwalking,' he says. 'The most difficult thing artists have to deal with is the crushing difference between what they know they can do with their dream being supported, and the reality they have to navigate with the business.'

Over the years, he has blamed his former record company, Sony, for the failure of his career, saying it refused to promote *Neither Fish Nor Flesh*. He drew parallels with George Michael, who fought a long battle with Sony in the same era, claiming it wished to keep him in a situation of 'creative slavery' when he wanted to branch out with his sound. But George Michael is still with us. I'm curious to know whether, with hindsight and a change of identity, Sananda Maitreya finds that his feelings about the causes of his career failure have changed. 'The good news is, most record company people are motivated by the same reason most of us are: greed,' he says. 'So, no, when you look back at it, it didn't make much sense for management not to want my second record to succeed.'

The alternative reasons he gives are a surprise. 'I came around at a time when myself, Michael Jackson, Prince, Madonna and George Michael, we were considered kind of dangerous,' he says. 'To the system, to the establishment, you become a rival politician.'

The establishment's urge to end his career was so great, he says, that there were debates about him in the House of Lords. His real nemesis was not the Thatcher administration, but 'the 800lb gorilla in the room, Michael, Master Jackson', who saw him as a threat and, having bought up the Beatles catalogue in 1985, held 'more power than the Pope' within the industry.

Every few minutes in our long conversation, Maitreya cuts away from dark realms of government plots and talks more candidly about the business. 'It's only a matter of time before a cheaper model of you comes along,' he explains. 'Record companies say, "Hey, if you like *this* asshole, you're going to like *this* asshole – plus we're making a higher margin on this asshole." They don't tell you that while you're getting smarter, commanding more for yourself, you're putting an egg-timer on your career.'

As a young man, he once observed, 'This industry doesn't like too many black faces around at one time. If someone puts me on the cover of a magazine, they ain't going to be putting another black face on the cover for a while because it wouldn't make commercial sense and that's the way of the world.' Already selling millions to a white yuppie audience, D'Arby could afford to be philosophical about genre pigeonholing, but the digs at his rivals abounded. He claimed that black artists before him – Lionel Richie, Luther Vandross, Michael Jackson – had emasculated themselves to get into the charts. He would be Jerry Lee Lewis, he once declared, rather wonderfully, 'the embodiment of the white man gone bad'.

Today he does not name the new, cheaper-to-run assholes who came up when the industry had 'successfully killed my primary image', so I draw his attention to a poem on his website, from 2002:

Note to Lenny K

Fear not,
Your girls are safe!
I've got an Italian girlfriend now
And my leash is pretty short
PS Also let me say to you now
How proud I am of you.
You took care of the tribes necessary business and moved it forward
And kept the light on. I know it wasn't easy. Bless you!

I ask him whether this poem was dedicated to Lenny Kravitz, who achieved success the year Terence died and was also, like him, a sexy black rock star who'd grown up listening to the Stones.

He says he can't remember writing the poem, but then concedes: 'At one point, I thought they would give Lenny my social security number as well. I think my greatest envy of him was that he actually did have a tremendous amount of support from his record company while I was always fucking arguing with mine.

'Much of what I wanted to do was moved over to him while I was going through my mortification period.'

In August, at a festival in Sweden, Kravitz's leather trousers split on stage and the unfortunate incident went viral. He was revealed to be wearing no underpants, and a cock ring. I ask Maitreya whether he saw the internet clip.

'No,' he says, and for the first time a spark dances in his eye. 'Choreographed for sure. The only thing I could think to do with a cock ring now is keep my house keys on it.'

In hindsight, it's impossible to imagine a *Game of Thrones* playing out in the late '80s and early '90s between a handful of black male rock stars – D'Arby, Kravitz, Seal, Michael Jackson and Prince. Yet Jackson, paranoid about everyone, indeed felt threatened by D'Arby; he was upset when his lawyer, John Branca, took D'Arby on as a client, and urged him to drop him.

'The hero factory is there to produce pop idols,' Maitreya says. 'We're fools, we wear the fools' hats. Our job is to be publicly flogged and beaten when it's time to do that. The price of fame is: when we need to crucify you, you need to be available to us. We'll give you a good burial, make some nice T-shirts. Each of them pays their own price. You don't just come through unscathed.'

Did he hold on to his publishing rights? Does he still get royalties?

'Yeah. I wasn't a total idiot.'

* * *

In January 2009, Lady Gaga told the world, 'I've always been famous, you just didn't know it.' The press enjoyed her nuclear sense of self-belief and the postmodern, almost academic way she talked about her music, borrowing a limb from all her heroes and setting herself alongside them. Five years later, Gaga was declared dead by various publications – but not before she had rendered Madonna irrelevant. In 1988, Terence Trent D'Arby declared he'd be as big as Madge, too. 'The worst thing she could possibly do is not to have died young like Marilyn,' he says. 'How considerate of Marilyn to have died, so we didn't have to deal with the reality of the fact that even our goddesses get older.'

In the afterglow of his first album's success, he declared he would finally break America – and shortly afterwards he turned up on the cover of *Rolling Stone*. But every long profile of him began with enthusiastic speculation about his inevitable fall. 'He created this monster,' Ware says. 'It started off as a giggle, an ironic thing. He understood the business of star-building and he became his own experiment. Then he fell out with journalists who were extremely eager to pull him down.'

Before he joined the army, D'Arby studied journalism for a year at the University of Florida. He records our interview and emails me afterwards. I'm half expecting him to retract some of the things he has said, but he's just improving a few of his quotes. The old self-belief is still there, but these days it is shot through with pain. Where does it come from? Can he explain, now Terence is dead and buried?

He has never told anyone this, he says, but on the night of 8 December 1980, he dreamed that he met John Lennon on the street in New York and extended his hand, and felt Lennon 'basically walk into' him. When he awoke, he heard that Lennon had been killed. 'From the age of eighteen onwards, I had a different confidence about what was meant to happen to my life. I can only say this with all relative humility: I saw myself as a Beatle.'

* * *

A few years ago, Sananda Maitreya's wife told him his attitude was that of a typical New Yorker. 'I thought about it, and I said, "Actually, that's right, you know," because New Yorkers have a chip on their shoulder, too.'

He was born in Manhattan in 1962 to a gospel singer and counsellor, Frances Howard, and raised by her and the man he now refers to as his stepfather, Bishop James Benjamin Darby. Pop music was banned from the household: hearing Michael Jackson's voice floating from a neighbour's yard was 'like my first kiss'. The family moved from New York to DeLand in northern Florida, where his stepfather became pastor of the city's Church of Our Lord Jesus Christ and chairman of the Pentecostal International Board of Evangelists.

Terry Darby, as he was known, was a successful pupil – he became managing editor of the school paper and sang in a student chorus called the Sound of the Seventies – but he got into fights. He had problems with black kids and with white kids ('Fuck the both of you – I'm green,' is how he once put it) and suffered his first fall from grace when, during one scuffle, he stabbed someone with his Afro hair pick. Boxing was an outlet for his anger – he won the prestigious Golden Gloves prize in Orlando at seventeen and caught the attention of army coaches. His parents persuaded him to go to university instead, but he was frustrated there, particularly by his lack of success with women. He dropped out and joined the army, but soon got fed up of taking instructions from people he considered less intelligent. After amassing a number of reprimands, he was discharged at twenty-one.

Maitreya tells me today that he was an illegitimate child, raised with five legitimate children. 'The circumstances of my birth were very embarrassing to my mother,' he says. 'My biological father was a married man, so basically, in any event, it was already a messy situation.'

I ask him if this biological father was white (he has often drawn attention to his light skin). 'Or an alien, or both. Point is, I came into the world in a very compromising situation, and because of my mother's religious upbringing, abortion was out of the question.'

He tells me that his mother 'made it very, very clear that Jesus was the most important thing in her life, and she did what she could not to project the fact that I was an embarrassment to her. I spent most of my life unconsciously competing with Jesus for my mother's attention. Which is kind of tough, because first of all, I couldn't see him, except for pictures, and second of all, he wasn't really there, and it's tough to compete with somebody who's invisible.'

Does he still talk to her? She can be seen on YouTube, singing gospel under the name Mother Frances Darby.

'I'm not sure she's even the same woman,' he says, vaguely. And then, as he has been given to doing throughout his career, he pulls his experience – and probably that of many other pop stars – into focus for a moment. 'If you have a chip on your shoulder, use it,' he says. 'In Latin, fame means hunger, and I'm hungry. Not a hundred people in my generation could have done what

I did, and the difference between us is that they got from their environment what they needed. There was no need for them to mount some huge, fucking life-destroying campaign to show the world, "Look, I am worthy of my mother's attention".'

Did he have a nervous breakdown?

'Of course I had a breakdown,' he says. 'It was clearly a breakdown, and all you can do is surrender and try to not put too many pills into your body. You could say, clearly this guy had some sort of bipolar crisis.'

And where was he when this breakdown happened?

'I was living in great fabulous fucking mansions in Sunset Boulevard on my own,' he says, sounding suddenly weary and tapping my tape recorder. 'Are you sure this thing is on?'

Maitreya says he has inherited 'a degree of family madness, some male schizophrenia issues', from his Scots–Irish bloodline. He talks about the connection between madness and creativity, comparing the management of demons to the delicate power balance involved in a man having successful dominance over a wolf. Yet the cast of characters in attendance during his breakdown – which occurred after he moved Los Angeles in the mid-'90s, feeling alienated by the British press – appears to have been more mundane.

'I can remember getting up in the middle of the night and sleepwalking to the bathroom, taking a piss, and having a quiet inner voice saying, "Don't worry. Some day, you're going to change both the music and the business,"' he says. 'I do believe that Master Lennon, being an angel of the Lord, is available to a lot of people in inspiring circumstances. I believe the same about Elvis, the same with Master Michael, even though he was a huge nemesis in that lifetime. Since his death, he definitely knows he owes me some karma.'

It was angels who named him Sananda, he says, in dreams during his depression. 'Then, later, I realised I think I need a second name, because I didn't want to piss Madonna off, you know!'

* * *

The singular ambition that burned *Neither Fish Nor Flesh* to cinders has only intensified over time. Sananda Maitreya puts out a new album every two years on his independent label, Treehouse. They usually feature two dozen compositions; his pun-tastic titles include *Nigor Mortis* and 'Neutered and Spade'. Each project is the fruit of finally having the space to 'completely regurgitate all the stuff that went into my becoming an artist in the first place'. For several years there has been talk of a film about his life, he says, but he is struggling to get involved because he can see three or four different ways of telling the story.

The new project, *The Rise of the Zugebrian Time Lords*, is a retro-futuristic concept album spread over two discs of 'bipolar' excess. Maitreya's decision to start with a Beatles song, 'You're Going to Lose That Girl', should come as no surprise. The energy of the project is almost exhausting. Instruments – he plays them all – form a noisy zoo of woodwind, blues guitar and a loose, jangly piano spooked by the spirit of Carole King. What is this record? A Broadway musical for one? A fantastic exercise in rock 'n' roll hubris? An aural exploration of mental health issues?

Surprisingly, he doesn't want to talk about it. I press him about the lyrics to 'Giraffe', a likeable, child-friendly melody that contains the lines: 'Giraffe/Can I have your autograph?/Please sign it to Sananda'. When I suggest that it sounds like a song from *Sesame Street*, he brightens. For the past five years, he has been listening almost exclusively to children's music with his two sons, aged three and five. Joe Raposo, who wrote many of the programme's best-loved songs, including 'It's Not Easy Being Green', is one of his favourite composers. His husky voice swells into a perfect, sparkly croon: *Can you tell me how to get – how to get to Sesame Street!* 'You know,' he says, 'I think Elvis Costello was also influenced by some of Raposo's stuff. You're not supposed to say that, as an angry young writer, "Oh yeah, I listen to *Sesame Street*", but I can hear certain devices of his that sound like that whole *Electric Company* style of songwriting.'

His boys love 'Giraffe', but he can't be around while they are listening to it; his wife later tells me she has to wait until he's out of the house to play it to them. He talks touchingly about love being 'something you have to work on – it doesn't just come to you'. As a young man, he scythed his way through women, partly because of his mother issues, he thinks. Then one day he decided to stop, 'because you're only going to wind up looking for the same thing anyway'.

He can't listen to anyone else's pop music these days. His only comfortable relationship is with 'Master Beethoven', who presumably is dead enough not to offer any painful competition. But clearly the man who makes a double album and then can't play it again is living daily with bigger enemies than 'Lenny Cockring Kravitz' (as he calls him in his follow-up email) or the ghost of Master Jackson. Across the record there are hints of the cinnamon-voiced psychedelic wonders that could emerge from the pen of Sananda Maitreya, were he to allow a producer or A&R team to get their hands on his work. 'His voice is even better than it was at the time,' says Martyn Ware, who still receives each new project in the post from his old charge. 'But he has no sub-editor.'

'Tell me about your new album' is usually the most boring prompt in the rock 'n' roll interview. The second – 'How has being a father changed you?' (Maitreya also has a grown daughter from a previous relationship) – yields similarly surprising results. 'Anything else at this point in life is a bonus, because I've already done the most important thing, simply to have passed my genes on to some other bitches,' Maitreya says, showing me a picture of two small boys who look just like him, only with blond, curly hair and blue eyes.

'I'm very confident that my first son is my biological father and it gives me the chance to finally have a relationship with him. My first son is also a continuation of the life that I left behind.'

His first son might be Terence Trent D'Arby? Does that not worry him?

'Preferably they'll both want to follow their mother and be architects,' he says.

As the afternoon draws to a close, he talks again of bloodlines. Originally all the world was black, he tells me: 'Bitches looked like me! Didn't look like you!' His own white, 'land-owning, slave-owning blood' is another reason Providence gave him his assignment, he says.

And once we're back on to that, something clicks down in him again. We're on to Jonah and the Whale, 'being spat out unceremoniously after three days', and thence, without pause,

to vampires. For a moment, he becomes agitated when he realises that the brown cotton scarf that was covering his dreads has
disappeared. It's true enough: one minute I was looking at it and
the next it wasn't there. So much magic has been talked in this
room today that I think, for a moment, that Sananda Maitreya's
headscarf might have vanished into thin air and I'll have to tell
someone about it afterwards. We search and find it down the
back of his seat.

'What was I saying?'

I want to tell him not to re-join his mystical thread. He was so
much happier talking about Elvis Costello. But we're back to the
industry, and death. The irony is, the industry he was raised in
is dead and buried, too.

'And in killing the messengers, they killed a whole generation.
Like Maestro Thom Yorke: they alienated him, and he was providing the answers they needed.'

Surely the point is that you're free now?

'Yeah, well, free is relative,' he says. 'The moment we're met
with too much freedom, we shit our pants.'

5
STILL OBSESSIVE AFTER ALL THESE YEARS

Bruce Hornsby

There is nothing more irritating to me than the phrase, 'Men want to be him, women want to be with him'. Most of the women I know who've had major creative obsessions with men have done so because the men have something they want for themselves, or already have and can't recognise. Bruce Hornsby, the man who had a number-two hit with 'The Way It Is' in 1986, was one of my big musical love affairs, and one of the headiest, but I didn't want to be married to him, although that would probably be nice. Where have you been all my life?, I asked myself, when I discovered him mixing Scottish reels into American rock songs, or getting Pat Metheny to do the guitar breaks on his records. Bruce was at the centre of all the music I loved, and gravitated to, tying it together. If I could compose – which I can't – this is how I would do it; these are the chords I would use. *Of course* it was him, playing the choked-up piano on Bonnie Raitt's 'I Can't

Make You Love Me', which I sobbed over, walking up the field with my dog, as a child.

I consumed his music in a six-month period between September 2014 and the following March, when I met him. I would walk the three miles home from Farringdon, where the *New Statesman* offices then were, to my flat in Kentish Town because my body was too full of energy to sit on a bus. I would play the same bits of music over and over, and once hurt my ankle jumping up and down in my room to a particular guitar break. I found it hard to sleep. I bought an electric piano and took up the instrument sixteen years after I had last touched it, learning the complicated jazz piano solo to 'The Way It Is' note by note from watching his fingers in the promo video.

There was one song I would listen to over and over – a live version of a track called 'Country Doctor', which was about a small-town physician who poisons his wife. At one point, the drums rise in a storm while a guitar solo rolls down on top: it felt like a plane trying to land in a strong wind. The skin on my arms turned to that of a plucked chicken and I could hear Bruce going 'whooo!' from his piano, apparently thrilled by his own band.

For months the creative obsession boiled away in me: it made me feel a few inches taller. I dated no men, and I didn't miss it. I began to recognise that I often felt a similar thrill in writing, though nowhere near as wild, and I wondered whether it might be a good use of my energies to try and find him in America, since he'd not been written about in the British press since about 1989. I wanted to write him as I saw him and felt him – something slow, and long-readish, in way too much depth. I also knew that if I was seen to have travelled 2,000 miles to meet him, on my own money, it would be very difficult for him not to invite me into his house.

In order to make the trip as long and ruminative as possible, I flew into New York and took a Greyhound down to West Virginia, through part of Appalachia, with the intention of working my way back up to Bruce in Williamsburg, Virginia, on the East Coast. I had saved some of his music for the journey: I will always see the steel town of Ashland, Kentucky, in my mind's eye, as the sun set, when I hear the opening chords to his version of the Grateful Dead's 'Lady with a Fan'. I caught a twice-weekly train up the East Coast to the town where he lived: it came so infrequently that it scared the cattle in a nearby field.

I stayed the night in a bed and breakfast in Jamestown, the first English settlement, owned by Hornsby's cousins (he has a huge family). I looked up a magazine he'd produced in high school in the local library in Williamsburg and rode a car ferry featured in one of his early videos. The more I delayed my meeting, and the more I trod the ground Bruce trod, the more I felt the distance between him and me as a journalist – those old feelings of shame and exhilaration all over again. I had created these conditions. It was exactly where I wanted to be in my life. Yet I sat in the hotel on the morning of the interview, with ninety questions on seven sheets of paper, feeling like I was going to die.

How Bruce Hornsby survived a hit song
New Statesman, 2015

In 1607, a galleon called the *Susan Constant* arrived in the New World from Blackwall, London, and established the first permanent English settlement of Jamestown, Virginia. Over the river in Surry County lies the land John Rolfe received as a dowry when he married Pocahontas. Today, up the road in Yorktown, the children of the fife and drum society make their evening parade around a monument marking the last great battle of the American Revolution, in front of a family-run bed and breakfast called the Hornsby House Inn. In Colonial Williamsburg, the heart of this historic triangle, distant cannon fire can be heard and every so often someone runs past in a tricorn hat.

A few years back, Williamsburg's best-known modern-day son put out an alternative settlement narrative for Virginia in the form of a punk-rock sea shanty called 'The Black Rats of London', in which he pointed out that it wasn't divine intervention that toppled the natives but 'parameciums' from 'imported English dirt'. Bruce Hornsby is the first person I've heard use the phrase 'American Holocaust' in casual conversation, but then his family goes back a long way. At the inn, his cousins explain that their five-times great-grandfather, Nathaniel Bowditch, wrote *The New American Practical Navigator*, the oceanography bible still carried on every US naval vessel.

Three hundred and seventy-nine years after the rats, London sent something else to the New World, in a roundabout way: a five-minute song with two jazz piano solos that was considered too out there by American A&R men to release as a single but caught the attention of a BBC Radio 1 producer, Mik Wilkojc, and became an international hit. Everyone knows 'The Way It Is' ('That's just the way it is/Some things will never change'), its air-punching riff off-set by an apparently gloomy prognosis for American race relations – though younger people think it's by the rapper Tupac Shakur, who sampled the riff and the chorus in 'Changes'. Bruce Hornsby and the Range hit the MTV video boom in the same year as Peter Gabriel's 'Sledgehammer' and Madonna's 'Papa Don't Preach'. He was a straight thirty-one-year-old in a white shirt with a strange ringlet ponytail and a Donald Fagen-ish voice of the kind Amazon now calls 'adult contemporary'.

In fact, Hornsby may be the only musician apart from Frank Zappa to have had a pop moment, a rock moment, a country moment (he won the bluegrass Grammy in 1990 and 'pissed off all the purists'), a jazz moment (ongoing) and a modern classical one: the '12-tone pop' he's writing now is a strange mix of Schoenberg and Broadway. He is also one of just two keyboardists from the Grateful Dead still vertical and above ground.

I first saw him do a solo piano show in Troy, New York, the day after Halloween last year. The city was hit hard by the recession in the '90s and still hasn't recovered. Many of the shops in town were boarded up and there was no one on the street. I sheltered from the incoming snow in the CVS pharmacy, which was where, as it turned out, the rest of the town seemed to be hanging out too. As the sky darkened, I couldn't help but wonder why a guy turning sixty and still bringing in royalties from half a dozen hits he'd bagged in pop's most lucrative era was putting himself through this – which Ramada Inn he was sitting in right now, waiting for night to fall. As he pulled up to the venue in a small, black car with no staff and no props, I thought of his fellow '80s piano man Billy Joel being helicoptered from Long Island to Madison Square Garden to play his old tunes for $2m a night.

'Y'all may be used to this temperature, but I am a pathetic southern weenie and I am not,' Hornsby said, seating himself at a Steinway in jeans and sneakers. He is 6 foot 3 and moves slowly, a bit like an athlete conserving energy. 'I'm serious. I was left standing at stage door for, like, twenty-three seconds.'

In 2009, the director Bobcat Goldthwait cast Hornsby in the Robin Williams movie *World's Greatest Dad*, a black comedy whose theme – auto-erotic asphyxiation – was only marginally less taboo than that of his previous film, about a woman who had sex with a dog. Hornsby was a running joke in the script, his music loathed by the teenage central character (a furious masturbator) and loved only by his sad-sack dad. He once described his audience as a collision between two groups: Dreadlock Dave and Stockbroker Stan, the first being the tie-dyed, bearded, jam-band crowd he picked up during his time with the Grateful Dead, whom he joined aged thirty-five in 1990, and the second a nostalgic audience who bought his first two records in an era of yuppie pop crystallised in *American Psycho*, when Patrick Bateman murders a fellow banker to the sound of 'Hip to be Square' by Huey Lewis and the News. (Huey had a number-one hit with Hornsby's song 'Jacob's Ladder'.)

Here's how it works. The gigs are request shows – write a song title on a bit of paper and take it up to the stage. At some, there are so many requests that it looks like someone has kicked over a trash can. The size of his hardcore fan base varies from state to state; he notes that he's not very big in the Deep South ('about 5 foot 2'). Request your hit, many of them branded on the American psyche – the rock lament 'Mandolin Rain', or 'End of the Innocence', the critique of the Reagan administration that he co-wrote with Don Henley – then surrender your desire to hear it as you want to hear it. Expect ten-minute detours: along with Bud Powell's 'Tempus Fugit' and extracts from Olivier Messiaen, he has made diversions into 'Three Blind Mice' and 'There's a Hole in My Bucket'. Expect sarcasm if you request something he doesn't play any more. And don't leave your mobile phone on. He has been known to get his own back on an inattentive audience by playing someone's favourite song in two different keys at the same time.

The solo tour – the most gruelling part of his repertoire by his own admission – is roughly a fifth of the Hornsby workload. It usually takes place between April and November (November to March is the basketball season, when he stays put). Then there's the ongoing bluegrass collaboration with Ricky Skaggs; his musical *SCKBSTD* ('sick bastard'); his rock band the Noisemakers, now in their seventeenth year; the twenty-year gig writing music for Spike Lee films; and the folk music (his next album is 'your long-awaited dulcimer record'). He will join the Grateful Dead for their last-ever gigs in California and Chicago this summer, playing to 380,000 people. 'You know about that?' he says. 'Mental.'

We're at his house in Williamsburg, a white weatherboard number his brother built for him when he moved back here four years after the big hit. It is set on a tidal creek and looks a bit like an Edward Hopper painting, which is appropriate since he has some: *Farm House at Essex* (currently on loan somewhere), *Sultry Day* and *Funnel of Trawler*, and many sketches, including train and waiting room scenes such as the enigmatic *Chair Car*, covered in Hopper's annotations. Hornsby's grandfather, an organ player, knew Hopper as a young man. His house lies in a patch of land he has named Tosser's Wood, complete with a sign that his wife made him – his homage to the phrases of the Old World. He was pleased on a recent visit to London to learn the rhyming slang 'thrupennies'.

He presents me with his left index finger to shake; too many firm grips over the years could damage his hands. I ask him why he drives round to his gigs on his own and he says, with an amused look, that it suits him as he gets further into his misanthropy. Then he walks me through the house, showing me pictures of his identical twin sons, Keith (after Jarrett) and Russell (after Leon), and digs out an ancient Casio synthesiser, fiddling with its batteries and bashing out the riff from 'Shadow Hand', his song about a man with imaginary friends. He is a big, rather stately figure in trackpants, given to bouts of Tigger-ish excitement. It is difficult to see this Hornsby in the one from 1986, furrowed of brow and tightly rolled of sleeve, looking less than comfortable at the peak of his sudden fame.

'When we first came out in the UK, oh, it was amazing,' he says, settling into a tiny chair and somehow managing to sit cross-legged. 'We broke worldwide and it was a very intense year. I had to learn how to be a public presence right away. The head of publicity at RCA said, "Bruce, here's some press" and handed me a pile of Xeroxes from *Melody Maker* and *NME*. One review said: "[*English accent*] This particular gherkin calls himself Bruce Hornsby. With any luck, we will never hear from him again!"'

He describes the moment he got famous as 'the least enjoyable year of my career'. The ascent had been slow. He can be seen in the video for the world's rudest song, 'Sugar Walls' ('Come inside my sugar walls'), written by Prince and performed by his protégée Sheena Easton. Hornsby toured with Easton for two years, playing keyboards in the mid-'80s. He says that his son Keith, a college basketball star, watches the video whenever he has a bad game.

'The Way It Is' was the second song he released and it remains his biggest hit. At the time, he'd been living in LA with his wife, Kathy, and his brother, John (who co-wrote many early tracks) for six years, trying to make it. They had moved from Williamsburg with $13,000 in savings; she worked as a junior school teacher and he got a salaried position as a songwriter for 20th Century Fox. He had (very sensibly) given himself ten years to get a record contract; if that didn't work, they were coming home. When he finally got one, he turned down the offer of a $40,000 advance in return for half his publishing rights and 'took a gamble on myself'. The small family industry took place against the backdrop of the Sunset Strip and hair metal. Hornsby worked the classic rock clubs – the Roxy, Madame Wongs, the Lingerie. 'We were doing just fine,' he says. 'In the middle of our year, we were a theatre act playing 2,500-seaters but then, by the summer of the next, it was 10,000.

'It was just too much. Such a full onslaught of attention and opinion. I never thought it was going to be that big a deal. I thought I was terrible at all of it and I was. I see old clips and frankly, that thing about youth being wasted on the young? Only I wasn't even a youth. I was thirty-one, but my level of ability at all this extra-musical business, interviews and how to act – I was twenty-one. I felt like an idiot so much of the time. I thought, *Is this what this is about? If so, I want off.*'

I ask him to explain why 'The Way It Is' was so successful. He says he can't possibly do that, then does. 'I see it as a novelty record,' he says 'There are things that set it apart. I feel the same way about "Sultans of Swing" by Dire Straits. It goes down easy and isn't that what a lot of pop is about? But at the same time, it's a completely different sound than you'd heard. Even the big piano guys like Elton and Billy Joel, they didn't really solo like that. A pleasing sound with solos. Like Mark Knopfler on "Sultans of Swing". That's how I explain it. But that's complete crap, too, probably.'

Like other 'novelty' mega-hits – Journey's 'Don't Stop Believin'', with a chorus that doesn't come until most of the record is over, or 'Bohemian Rhapsody' with its opera section – 'The Way It Is' demanded more of the ear than regular songs. It was proof, perhaps, that the guy stuck in traffic with the radio on picks up, as the songwriter Eg White once told me, on the deliberate dropped stitch, missed beat or melodic twist that marks a record out from the mainstream. Hornsby has always said he couldn't believe some of the things he managed to slip under the wire on the top forty, but the hits didn't last. He moved back to Williamsburg in 1990 and two years of touring with the Dead threw him back into improvisation (they could play one song for an hour). As his chart presence faded, his critical standing increased. For subsequent records, he pulled in everyone he wanted – Pat Metheny, Béla Fleck, Ornette Coleman, Charlie Haden, Chaka Khan, Eric Clapton. Bonnie Raitt tells me she considers Hornsby to be set apart from other artists by his 'level of devotion to his instrument, to his writing and to the sheer joy of being totally spontaneous onstage'. Two years ago, Elton John said that Hornsby's piano playing on Raitt's 1991 hit 'I Can't Make You Love Me' made him 'seek perfection. It is sublime. He is one of the best pianists – if not the best – out there.'

* * *

BRUCE HORNSBY

The College of William and Mary is the second-oldest university in the US. In its library can be found bound copies of a periodical called *Piano Monthly*, which Hornsby edited between the ages of seventeen and twenty with his brother and two friends. One afternoon, he slipped several copies into the education section between *Phys Ed Weekly* and the *Princeton Review*. They later migrated into the music periodicals along with the jazz title *Downbeat* and finally, after he'd had his hits, they were placed in 'rare books' alongside the Thomas Jefferson papers.

Piano Monthly was not about pianos. The first cover featured two all-star wrestlers; another, a Vietnam commando (the 'Blood & Guts' issue). There is an advert that reads: 'Learn the harpsichord in seven days and impress the ladies'. There are reams of adolescent rock dreams – phoney reviews of records that appeared in the hazy early '70s ('It's been quite a while since Harry Nilsson spent hours in a cubby hole with Bruce Hornsby licking and pasting labels on his albums'). In a telling moment, Hornsby reviews a release by the New Orleans piano titan Professor Longhair and irony is suspended. 'Longhair can probably do more with the 1–4–5 progression than any other piano player.'

At this point, he had been playing piano for less than a year. Within two, he was at the prestigious Berklee College of Music in Boston. I ask him how this happened and he says Berklee took anybody in those days. His father, who ran a real-estate business, told him he must pay his own way through college if he wanted to do music, so he played cocktail jazz in hotels at night. Aged twenty, he failed to get into the New England Conservatory because he chose an impossible audition programme of Chick

85

Corea and McCoy Tyner, which he 'had no business playing'. Then he bought an upright piano, moved out to a farmhouse in Toano, Virginia, and practised for six months, eight hours a day. He entered the University of Miami School of Music to study jazz in 1975 at the end of its 'golden era'; in the years above, or already teaching, were Jaco Pastorius, Pat Metheny, most of Metheny's first band and the guitar whizz (and future member of Deep Purple) Steve Morse. These were the fragrant, long-haired legends of '70s jazz rock. Something tells me Hornsby didn't cut the same figure.

'I was a geek! Oh, totally. I looked hilarious,' he cries. 'But it's a beautiful reason why I was a geek and why anyone is a geek. I was so *consumed* with it. You are so interested in what you are doing that you don't even think about the fact that you've worn the same white T-shirt for a month without washing it and the same jeans and you probably reek from twenty yards away.'

But this was '70s Miami, I say, the hippest place on earth. 'You can have your own little world,' he says. 'You can be completely oblivious to, I guess, what was happening then – the TK Records phenomenon, the disco era, KC and the Sunshine Band, George McCrae, [*sings*] "Rock me baby!" I stayed in the practice room. And at night I earned money playing in a band with a gay Spanish singer who shook it while we played: [*sings*] "That's the way, ah, ah, I like it!" By day I was in classes, then the practice rooms. So, really, I had no time to know what was happening in Miami.'

Hornsby's ascetic streak didn't die with his student days. 'It was around Christmas time. I had just turned forty,' he tells me. 'I thought, *Right, what am I going to do now?* Most of my singer-songwriter friends kind of stop at that point. They're not interested in improving on their instruments and that's fine, I get it. So many of the people who were lionised in that era of pop music I came out of, chances are they don't even play any more. I thought, *What am I going to do?*

'I used to find myself in solo piano contexts occasionally and I always felt inadequate. There's this area of piano playing that has always been represented for me in its most amazing, fullest form by Keith Jarrett, which is the independence of the hands – being able to "split your brain" as an improviser. There were things Jarrett could do and I'd think, *This is so amazing, I can't even sniff at it, I can't even start to replicate this.* So I decided to re-dedicate myself to the study of the piano aged forty, around holiday time, when the boys were out of school. Kathy was pretty bummed with me. She said, "You spend enough time out there as it is."'

I ask him to demonstrate what he was teaching himself to do – the piano equivalent, he says, of 'rubbing your stomach and patting your head'. We go next door to his studio and he starts thundering away on a complicated left-hand passage from a 1998 song called 'King of the Hill'. With his right, he hits one note repeatedly on the beat, then turns it into triplets, then syncopates it. 'You have to crawl . . . before you can walk . . . before you can run,' he shouts. I feel like we're in a ballet class. By the end, he is playing a completely different rhythm and melody with each hand. I ask him how long the passage took him to learn and he says a couple of months.

'People say, "Ah, you just want to show off",' he says, rising from the piano stool and floating back into the other room. 'That is always the argument about virtuosity. The punk aesthetic dictates that it shouldn't have to be about playing your instrument well. It's all about the emotion and the spirit of it. And I get that.

I don't dismiss it. The accordion is my punk instrument, because I'm terrible at it but it doesn't stop me. I don't mind sucking on the accordion in front of thousands. Same with the dulcimer.

'But to dismiss virtuosity as musical masturbation is to dismiss Evgeny Kissin, the great classical pianist, playing Rachmaninoff as a show-off. I know Joni Mitchell used to really take umbrage with this mindset because she had Wayne Shorter playing with her and people would dismiss him as this "jazzbo". Shorter was *not* a guy about musical masturbation. He is a guy who will play one tone for twenty seconds. If you want to limit the range of the colours you can paint with, then be my guest. But to me, I just think it's too bad.'

On the piano, laid out in preparation for the second leg of the solo tour after the basketball season, is a copy of *Caténaires* by the New York atonalist Elliott Carter (1908–2012). It is a mad, mad piece – a terrifying scud of black semi-quavers laminated and stretched out over umpteen pages. Hornsby finds Carter inspiring because he composed until he was 103. What does Stockbroker Stan think when he requests 'Every Little Kiss' and gets Elliott Carter instead?

'Well, look, I'm sure he hates it!' he says. 'And I totally understand. I feel his pain. But I just can't let it stop me from the pursuit of the new and the pursuit of developing myself further. No scientific study has been made of this, but I am almost sure that what I call the "softcore" fan, the person who just knows those four or five or six songs from the 1980s, they're not that deeply involved. They come to see me because they used to make out in the car with their wife to "Mandolin Rain" and they're there for a nostalgic night out. That's the way of most concerts, if you have created a certain body of work that means something to a sizeable number of people. So I feel his pain and I try to placate him in my own way. For instance, I play "Mandolin Rain" a lot, but I play it in the minor key because that's what resonates with me at the moment. And as for "The Way It Is", I really like playing that.'

I suggest that he likes playing Bach's *Goldberg Variations* with a bit of 'The Way It Is' thrown in the middle. He giggles.

'Look, I am a different person from that old guy from 1986,' he says. 'I really am, in every single way, and it is so obvious. My feeling is, I'm trying to give it to you – and I am giving it to you – and I just hope you can meet me halfway. In the end, it's simple. If you really hate it, just *don't* come back. You should *not* come back, because I am not going to be a vehicle for your stroll down memory lane. The people who have their pop moment and spend the rest of their lives replicating that – the people who can do that and really mean it – I admire them. For me, it is a prison and I just refuse. I know I'm asking a lot, especially now that I'm inflicting the modern on them. But if you don't like it, don't come. I am fine. I've been playing these places a long time. Some people will go. Others are discovering it.'

At Troy, Hornsby seems to amuse himself most by his experiments in pointillism – the technique of hitting a rapid spray of notes across the keyboard, the musical equivalent of flicking a paintbrush across a canvas. He appears to be tickled by discords and moved by lush melodies, giving a small whoop of pleasure when he hits something he likes. He has called these his 'ecstatic' moments. It is something I've generally only seen in jazz musicians, that sense of musical surprise, something out of the player's control. I ask him if every musician gets it.

'I think some people get it because of the amazing arrangements they have created, whereby every night the thing feels transcendent,' he says. 'A perfect example is Joe Cocker's "With a Little Help from My Friends", that incredible version. I get chills just thinking about it. I saw him do it at Woodstock '94 – I was at the side of the stage and I was just going . . . [*He screws up his eyes and gives a little silent scream.*] Now, there are not that many transcendent arrangements like that around, but most of the greats will have a few of them and I imagine that they've created something that will achieve that height every night. It's just built into the music.'

He appears to get his own thrills out of something as tiny as a chord change. 'Or sometimes it's just the sound of the hall. I am an acoustic musician, so I am at the mercy of the instrument and the venue and sometimes the way I played it, the way I struck the chord, the dynamic and the sound of it will just make me go . . . [*He shivers.*] It's intangible. And I wish I could do it every night.'

* * *

Hornsby was raised in Christian Science, the sect founded by New Englander Mary Baker Eddy on the principle that sickness can be healed by prayer. 'Let's see . . .' he says, when I ask him what that meant. 'I went to the doctors in second grade when I needed glasses. And I went to the dentist, too. But, sure, there were times when we would have maladies as children and we were able to lose those maladies.'

His mother is a prominent figure in Williamsburg; there is a school named after her. As the church's community liaison, Lois

Hornsby invited patients from the Eastern State mental hospital into the family home. Hornsby and his brothers grew up with people who were, 'you could say, way, way out there'. She was also, he adds, 'one of the few white hands clapping in applause for integration in this generally conservative town', though she was not the only family matriarch to campaign against segregation. Hornsby's aunt, a teacher who served on the York County school board, vetoed the transfer of condemned bleachers from a white school to a black one and was involved in the campaign against the so-called massive resistance movement in the late 1950s, when Senator Harry F. Byrd tried to oppose the merging of Virginia's public schools. Hornsby says that, given his liberal upbringing, he had 'no excuse for sucking'.

A friend saw the Grateful Dead at Wembley in 1990 and recalls sonic chaos with 'this beautiful, crystalline piano floating over the top'. Three of Hornsby's keyboard predecessors in the near-mythic band had died in the saddle. 'Pigpen' McKernan died of booze; Keith Godchaux, a heroin addict, was killed in a car crash shortly after being ejected from the group. Brent Mydland died of an overdose and Hornsby was brought in to replace him, having struck up a relationship with the Dead when he supported them in the late '80s. Vince Welnick, who took over from Hornsby when his twins were born, committed suicide in 2006. Hornsby looks bored talking about the rock 'n' roll lifestyle ('I always thought it was a little . . . trite,' he says). He never got into drugs and doesn't like the taste of alcohol much. He tells me he gets drunk once every two years, on the tour bus for the amusement of his band, but beyond that he has no need. You suspect that his trouble-free lifestyle was an attractive thing for the Dead.

He had seen them aged eighteen in the sports hall at the College of William and Mary. They played a five-hour show, then took out the bleachers and did a second night for free in which, he was impressed to see, they didn't repeat a single song. In one sense, he was a shoo-in for the job because he already knew a lot of the music. But there was a less tangible connection. It is generally acknowledged among Deadheads – the world's most analytical fan base – that Hornsby's playing rejuvenated Jerry Garcia's guitar work at a time when his health was in sharp decline (he died in 1995 after an epic struggle with drug addiction). Hornsby says that on the tour bus, Garcia, whose knowledge of folk and bluegrass was encyclopaedic, in effect gave him a music lesson every day. Then there was the improvising. Onstage, he often had no idea what song the Dead were about to play. He transferred the approach to his own band. The Noisemakers don't get a setlist and are required to read a spontaneous arrangement communicated by his hand signals, or sometimes just the raise of an eyebrow.

In a recent episode of *The Looney Tunes Show*, Daffy Duck has a piano delivered to his house. 'I will fill our home with Beethoven and Rachmaninoff,' he splutters – 'and [*hands clasped*] Bruthe Hornthby. Thhho much Bruthe Hornthby.' The sound of the duck's flippers on the black notes is not unlike some of Hornsby's more experimental moments today. It is interesting to think that all over the US, existing 'soft-cores' might be undergoing a modest, case-by-case conversion to this music, whatever it is. For years he would describe his style as 'Bill Evans meets the hymnal', but the coordinates are changing. The vague course remains the same: the thousand-seaters of Prescott, Arizona, and

Cleveland, Ohio, are his practice rooms. A brief soundcheck to 'make friends' with the piano at the venue, a gig, then back in the car and on to the next.

The day after Troy, I made my way to Ridgefield, Connecticut, for the last night of the tour. I had a feeling the menu wouldn't be the same two nights running. I arrived late at a venue tucked away in the woods in a town of picket fences and SUVs, and walked in on the same guy in the same clothes hammering away on a Steinway with the same intensity as the night before. But, sure enough, we got music from the composer Charles Ives, because he was a 'Connecticut boy', and songs that (Hornsby quoted Leon Russell) offered 'maximum "Shenandoah" factor', meaning lush folk tunes – wrung through an East Coast intellectual sensibility, a uniquely American synthesis passed from Copland, to Gershwin, to Jarrett, and now this.

The good people of Ridgefield had turned out with children in tow, possibly to hear 'The Way It Is'. In the darkness, a woman slipped out to the toilet. When she returned, as his left hand worked away on one of those complicated bits and his right played a flourish over the top, Hornsby cried out, 'Tell her what she missed!'

Afterword

As soon as I had finished this profile, the edge of my Hornsby obsession faded. When I first met Roger Taylor as a teenager, the same thing happened, because I had temporarily left my bubble of shame and stepped into his world. But with Hornsby, who came to me in adult life and whom I was able to write about, it was something else. I no longer yearned to 'be' him because, in a way, I'd just worked with him, or so I told myself: the musical love affair, unlike that with Roger, had taken on a creative energy and there'd been a degree of interaction between us.

Because he was, at that point, largely ignored in the UK press, Bruce felt like he was mine. I recognise a similar possessiveness over Queen in retrospect, as though I had to believe that no one else was listening to the act for my own obsession to flower. But when I think of the people I've got like this about – the ones who've truly taken over my life for a period of time, and there have only been a handful – I feel something else connecting them, too. I have never become obsessed with a tortured soul: a Jeff Buckley, an Elliott Smith, a Nick Drake. These people do so often inspire an intense attachment because of the sense of a life cut short, the feeling that their music was driven by a pain that it was ultimately unable to heal.

Queen, Glen Campbell and Bruce Hornsby, on the other hand, are three most un-tortured artists. Roger Taylor once described his band as 'fun ambassadors'. Glen Campbell was a covers guy whose extraordinary talent could alter the whole meaning of a song, but the chaos of his private life never had a creative expression, and he didn't appear to need it.

Bruce Hornsby goes a little further, operating a kind of musical existentialism within an industry that has often failed to understand him, driven by the pursuit of goosebumps, and deriving from a chord sequence the kind of highs other people get from drink and drugs. Hornsby was a kind of magician to me, a sort of cosmic father figure, confirming what I already knew about music: that it can transport you, change your state of being. That was how I always felt, running down the edge of the field behind our house in the '90s with the Discman balanced on my palm.

These days, if he's in town, Bruce emails me, and I go backstage at his gigs, and reach up and give him a hug. I saw him play a show in Knoxville, Tennessee, a few years ago, and he did one of my favourite songs, 'Shadowhand', dedicating it to 'our friend from England'. He always talks in the royal we.

6
WHEN THE WHEELS COME OFF

Jon Bon Jovi and Steve Perry

Somebody once told me we're made up of two parts, the Viking and the wounded child. The Viking is the persona, the wounded child what lies underneath. Every journalist believes that their job is to tear away the Viking and expose the wounded child: this, of course, is impossible, and anyone who thinks they have achieved that in the space of a forty-five-minute interview is deluded. I was convinced that Jon Bon Jovi, the Bill Clinton of rock, would be frustratingly smooth. I knew my editor at the *New Statesman* wasn't keen on featuring him in the magazine, and not for the first time I'd be struggling to justify the existence of my piece in the flatplan on press day.

Before I walked in, Bon Jovi had just spoken to the *Big Issue* and when I perused the piece a few days later, before I'd written my own, it was very much on brand: he spoke of charity work, poverty and the welfare state. But for some reason I will never know, he decided to do two completely different interviews back-to-back that morning, and to present a side of himself to me that I had not seen him show before. We spoke six days before the US presidential election in 2016 and he, a Hillary supporter, also predicted the triumph of Trump, which few did at the time. As I left the *NS* office on press day, I watched them preparing the Hillary cartoon for the cover. Two days later, the magazine came out with a hastily sourced photo of a nuclear explosion on the front.

During research for this piece, I had become fixated on the relationship between Jon Bon Jovi and his guitarist and co-writer Richie Sambora, who had recently left the band. I kept a small file of snaps of them together on my desktop, with their arms around each other, or hugging in a conga line of two. I found them very beautiful, but ideally, I'd have both at the same time: Jon blond and small, Richie dark and rough around the edges. I was edging into fan fiction territory, the kind where teenage One Direction fans used to write love stories about Harry and Zayn.

The only key to longevity in rock bands is finding a way to stay together. At the point of my interview with Jon Bon Jovi, Richie had left the band after thirty years because of frequent alcohol abuse. He had gone to rehab several times, but it was always rehab paid for by the band and that struck me as chilling: that your mental health was ministered to by the company that had you in bondage. Their split was a rift akin to the break-up of the silver wedding anniversary parents who'd met at the dance aged sixteen. It effectively ended the band, but because Bon Jovi have never been subject to interest by the music press – too polished, too constant – the sad, seismic disaster has gone almost unnoticed.

Bon Jovi himself, despite valiant attempts to go on, was musically buggered and he knew it. At the time I spoke to him, Richie was on tour with his younger and equally wild girlfriend, the Australian guitarist Orianthi. My initial intention – *oh, how wonderful this would have been* – was to interview both Richie and Jon separately, without the other one knowing, and *then* bring them together in the same interview with their therapist Lou Cox, who spoke to me surprisingly willingly for the piece. I still dream of that feature today: rock couples' therapy. It would have been majestic. Unfortunately, Richie was not to be pinned down.

'I have earned this grey hair': the agony of Jon Bon Jovi

New Statesman, 2016

It's something unheard of in the modern PR junket, but Jon Bon Jovi interviews are running early. Breaks have been built into his day, but he doesn't want them. He's somewhere in this suite at the Savoy Hotel in central London: remnants of black tea steam in a delicate china cup next to a recently vacated chair. Soon his compact frontman's frame appears in the doorway, stomach flat as an ironing board – and, to my dismay, it becomes apparent that this will be a *sunglasses* interview. They're removed just once, thirty minutes in, for a weary pinch of the nose.

It's been a terrible three years. 'Turmoil,' as he put it to Jo Whiley the previous afternoon during a three-minute chat at an album launch. He didn't get time to say why but everyone knows. His compadre Richie Sambora – partner for thirty years, co-writer of their four number ones, fellow New Jersey boy and guitarist in one of the biggest bands in the world – is gone. He stopped showing up for work in 2013 and now tours the world with his girlfriend in an act he describes as 'Sonny and Cher on steroids'. Jon, who has played to 32 million people, launched a new album cautiously with a string of gigs that could be described as 'boutique'. Neither mentions the other on stage.

Other things went wrong for Jon Bon Jovi. The band fell out with their record label. And, two years back, he tried and failed to buy the American football team the Buffalo Bills. He already had one team – and when it was rumoured he would move the Bills from Buffalo to Ontario, Canada, there was uproar. Whole areas of the struggling city declared themselves 'Bon-Jovi Free Zones'. His music was banned from bars and strip clubs. It must have been painful for the man who's spent thirty years, like a kind of blockbuster Springsteen, reflecting the blue-collar worker in the American musical psyche. He and Richie's biggest hit, 'Livin' on a Prayer', followed the fortunes of a young couple during the union strikes of the Reagan era. Fans debated whether the song's fictional Tommy was a strike-breaker. 'No, no, Christ no,' said an anxious Jon in 2009. 'He just lost his job. It wasn't that he crossed the picket line!'

In discos, dives and weddings across the planet, floors still fill to his anthems' opening bars. From the philanthropy career (he builds homes for low-income families) to his campaign work for Al Gore, John Kerry, Obama and both Clintons, Jon Bon Jovi has been a model citizen. He spent two years on the White House Council for Community Solutions, which, he assures me, actually 'meant we had to show up for meetings and do things'. He has said, however, that he'd never go into politics full time 'because fifty people hate you before you've even walked out the door'. He called it a 'shit job'.

'No,' he qualifies. 'They asked me who had the *better* job, me or Bill Clinton. I said "Me, because I get to keep the house and the plane".' So he'll never run for office. What about Springsteen?

'Bruce isn't a politician,' he says. 'Bono is more of a politician than Bruce.'

He stands up and moves across the room, throwing open the floor-length windows that look out over the Thames. Tour boats are moving up and down the river, and he's been bugged by a particular one all morning – someone is singing through a Tannoy in a high, male voice. 'Did you hear that? At first I thought it was someone falling off the bridge. I thought it was someone jumping. Heh heh.' His gloominess is strangely performative.

'Here's my take on Trump,' he says, getting back to work. 'The one demographic he's currently leading in is the white, older, *somewhat* educated male. That demographic are coming from a place of disappointment and fear. Fear because they don't know where their pot of gold went. Disappointment because they have now realised the American Dream isn't going to happen.

'Hillary has to embrace the voices of the Sanders millennials who are resolved to the fact that they are *not* going to own a home or have two cars, but are very concerned about the environment and their own futures. The Trump demographic, they're probably non-believers in global warming because they're uneducated and they're not paying attention. With regard to the Republican candidate, I wish there were a better mouthpiece to speak up on behalf of those people.'

When Jon Bon Jovi was twenty-six, he was hurt by a review that made fun of his inspirational music, which celebrated the simple values of loyalty and friendship and, as the writer put it, appeared to believe in Rocky Balboa running up the steps in Philadelphia. Then Jon had a realisation: 'I *live* that life,' he said. 'If I went to Washington tomorrow, I could probably meet the president. I *was* Rocky.' The American Dream happened for him.

Rock 'n' roll was not an impossible fantasy for the son of two ex-marines growing up in Sayreville, New Jersey. 'Thirty miles south from where I lived is this beach town [Asbury Park] that Bruce was able to make famous. The biggest place he could play at that time was literally a 3,000-seat theatre. He made the unattainable accessible.'

In 1973, the state of New Jersey lowered the drinking age from twenty-one to eighteen, largely to allow soldiers returning from Vietnam the right to purchase alcohol. He says the new drinking age helped him break into the music scene. 'At sixteen or seventeen, I could get into bars and play.' His parents were supportive, he explains: 'They said, "If you're going to be in a bar until three in the morning, at least we know where you are."' Like most of his peer group, he had no college aspirations. His cousin Tony ran a recording studio in Manhattan where – sweeping floors, like a hair-metal Kris Kristofferson – Jon was able to cut some demos. He got a record deal at twenty. 'Then it got a little bigger, and a little bigger until it got to the place where I am, and no one had dreamed of that.'

Like any good Italian boy, when he started making money, he tried to put a bit back. He bought expensive things for the family, such as holidays and cars. He warned them about a trip to Italy a year in advance so they could plan time off work. How long did it take his family to get used to their son having more money than them?

'They didn't get used to it,' he says grumpily. 'They still aren't happy with it. They're still resentful of it sometimes. They were like, "Of course I want it", then they got it and they were like, "I hate this fucking house". Really? You don't have to stay here . . .' At several points in our conversation, he slips into imaginary dialogues.

'We weren't the first and we're not the last. Elvis did it fifty years ago and I'm sure that Harry Styles did it two years ago. It's a confusing time when you become that guy and have the ability to share with your family the fruits of your labour. People think that money makes you smart. It doesn't. It makes you rich.'

His cousin Tony sued the band, claiming he'd had a part in developing their sound. His brother – another Tony – worked within the touring entourage in the early days. '*Two* of my brothers, actually,' he corrects. Are they still employees?

'Yes and no . . . Sorta . . . *Anyway.*'

* * *

It's not fashionable in the UK to talk about your rock band as a business. Sambora once explained that Bon Jovi 'created forty-two markets' by touring forty-two countries. 'I think you'd be hard-pressed to get someone to even fucking *name* forty-two countries,' he added. In 1989, they were guests of honour in Gorbachev's Russia. I ask Jon to recall his experiences of this historic moment. I can see his eyes through his shades and he's staring into the middle distance.

'Records were still on the black market. Even having a *list* of the records you owned could get you put away. The hotel rooms were definitely bugged. The bottled water was very salty and the meats were dried.'

He is starting to enjoy this. 'The entire Aeroflot fleet had glass noses so they could be converted at any moment into military aircraft. And they didn't have brooms. They're trying to sweep out the stadium on the first night, and it was a bunch of sticks tied together. I've not been back since.'

Jon Bon Jovi sees himself – as his band's name would suggest – as 'the CEO of a major corporation'.

The group is not, and has never been, a democracy. Once, the band's curly-haired keyboard player, Dave Bryan, was asked whether this bothered him and he said, 'I'm semi-bothered about it but not enough to ruin my life. You can't fight City Hall.'

Jon says it's the Henry Ford theory of management: someone's name has to be at the top of the paper. However, the group's appeal was always a double act – that brittle romance between lead singer and guitarist that lies at the heart of many classic rock bands, from Mick and Keith, to Steven Tyler and Joe Perry of Aerosmith, who may grow to loathe each other but stay together for the sake of the songs. Sambora – multi-instrumentalist and a flamboyant guitar hero – explained his role in the band like this, in 2009:

'I've always had it in my head that the success of our band was going to be our leader being very, very happy – and I tried always to be there for him as a friend, and from a musical level, and from a business standpoint. If I can help Jon be in a great mood as much as possible, I'm going to do it and that's what I've put on myself as a responsibility.'

Jon, who is clean-living, and Richie, who is not, kept it going for a long time. In the early '90s, Bon Jovi nearly split but were saved by group therapy at the hands of the psychologist Dr Lou Cox, who runs a company called EgoMechanics in New York.

'It was fabulous,' says Jon. 'We got the idea from Aerosmith. He wasn't like Brian Wilson's guy [the Svengali Eugene Landy]. He got his hourly fee and he left.'

I called Cox at home: he was a kind, avuncular voice on the end of the phone. He told me he made Bon Jovi act out their feelings for one another. 'I would have them be angry at each other in a kind of role play, just to find out they could do it safely and not kill each other.' He talks about family dynamics being laid down early – certain prohibitions against 'speaking up'. And about the honeymoon phase in the life of a major rock band 'when they are literally in love with each other . . . Then you have your first fight and the air goes out of the balloon. How do you manage, going forward, when it isn't all wonderful feelings?'

Cox describes the relationship between Bon Jovi and Sambora as 'such a strong bond, and such a painful one in the unravelling of it'. They have not spoken in three years. On 3 April 2013, Sambora failed to turn up to a concert in Calgary because of alcohol problems. Jon donated £100,000 to Calgary's homeless to atone for his partner's behaviour. Richie was told, sources claimed, to clean up or get out (he was also told, in the source's words, to lose his 'stream of Hollywood bimbos'). So he got out. And the turmoil began.

'Would you like a cup of tea or a glass of water?' Jon says. He stalks out of the suite and returns with a cup of green tea and a cup of black tea in two more fine china cups. Then, standing above me, he executes a strange stretch, arms above his head, and says, a deep yawn in his voice, 'I'm sorry. You were saying. Turmoil and stuff . . .'

The cover of his new album, *This House is Not for Sale*, the first he's ever recorded without Sambora, depicts a striking black-and-white photo of a Gothic house with colossal roots going deep into the soil.

'The house is a metaphor for my band and my life. This big, proud, rock of a stone house with deep roots that's in disarray. It's tired, it's beat up – this was symbolically *me*. Milk and sugar?'

Did he think, when Richie left, that Bon Jovi would end?

'Absolutely not. In all deference, God bless my friend Richie, there was *never* a question. No. No. We wrote some great songs together, and I love the guy, and our voices together were absolutely magic. But there is a very definitive line between wanting somebody in the band and *needing* somebody in the band.' Ouch.

What about the mechanics of physically writing songs without him?

'It's of no consequence to me. I have either written or co-written every song we have ever done. There's never been a question of: *am I able?* I've written number-one songs on my own [the theme from *Young Guns II*]. I know how to do this. There is no *question* that I know how to write a song.'

It is part of the business plan of all the biggest rock bands to stay together –

'– I know.'

– no matter what –

'– I know. And you know something? It is *beautiful* to be in a band when you are a young man. But when the day comes that you choose not to share your art any longer, then, *amen*! I'm okay with it!'

But he's not finished.

'The *circumstance* was what jarred. The *way* that he did it. Nobody saw *anything* coming – unfortunately for us, we had to play that night. He *couldn't* show up. The guy that filled in the last time Richie was in the rehab, I called him up and I said, "Do you still have that notebook with all the chord changes in?" He's been there ever since.'

In his younger years, he tells me, optimism was a 'cloak I felt comfortable wearing'. He'd be so pumped with adrenaline, he once said the reason he couldn't stand still on stage was that if he did, he'd soil himself. Does he still benefit from that kind of stage fright?

'I'm not scaaaaaaared . . .' he muses. 'I've never been *scared*. I was so *über*-focused on wanting to be 101 per cent that you could probably drive yourself mad. But *never* fear. Life for me was never ever motivated by fear.'

What was the motivation?

Long pause. 'The exuberance of youth gave me blinders,' he says. 'But that exuberance could be perceived as cockiness, when it's really just confidence. Not cockiness.'

Does he still have it?

'I don't lack for confidence . . . No, wait. [*Really* long pause.] Maybe I *do* lack a little of my old cockiness. I should get a little more of that swagger back. I'm a little different now than I used to be.'

Shortly after Sambora's departure, his drummer, Tico Torres, needed an emergency appendectomy before a gig in Mexico ('No big deal. I mean, we've got 100-plus people on the crew who had to be sent home for a couple of weeks but fine . . .'). The rescheduled date came around – and Torres had a gallbladder attack on the way to the airport.

'Imagine what was going through *my* fucking head,' he breathes. 'Richie doesn't show up, and then I turn around and there's no drummer either? And it's just me and Dave? I feel like I'm the monkey and he's the organ grinder. God. Fuck!'

He sighs deeply. Then pushes on.

'Think of the *backbone* it took for me to play twelve stadiums like that. We were in Rio – and I was one night, and *Bruce* was the next night. But I was like, yeah, let's fucking *go*. I ain't afraid of *any* band. And we went out there with a drummer from a cover band, and a guitar player that I barely knew, and I said, "Let's fucking go, 80,000 people!" That takes *backbone*. I should have cancelled. But there was not a chance in hell. The *shit* that I had to go through on that last tour. I have *earned this grey hair.*'

The Jon Bon Jovi/Richie Sambora dynamic was extremely physical. They would occasionally kiss on stage. Jon spent three decades with an arm draped around Richie's neck. He drapes his arm around the neck of the new guy now, but it doesn't look right. He struts and whirls a bit less, seems more aware of himself. How did it feel to look up and see that Richie was no longer there?

'It sucked.'

Did you miss him?

'Yeah. I swear on my career, and on my children, there was no fight. He has [he waves an imaginary bottle] issues and he can't deal with them. There's *obligations*. You're not twenty. You *have* to show up. Get help, okay? I'm here to help. You don't want the help? I can't force anybody to make lifestyle choices.'

Increasingly, pop stars pull out of gigs for reasons of personal chaos. Last month Justin Bieber walked off stage because fans were annoying him. Zayn Malik cancelled shows due to anxiety issues.

'There is a generation of anxious young men and women who are being diagnosed for the first time – and maybe it was always there,' Bon Jovi begins. 'I get it. But let me give you a little education, motherfucker. Jane just saved up for three months to buy that ticket. She travelled on a train to get there. And she is not going to be able to get a refund for her hotel room, or her travel, or the day she took off from work, or the babysitter she paid for. And the 120 families that are affected when they didn't get their pay cheque at the end of the week because you didn't show up for the fucking show . . .'

* * *

A few weeks later, on the other side of town, Richie shows up for his own gig at the O2 Arena, as part of the BluesFest weekend. The performance is spontaneous, to say the least. He stops to tie his shoelaces, swigs from a mug and switches his famous hats at random. He brings on Bruce Springsteen's guitarist Steve Van Zandt for 'Livin' on a Prayer' and they screw it up. (This is downtime for Steve: Springsteen, at sixty-seven, has recently started doing four-hour shows.)

Richie's hair is wild like a bird's nest. His girlfriend, the guitarist Orianthi – who was booked to play on Michael Jackson's doomed final tour – is a strange figure under a red hat, polished but remote. There are twenty-six years between them: whether it's a full-on Sid and Nancy affair or a business arrangement, no one quite knows. Sambora roars out blues standards he learned as a boy. 'Steve is playing again afterwards! Come! I'll chip in for tickets! I'm playing too, by the way!'

There is a certain chaotic freedom in it. He kicked off this tour by saying he intended to go without underwear. 'Richie is pushing the need to be his own separate self,' the psychologist told me. The band came back to him for help again when the 'Richie thing' got to a certain level. 'We had meetings and tried to work that through . . .' They went as far as they could. Perhaps, when your therapy and your rehab all comes as part of the package offered by the company you work for, the only way of changing your life is by becoming unfit for service.

For Jon Bon Jovi, it all seems to have come a bit too soon. The future feels uncertain. There is always politics, if he can get his head around not being liked. I ask him whether he will get a role in Hillary's council. He has appeared at half a dozen campaign events with her and is currently on the cover of *Billboard* magazine with Bill.

'I will be the secretary of entertainment,' he predicts ironically. 'I've been blessed to know them for twenty years now. I call her Mrs C out of respect. I would never dare call her Hillary and him Bill.'

Do they call you Mr B?

'No.'

I ask him if he knows Trump personally.

'I've met him a number of times,' he says. 'He's always been like that. He has played this like an episode of *The Apprentice*. All he had to do was get rid of the other contestants, and like the host of any TV show, he doesn't have to know a lot.

'This is *my* fear,' he says, standing up and addressing me with great focus, as though preparing to drop the mic. '*My* president, Al Gore, was SO much smarter than George W, but everyone walked away and said I'd rather have a beer with *that* guy. Holy fuck. If that happens on Tuesday morning, it's the end of the world.'

Poor Steve Perry of Journey had different emotional baggage to Jon Bon Jovi. He had suffered a rejection of the type that only ruthless commercial prog bands inflict on their high-singing frontmen. What happens when your body conspires against you, and then your bandmates pile in too? Perry, co-writer of 'Don't Stop Believin'', once the most-downloaded song of all time, had been ejected by Journey when he refused to have a hip operation on their advice. They carried on without him and enjoyed a global renaissance with a replicant twenty years younger whom they'd got through a YouTube audition. The same thing happened to Jon Anderson of Yes: his replacement's name was Benoit David, and he was also twenty years younger. He could not only hit the high notes but run around in adidas trainers too. (Eventually, Benoit stopped being able to hit the high notes. He quit in 2012, after Chris Squire mocked him about it on stage, playing an ugly bit of bass to mimic his wobbly voice.)

I was drawn to Perry because he'd been living reclusively while his band milked their big tune around the planet. An odd fellow, he made much of his wounded child. He was wistful and persuasive. I found it fascinating that he'd left Journey the first time, in 1987, to take care of his dying mother, and that he had recently begun a relationship with a woman who'd come to his attention because she had terminal cancer. Yet he was also a technician, dispassionate and ruthless about his music and the industry. The *New Statesman* photographer shot him in a record company office, at a leather-bound desk with gold discs on the walls and his fingers steepled like a media mogul. I was drawn to him for his ageing vulnerability, his giant ego and his extreme oddness. It is the perfect combination for me, and it features more than once in this book.

I could never quite work out why the piece was consistently in our 'most read' list, given that it fell so far outside the usual content of the *New Statesman*, but I got my answer when, putting this book together, I came across a viral YouTube video all about my interview, presented by a man in sunglasses in front of a stars-and-stripes flag. The video was enigmatically titled 'The New Statesman Interview is Not Typical': my article, the presenter reassured, was 'an outlier and not one we need to focus on'. Steve Perry's interviewer (a man, they assumed) was 'notorious for taking things out of context' and making stuff up, he'd been advised. My article 'reeked of horseshit' wrote one fan, in the comments below.

I watched on, heart racing, to see what I'd got wrong. One major grievance, explained the presenter, was the fact that Steve had said 'fuck' in the interview, though on this, he defended me, pointing out that Steve also said 'fuck' at his induction to the Rock and Roll Hall of Fame in 2017, so that particular word was not necessarily added into the transcript by the writer. It transpired that the main objections to my piece were from fans incensed at how Steve had talked about his bandmates: was it fair to compare being kicked out of Journey to being bullied at

high school? 'At least clarify,' said the presenter, to an imaginary
Steve, 'and say, I'm completely over that now!'

Steve Perry: 'Songs should be like pancakes'
New Statesman, 2017

In the small hours of 14 June 2007, the Queen guitarist Brian
May sat worrying at his computer. The American rock band
Journey had fired another lead singer. Forty-one-year-old Jeff
Scott Soto had been erased from the group's website – shed,
Brian observed in his blog, like a used pair of boots.

It wasn't that Brian didn't sympathise with the pressures on
a middle-aged rock band burdened with touring millions of
dollars' worth of hits when their original frontman was indis-
posed. He laid out Journey's options. 1. Throw in the towel.
2. Find a look- and sound-alike. 3. Go out under a different
name ('unrewarding'). 4. Find a new frontman who steals a bit
of the limelight for himself.

Journey are responsible for 'Don't Stop Believin'', the most-
downloaded song written in the twentieth century. They have
had five lead singers to date. The single component they've spent
three decades cyclically seeking to replace is the voice of their
frontman, Steve Perry, who came and went, and came and went
– then disappeared. Any Journey singer needs to sound *exactly*
like Steve Perry, and that is not easy. He must have a high 'tenor
altino', reaching F#2 to A5, with a tone somewhere between
Sam Cooke and Aretha Franklin. The first time Perry quit the
band was at the height of their fame, in 1987. He'd been nursing
his dying mother, and considered retraining as a neurologist.

The second time he left, ten years later, was because the band were pressing him to have a hip operation, and he refused. The girlfriend of keyboard player Jonathan Cain dimly recalled a guy from another group she thought could hit notes as high as Perry could – so founder member Neal Schon tracked him down and found him working as a maintenance manager for Gap, enjoying the security of his first pension plan.

The new singer, Steve Augeri, became known as 'Steve Perry with a perm'. He took Journey's hits to the arenas of middle America. As he did so, the real Steve Perry – who'd co-written those hits – rode a Harley-Davidson through the San Joaquin Valley in California, back to where he was born.

Perry has been a virtual recluse for twenty years. He sits before me in a Whitehall hotel, dissecting a chocolate muffin and carefully dabbing crumbs from his lap. He speaks in metaphorical language: he once said that leaving his band was like 're-entering the earth's atmosphere with no heat tiles on my face'. The San Joaquin valley reached 43°C in the summer, with fields of almond trees, cotton and alfalfa. The alfalfa became a symbol of his escape. 'It holds so much moisture that when you come to an area where there's an alfalfa field on the left and right, the temperature drops 15 degrees. So I'm out on my motorcycle, and those were the days before "helmets" [he makes quote marks in the air] and the wind is in my hair and all of a sudden, well, I cooled off.'

No one knew what Perry did next. There was a rumour he'd invested in a small bovine insemination business in California's Central Valley, but it turned out to be a rogue edit on Wikipedia. In what some might call a terrible irony, the band he left behind enjoyed an unexpected, international renaissance without him, attracting a new generation of fans. In the twenty-first century, 'Don't Stop Believin'' was used on the soundtracks of the Oscar-winning 2003 film *Monster, Scrubs, Family Guy, Glee* and perhaps most memorably, in the final eerie moments of *The Sopranos*. It inspired long-read journalism on the magic of song craft, and it even formed the plot of the Broadway hair-metal musical *Rock of Ages*.

Perry banked the cheques, but he missed the shows, because there was a *new* lead singer in the band who sounded just like him, and this time everyone was talking about it. Arnel Pineda was a Filipino fan who'd spent two years living homeless on the streets of Manila as a child – Neal Schon had found videos of him singing Journey songs on YouTube. Pineda has enjoyed the most successful stint in the job since the man he is imitating. Find a frontman who steals a bit of the limelight for himself, said Brian May, and 'the sky's the limit'.

When not riding his motorbike through the San Joaquin Valley, Perry attended the local fair, which came to his hometown in June as it had done in his childhood. 'I was drawn to the circus life, because they'd come into town – it was lights, Ferris wheels, it was moving, it was fantasy – and the next thing you know they're gone,' he says. The circus was, he admits, not unlike a rock band.

'I saw *Pinocchio* as a child, and there was something *evil* about this special place where all the children could go. They'd go on the rides, but their ears would grow – and they turned into asses, actually, I guess.'

Rock bands are a ruthless business, but in Journey it's hard to say who holds the power – the mutable frontman who forced the band in and out of hibernation for a decade, or the founder member who turned the frontman's voice into a million-dollar franchise. Perry once claimed that he'd never felt part of the group. Schon replied: 'How can you "not feel part" of something you're almost *completely* controlling?'

They only communicate through their lawyers now. But their songs play in every sports bar and mall in America, instantly and innocently evoking the pain and passion of ordinary human life.

Perry has watched his replacements come and go, but once, he was the replacement himself: in 1977, aged twenty-eight, having failed in several bands, he'd returned home to work, mending coops on his uncle's turkey ranch, when *he* got the call from Neal Schon, asking him to join a jazz fusion band who couldn't get a hit. Perry asked his mother and she advised him to go for it. Schon tried him out by bringing him on the road and telling everyone he was the roadie's Portuguese cousin. He sang a song at soundcheck when the official singer was away from the stage.

The clichés – 'married to music', 'a band is like a family' – are well worn, but for the generation of men who became millionaire rock stars in the '70s and '80s (for it is men, and it is one generation), they are the only way to understand their motivations, not least because it is a language they invented themselves. Solo albums were referred to by Journey's manager Herbie Herbert as cheating on your wife (both Schon and Perry cheated). Of the hip operation stand-off, Perry says: 'When they told me they checked out some new singers, it's like *your* boyfriend saying "Look, I really love you, but I need to know if we're getting married or not because I've checked out some other chicks."'

But it was more than that, wasn't it? They were telling him they'd only take him back if he underwent major surgery.

'OK,' says Perry. 'It's like saying, "By the way, drop a few pounds, too. Get your nose fixed at the same time." FUCK OFF.' He then asks if we can talk about his new record, *Traces*, his first in twenty-five years.

When Perry was sixteen years old, he heard 'I Need You' by the Beatles, released on the *Help!* album, and he felt they could have done better. Why had they done a kind of bossa nova he wondered, when it clearly cried out for R&B? He has reworked the song on his new album, which he wrote and produced on his own. 'No one had their foot on my neck saying, "Are you done? Are you done?" FUCK OFF,' he says.

When he was very young, Perry would 'mumble hook lines' for potential songs, and it was in Journey that he was able to 'apply everything I had ever dreamed of'. Their audience – suddenly full of girls – had a new and emotional relationship to the band via their commercial power ballads.

'You can't solo for eighteen bars,' he recalls telling Neal Schon, who was such a good guitarist that he'd been recruited by Carlos Santana aged fifteen, in the summer of 1969. 'You can have about *eight* bars. And if it's going to be eight bars, it has to be something beautiful.'

The first time the pair were put together to write, they finished Perry's love letter to San Francisco, 'Lights', in about ten minutes. He describes a song idea as a 'sketch' – a framework of chord changes, a couple of melody ideas and a loop for rhythm. 'But *my* problem is, I hear it completed already.'

Songs, he says, should be 'like pancakes – stacked high with layers of feeling'. Modern writing is an 'industrial assembly line because everyone's on the grid. There's twenty people writing these songs. They're trying to maximise the individual assignments, like when they're making a film, to increase the opportunity for a hit. But a song should be all about selling a *feeling*.'

Selling a feeling – is that the essence of power ballads?

'It's the essence of music,' he says.

'Don't Stop Believin'' has had a lot of analysis in recent years, as interest has grown in the industry's backroom magic. It is a power ballad with a strange minimalism, full of barely-there figures – 'strangers waiting' and 'streetlight people'. Unable to sleep in a Detroit hotel room, Perry had looked down to the street and noticed the way in which walkers would pop up suddenly in circles of light. The lyric's 'midnight train' was a musical madeleine, designed to take you back to Gladys Knight. The song was self-consciously cinematic, but states that life is a movie that never ends. Its thin but powerful sense of hope was so abstract, it applied to everyone – from the gambler in the lyric, rolling the dice 'one last time', to the real John Doe hearing 'Don't Stop Believin'' in a bar on a Friday night. It started with a refrain written by Jonathan Cain: what Cain heard as a chorus, Perry heard as a 'pre-chorus' – suggesting that a 'chorus of choruses' should be held off until the very end. It does not appear until three minutes and twenty seconds, delaying the climax. Perry gets a bit antsy discussing it.

'I don't want to talk about the music because then you won't listen, and it won't be yours,' he says. 'Your definition – what the song does to you, and the next person – are totally different. You hear music differently based on your life, your experience, what you are. When something resonates with a massive number of people, that is exactly what is happening.'

In 2007, he was approached by HBO for permission to use the track in the final seconds of *The Sopranos*. He refused to give it over without knowing what scene it would accompany, concerned that the entire Soprano family were going to 'get whacked' to the song. For a few weeks, he was one of the only people in the world who knew how the series ended.

Another equally effective, modern-day licensing of the track was in Patty Jenkins' *Monster*, when the serial killer Aileen Wuornos, played by Charlize Theron, meets her lover at a roller rink. A jukebox and a skating rink were just the kind of places you heard Journey every day, growing up, reinforcing the sense of their music as part of the wallpaper of American life. Perry, now sixty-nine, loved high school, 'a magical time, when innocence is running your life'. Its memories are his songwriting metaphors: a concert venue, he says, rather strangely, is 'the backseat of a car'.

'Everything I write comes back to high school. I know it sounds funny, but everything. It all comes from the emotions I grew into during my adolescence. Those moments are not to be tossed away.' He becomes emphatic. 'If something means something to you, go back and get it and make it part of your life. And anyone who doesn't understand how important that is, you tell them to FUCK OFF,' he advises, before breaking off to reveal he is desperate for the bathroom.

Perry was born to Portuguese parents in 1949. His father, Ray, was a singer – a baritone – who had tried to break into the business, and performed in the local theatres of his hometown. What kind of music did he sing?

'"Pennies from Heaven",' Perry replies.

His parents eloped because his mother's father didn't approve of a singing career. He tells their story as though music were some kind of hereditary condition or family curse, which in the case of Perry, you kind of feel it might be. His parents split when he was eight years old, and he, an only child, moved with his mother to his grandparents' dairy farm – which might explain the rumours about his subsequent career. As with many rock stars, from Roger Waters to Lennon, the absent father was significant. I ask him why he became a singer.

'People don't become performers because they don't have needs,' he says. 'Singing, though it can be very lovely, is essentially a primal scream. And I was screaming pretty loudly – and quite big.'

He was an invisible child, he says, but also a silenced one.

'There was a lot going on but nowhere to take it. Things happened to me as a child that I still can't talk about – nothing to do with my parents, but things did happen. It happened to a lot of kids, as I find out.'

How old was he?

'About nine. But there was nowhere to take that stuff back then. One of my needs to perform was the need to get myself heard. Now, please, do understand, I'm not complaining, but there was nowhere to talk it out, so I got to sing it out instead.'

He spoke to a professional at the age of sixty-three about what had happened to him at nine. He was advised to do so by the woman he calls the love of his life, Kellie Nash, a psychology

PhD candidate. But like everything else that has happened to Perry, theirs was not a conventional story.

During his mysterious, fallow years, Steve Perry seems to have investigated an alternative career in film-making. He was 'shadowing' *Monster* director Patty Jenkins. 'I love editing, I love directing. So with Patty I watched and learned a lot.' Jenkins was working on a TV film called *Five* for the Lifetime Network, exploring the impact of breast cancer. Being a methodical director, she surrounded her cast with real patients in remission. One of them – Nash – caught Perry's eye. Jenkins then told him that Nash's cancer had returned, was in her bones and lungs, and that she was fighting for her life. He went ahead anyway.

'I'd lost my mother,' he says. 'I'd not reconnected with my father – which was another clean-up waiting to happen. I'd lost the grandparents who raised me. And I'd lost this career that I'd wanted so much, because I'd walked away from it.'

Was he so accustomed to losing things that a date with Nash didn't scare him?

'I don't know,' he says. 'I justified it by telling myself, *Well, she's a PhD psychologist. Maybe I need another shrink?*'

They had a year and a half together before Nash died in 2012. One night, she said, 'Promise me you won't go back into isolation, for I feel that would make this all for naught.' He repeats the strange words, wide-eyed: *all for naught*. It was then that he decided to return to music.

'Life gets undone,' he says. 'You try to come up with a plan, but it's good for ten minutes a day. Some people have an ability to make belief systems work for a lifetime, but I think they're hard to keep up.'

In 2014, he made world news when he turned up unannounced at a gig by the indie band Eels and performed their song 'It's a Motherfucker' along with two of his own. He'd not sung live for nineteen years but, explained the band's Mark Everett, 'for some reason only known to him, he feels like tonight in St Paul, Minnesota, it feels right'.

Perry, the once-invisible only child, still talks about Journey as a 'nucleus' he could never break into. It is fair to say that the band didn't want him at first – it was only under the orders of their manager that he was hired at all. They came to epitomise corporate rock. 'There are still things I don't like about it,' Neal Schon once said, 'but this is the way I make my living.'

You suspect that, creatively, both men might have been better off without the band – the jazz rock boy-wonder, and the hit-writing soul mogul who really wanted to be on his own. But you take whatever route to fame is presented to you – and you follow the money. 'I'd rather fail at being what I wanted to be,' Perry says, 'than be successful being someone I didn't.'

7

ONCE YOU ESTABLISH THE BRAND, YOU'RE A SLAVE FOR LIFE

Paul O'Neill

A year after I met him for this piece, Paul O'Neill, the mastermind behind the American rock band Trans-Siberian Orchestra, was found dead in the same hotel that he had put me up in, on the campus of the University of South Florida. I always thought it was odd that the band came to me at the *New Statesman* – that they'd sought out such a serious publication, and thrown so much money at the trip, when they made a living playing Christmas music to middle America. On reflection, O'Neill knew that he was dying – the band's website reported an unnamed chronic disease – and he was working on his legacy: a couple of big pieces, with us and the *Wall Street Journal*, and his Christmas prog odyssey, the first real rock 'n' roll franchise, wouldn't look so odd in years to come.

O'Neill's concern – his obsession – went far beyond the personal: he wanted to know where rock 'n' roll would go after its originators were turned to dust, and how this music could continue to make its way around the world in two centuries' time, the way Beethoven's still did.

Thirty prescription pill bottles were found with his body. He had all sorts of conditions, including a fused spine, and although the coroner's ruling was accidental death caused by a collision of methadone, codeine, Valium and various other things, I've always wondered if he went to the hotel to dispatch himself. His family home wasn't far away in Tampa Palms. He talked constantly about his daughter, Ireland Wilde, named after Oscar, whom he'd written into a lot of TSO's adapted fairy tales. She was to be the band's guardian after his time on earth, he said: she dropped him at the hotel in the morning and had to break into the room in the afternoon, where she found him on the floor.

I still remember the feeling of being around O'Neill, with his soft, high voice and his rabbity teeth: he only once or twice took off his shades, and his eyes were milky pale. He gave me a silver dollar from 1825, for good luck, which until recently lived in the pocket of my denim jacket (a jacket that eerily came back to me, whenever I left it on a train or park bench). I genuinely think that if I'd asked him for a deposit for a flat, he would have given it to me. O'Neill was unlike anyone I've met. He was armed, yet harmless; paranoid but overly trusting; weak, yet hugely powerful; clearly a genius, but he couldn't play a note.

He gave a total stranger $50,000 in cash: the strange, multimillion-dollar empire of Trans-Siberian Orchestra

New Statesman, 2016

He calls it 'whacking'. It began near his property on 12th Street, Manhattan. He'd get his driver to circle Union Square while he identified a suitable beggar, then he'd jump out, shove a hundred-dollar bill into their hand, jump back in and drive off. Soon, he realised that many of the people he was giving to were schizophrenic and he was scaring them out of their wits. So he started passing the money to his daughter because, he reasoned, they were more likely to accept it from a three-year-old girl. He gradually increased the amount he gave – from a hundred to ten, twenty, fifty thousand dollars in a roll of notes. Paul O'Neill and his daughter would drive around the square and she'd say: 'Let's whack 'em, Dad, let's whack 'em hard.'

*   *   *

One of the biggest bands on the planet remains unknown to much of the world. Trans-Siberian Orchestra (TSO) have spent much of the past decade on *Billboard*'s annual list of top music money-makers; they now play to a million people a year and have grossed more than $500m in concert revenues since they were founded twenty years ago. In 2014, they made almost $52 million in fifty-two days. They tour for seven weeks only, from November to January. To maximise profits, they split into two halves – one band for the West Coast of America and the other for the east – and play matinees as well as evening shows.

Their genre? Heavy metal Christmas music. TSO are a glittering chorus line of rock chicks and axe heroes in black tie and tails, suspended on wires or balancing high above the stage on hydraulic platforms playing rock 'n' roll mashups of 'Deck the Halls' and 'Dance of the Sugar Plum Fairy'. There are eighteen people on stage, 240 staff and forty trucks to transport them. The show, which looks like Pink Floyd-meets-Meat Loaf's *Bat Out of Hell*, employs eighteen lasers and 750 pyrotechnics. The band travels with two trailers of generators: they once blew out the electricity grid in Jackson, Mississippi.

TSO's creator, O'Neill, divides his time between New York City and Florida, where the band began. I speak to someone at a UK rock magazine who once had a phone call with him. 'Just don't get him on to Churchill,' he says.

The Morrisound Recording studio in north Tampa was once the nerve centre of Florida's legendary metal scene, playing host to many of the genre's nastiest acts, including Sepultura, Cannibal Corpse and Napalm Death. Like most luxury recording spaces, it hit hard times in the past decade. Then, in 2015, TSO bought it and turned it into their headquarters, Night Castle. It lies behind high gates and is staffed by polite young engineers with russet beards. Visitors are met with a large food centre stocked with six different kinds of mineral water and a pine-fresh smell not typical of the recording studios of the past.

O'Neill has taken on a slightly mythical status within TSO. The official photographer tells me that you rarely see him because he is 'so protected'. When in Tampa, he is accompanied by a driver-cum-security guard with the physique of a wrestler, whose name is Tracey.

O'Neill emerges grinning from a darkened doorway. He has the little, anthropoid legs of Jeff Beck or Mick Jagger (finished off with heavy biker boots) and the sprung stoop of one who has great nervous energy – a coiled way of moving along, like someone who is ready to help but equally ready to flee. He sits down, throws one knee over the other and gestures at a large analogue mixing desk, saying 'You don't see too many of these any more' in the quick voice of a native New Yorker.

He was born in Flushing, Queens, in 1956, one of ten children of second-generation Irish immigrants. His father, who had fought in France, worked for a telecoms company, put himself through night school and qualified as a history teacher. O'Neill's siblings are high achievers. He was 'always the dumb one'. At seven, he still couldn't read, so his mother kept him in the house for the summer and 'forced phonics down my throat' until he could.

As an adolescent in the early '70s, he performed at Manhattan folk clubs, though he is not nostalgic about it. He played guitar in productions of *Jesus Christ Superstar* and *Hair* – 'Well, illegal touring versions,' he qualifies. 'Everyone was doing it at the time.' He entered Jimi Hendrix's Electric Lady Studios at 52 West Eighth Street to produce a progressive rock band called Slowburn, but failed to translate the baroque melodies in his head into playable music, so he gave up and went to work for the infamous management duo Leber and Krebs, who broke Aerosmith and AC/DC. These were tough times – Sharon Osbourne's father, the manager Don Arden, would assert his power over rivals and clients by hanging them out of windows. O'Neill worked for Aerosmith as a tour manager and 'settler' – meaning, he explains, that he would carry a fee of up to $50,000 in cash in a briefcase that, for security reasons, was handcuffed to his arm.

He has the disconnected synapses suggestive of years of hard living and his soft voice flits between business, American sentimentality and early twentieth-century warlords at alarming speed.

'I'll tell you why Aerosmith don't play the UK,' he says. 'They can't stand the plumbing. They can't believe you don't have the mixer taps. You know Churchill was a fan of American plumbing, too?'

His long chin gives his face a perpetual expression of mischief. When he is not wearing his sunglasses, he keeps his pale, grey eyes shut. He says things like, 'The one rule of work is: don't do anyone any favours, because then they've got nothing on you.'

In the mid-'80s, he was booked to produce a band called Heaven but was ejected halfway through a project that could have been huge – a heavy-metal version of Bob Dylan's 'Knockin' on Heaven's Door', five years before Guns N' Roses did theirs. He'd also wanted to try out something else with the band – a mashup of 'God Rest Ye Merry, Gentlemen' and 'Carol of the Bells', played on electric guitars.

It wasn't your average business proposal: 'six rock operas, a trilogy about Christmas and one or two regular albums'. O'Neill put it to the Atlantic Records mogul Ahmet Ertegun in the mid-'90s and claims to have been written a blank cheque. 'Christmas is the holy grail,' he tells me. 'Dickens wrote five books about Christmas. So I said, "Then it's too big for one album, too."'

On TSO's first Christmas album, *Christmas Eve and Other Stories*, a young man wanders into a bar and learns the magic of Christmas from a mysterious old man; it has sold 3.4 million copies. Then there's *The Christmas Attic*, in which a child explores an attic on Christmas Eve; *The Lost Christmas Eve*; and the DVD *The Ghosts of Christmas Eve*. Sleevenotes include short stories written by O'Neill. A few years ago, he even produced a fifty-page novella called *Merry Christmas Rabbi*, which featured Nazis. Atlantic wouldn't let him turn it into an album 'because they were too freaked by it. Now it's on Amazon for, like, a buck ninety-nine.'

His plan was to create a modern-day *Nutcracker*, something whole families would come to see, year after year. 'I think we were in the right place at the right time,' he says. 'Even Grandma has been to Woodstock. It made it a lot easier for us to jump the generational wall. That's what I wanted to do with the Beethoven and Mozart, too. People treat the symphonies like they're museum pieces, but I think they scream out for electric guitars. The record industry acts as if people only like one kind of music. In truth, they like variation, which is why we have hamburgers *and* chicken nuggets.'

Symphonic rock was not a new idea. Emerson, Lake & Palmer threw Bach, Mussorgsky and Grieg into their prog concoctions forty years ago. 'I worship Greg Lake,' O'Neill says. 'Greg is the Obi-Wan Kenobi – he is the Socrates of prog rock.' Both Lake and Jon Anderson of Yes have joined TSO on stage, as have the Who's Roger Daltrey and Aerosmith's Steven Tyler.

I call Lake at his home in Guildford to find out what it was like. His version of the band's inception is different from O'Neill's. 'They are the most *peculiar* operation,' he says. He is sixty-eight and sounds a bit like Ray Winstone. 'I heard they came up with the idea of doing a prog-rock Christmas show and took it to the promoters, who told them it was a dumb idea. They have a friend in Cleveland, a small-time promoter, and they basically bullied him into doing it. And they got away with it. The more I talk to them, the more I realise that *they* don't really understand what the phenomenon is. On paper, it looks like a bad idea. A prog-rock Christmas show? Stop it. But it's like a cult.'

Backstage at Long Island, before the TSO show, Lake's new iPhone disappeared from his dressing room. He told a security guard, and ten minutes later the device turned up next to the urinals. O'Neill had gathered the entire crew and told them no one would receive their Christmas bonus if the phone was not surrendered. 'That's Paul for you,' Lake says. 'He is like the Mafia.'

Back at the studio, O'Neill plays me a YouTube clip of one of his West Coast singers, John Brink, doing a TSO showstopper called 'Back to Reason', a ballad about a father searching for his son. By the end of the song, Brink is crying. I ask where he sourced the tenor. '*Les Mis!*' he says brightly. 'I always go to Broadway shows to steal!'

Though TSO might sound like a racket, they could be making even more money. Tickets are capped at about $75. 'There is enough money for everybody,' O'Neill says. 'You don't have to gouge every last penny out of people.' With a $20m production, they have to sell out every night. When he started out, he could see Led Zeppelin at Madison Square Garden for $7.50, he says. 'And here's the sad thing – nowadays, the first twenty rows are empty because the only people who can afford them are corporations, and they're in the bar the whole time, making business deals.'

He says that Florida was destined to be the birthplace of his group because it is the home of both heavy metal and Disney World. 'I worship Walt Disney,' he says. He decided he was going to build an amusement park so clean that if you lost your three-year-old, you wouldn't worry. And you would just pay one price and all the rides were free. TSO is an ideal, too – charge the fans the lowest price and make them feel emotions they have never felt before.

'Aaaaanyway,' he says, spinning on his chair, 'time for more swag. It's all about the swag.' He heaves the four-disc vinyl version of TSO's 2009 concept album, *Night Castle*, on to his lap.

While Yes had their in-house artist, Roger Dean, TSO have Greg Hildebrandt. 'He did the most iconic painting of the twentieth century,' O'Neill explains. 'The original *Star Wars* poster.'

He opens a glossy tour programme. 'I said to Greg, "I want multiple pictures of Beethoven." And then I said, "I need you to Churchill him up a bit."' He shows me a sorrowful, white-haired Beethoven, thickset like a Disney character and bulldogish around the jaws, crouching over the body of a fallen woman. His index finger flies over the images. 'Here's the condemned banker who cooked the books. Here's the carousel from Coney Island, all broken. And here's my daughter, Ireland, on her unicorn. And here's the castle – I'm gonna build that, one of these days.' I ask him whether the fans know what all these symbols mean.

'That is one of the things we need to do,' he says. 'I *need* to explain this to the fans!'

* * *

Cut to a café in Tufnell Park, north London, on a cold February day. Anna Phoebe lives nearby with her children and husband, the BBC presenter Gavin Esler. She studied social policy and government at the London School of Economics. She was also a member of TSO for six years, from 2004 to 2010, eventually becoming the lead violinist.

Phoebe had played violin at university. On graduating, she went to New York for an audition where a woman in dark glasses said, 'There's someone I want you to meet.' She was twenty-two years old when she joined TSO and suddenly found herself performing to 20,000 people a day, executing knee slides while cranking out rock versions of 'Ode to Joy'. 'You're playing the same size stages as Springsteen or Bon Jovi and you're paid as a rock star, too,' she says.

The fee for the three-month TSO season covered her living costs for the rest of the year; it bought her a flat in Berlin and financed two solo albums. 'We'd be given $5,000-worth of Bloomingdale's vouchers at the start of every tour. Paul would say, "If you're gonna be a rock star, kitten, you've gotta look like a rock star."'

She explains that part of the business model was signing merchandise and meeting fans: between 700 and 1,000 people each night, after every show, and double that on matinee days. She mentioned in a blog that she liked banana bread; at a gig soon after, a fan turned up with several slices of the cake strapped to his torso ('I've been trying to get this into the venue for, like, three days,' he said). She received other gifts from followers: an ice sculpture carved in her image and CDs of TSO fans reading the Bible.

Middle America is the band's heartland; they don't often play college towns. In 2004, an electrical engineer from Mason, Ohio, programmed 16,000 Christmas lights on his house and had them flashing to TSO's song 'Wizards in Winter'. When a video of this was put online, it became an internet sensation. Two years ago, sixteen households in Yucaipa, California, synchronised an entire neighbourhood to the song, filming it from above with a flying drone.

'I learned more about America in that signing line than anywhere else,' Phoebe says. 'The people we were playing to, they were Sarah Palin voters at the time. The poorer the state, the bigger the audience and the more men in military uniforms. This was the height of the Iraq War. They're saying, "Can you draw a star for my son? He's seventeen years old and he's passed away in Iraq.'"

She says that O'Neill is 'kind of insane, smart, extremely kind – and in a very privileged position to be like that and be able to follow it through'. There are musical directors, Al Pitrelli and Bob Kinkel, to make his unplayable melodies a reality, and a business manager, Adam Lind, 'to take his twenty ideas and home in on the one that is going to make money – or not *lose* money'.

Once, in the studio garden, she saw what she thought was a crumpled bag of rubbish and realised it was a bundle of hundred-dollar bills that O'Neill had dropped by accident. At Christmas, the whole band would be given money in an envelope and were told to give it away within twenty-four hours to a member of the public. 'It's quite an addictive feeling. It makes you feel like Mother Teresa,' Phoebe says. 'He has created a world, and whether he sees an idealised version of himself, or what the world should be, or what the people around him should be, I don't think anyone really knows exactly what is going on in his head.'

* * *

When O'Neill and I finish going through Hildebrandt's artwork, it is dinner time. We move out to the car park, surrounded by staff, and he heads over to a BMW i8, which can go from 0 to 60 miles per hour in 4.4 seconds and retails for

$150,000. It resembles the Batmobile. Its doors peel upwards and O'Neill, as bendy and black as the machine itself, deposits himself in it, then changes his mind and joins me and Tracey in an armoured SUV.

'Have you got the baby?' he says.

'Don't worry, I've got the baby,' Tracey says. The baby is a large, black briefcase. It is too full to close and weighs at least 45lb. He tells me it contains the only copy of a forthcoming TSO project, *Running in the Passions of the Fairy Tale Moon* – the music and the full libretto.

'I still handwrite everything,' he says. 'I can barely master email. I learned to text two months ago.'

Our car is overtaken by the Batmobile, driven by one of the young engineers. O'Neill will follow us back in it. 'I know how to get home from the studio, but not from the restaurant,' he explains. 'I'm sorry. You're thinking, "I've come to America to interview a retard."'

We arrive at our destination and he takes the baby from the car. Its huge weight makes him lean to one side, like a thin tree in the wind. We enter a dark, nondescript restaurant in the basement of a hotel. He whispers something to the hostess that ends with: 'It's non-negotiable.' He orders a large steak that remains pretty much untouched and asks for an extra salt cellar, which he lines up next to the other one. He does not remove his sunglasses. He listens to everyone else talk and asks me how my bacon cheeseburger is, adding shyly, 'I have bacon-flavour toothpaste and bacon floss.'

He is less than comfortable. I cannot believe that he fears being recognised when few know what he looks like. I wonder whether the baby causes his anxiety, whether carrying the next multimillion-pound project in his hand at all times sends him back four decades to the briefcase handcuffed to his arm. He hesitates, grinning, then leans over and takes my wrist, plunging it into the left-hand side of his leather jacket and pressing my fingers around the thick, bobbly grip of a Glock semi-automatic pistol.

* * *

It was summer 1986 in Los Angeles. O'Neill's friend Ray Gillen was standing in for Glenn Hughes as the lead singer of Black Sabbath, after Hughes had injured his throat in a fistfight. It was early morning and the Rainbow Bar had chucked out, so O'Neill got his Ferrari and the two of them went to the twenty-four-hour Tower Records store on Sunset Strip. They bought a tape of Andrew Lloyd Webber's *Phantom of the Opera*, which had just opened in London, and drove around until 6 a.m. listening to 'The Music of the Night', saying: 'He's God, we suck, he's God, we suck.'

The idea of a rock band as a stage musical may be a desperately unromantic proposition, but it has taken root among a generation of rock stars trying to ensure that people play their music way beyond its creators' natural lifespan. O'Neill whispers that Queen came to see TSO shortly before they launched their West End musical *We Will Rock You* in 2002. Then came *Rock of Ages*, in which young musicians acted out the glory days of the Sunset Strip in a plot based on the narrative of the Journey song 'Don't Stop Believin'', which in turn has enjoyed a second life through the TV show *Glee*.

Journey now tour not with their original singer, who had hip problems, but with a Filipino fan they found on YouTube. Yes recruited a younger Canadian vocalist, Benoît David, to take the place of Anderson, another singer known for reaching notes that others cannot reach. Singers are always the first to go, says O'Neill, who has little attachment to individual rock stars. 'The human voice is just these thin Kleenex tissue muscles. They're not designed to scream on top of amps five nights a week. It's not a matter of *if* you are going to destroy these guys' instrument but *when*. That's why we have multiple lead singers – to allow the vocalists to rest. TSO can go into their eighties.'

There's an old-school heavy metal band scattered among the TSO chorus line, whose story is a litany of all that can go wrong in rock 'n' roll. Two brothers, Jon and Criss Oliva, had grown up playing Kiss and Alice Cooper covers in the car parks around Clearwater, north of Tampa. Jon had a voice that could do Robert Plant one minute and Freddie Mercury the next. 'I call it the Mel Blanc gift,' says O'Neill. 'You know, the guy who does all the sounds in *Looney Tunes*?'

They called themselves Savatage and, with O'Neill as producer, they conquered MTV in 1987 with a video filmed in an underground cavern featuring a dwarf ('Hall of the Mountain King'). But demons crushed the band. Jon wrote most of their second album in rehab. In October 1993, Criss was killed by a drunk driver on the way to a livestock festival in Zephyrhills, Florida, and Savatage went into a state of suspended animation.

'I knew we needed something to justify a band with no original members left,' says O'Neill, with no sense at all of how strange that sounds. 'I didn't want to see all those albums disappear. It's not about getting caught up in the person or the individual.'

In 1996, Savatage's 'Christmas Eve/Sarajevo 12/24' – O'Neill's longed-for mashup of Christmas carols – was picked up by a

New York radio station and metal band morphed into TSO. Their name comes from an unfinished rock opera about the Romanovs, just one of fifty Broadway musicals O'Neill claims to have conceived.

'Look, this band doesn't make sense on paper,' he concludes. 'When I started out with Savatage, I thought it would be like the Eagles. I thought I'd be living off the royalties by now. I did not foresee the collapse of the record industry. I had to find a way to make it work. I worry about the next Steven Tyler or Janis Joplin – where are they going to go? What a thousand generations took to build, a single generation can lose. I'm sure Washington and Alexander Hamilton worried about the future, too.'

Last July, TSO played the Wacken Open Air festival in Germany – a heartland for them, because of all the Beethoven. After dark, the site was hit by a storm, knocking down the sound system. While the stage was being repaired, O'Neill wandered around the camp, talking to punters, possibly in a cloak, like Henry V before Agincourt. He found two young men of nineteen who turned out to be Sunni Muslims from Iraq. About ninety feet away, he talked to two men from Iran who were Shia Muslims.

'During those three days of that festival,' he says, 'I can't imagine those four young men didn't bump into each other. And God forbid, two years from now, they end up in two different militias and they recognise each other, I'd bet everything I have that not only would they not pull the trigger, they would un-chamber their weapons and say, "Hey, weren't we together at a TSO concert?" It's hard to hate – let alone kill – somebody that you went to a concert with.'

* * *

The next day, O'Neill is jumpy. We're travelling to one of his properties to look at his treasure collection. He shows me CCTV footage filmed from the main entrance of the band's former studio in Tampa. On the noiseless laptop screen, in broad daylight, the stockinged head of a robber slides into the frame; he gets to work on the studio doors with a pair of bolt-cutters. '*Three* pairs of lady's pantyhose,' says O'Neill in horror, pointing at the robber's disguise. 'We were inside the whole time. I had my Glock and I didn't want to use it, but I would have.' When the burglar realises that the band is home, he beats a speedy retreat.

O'Neill has had problems with aggressive fans, too, which he passes over with a shudder. 'I hate evil,' he says, more than once. TSO's product manager Thomas Ayad, of Universal Music Group, was killed in the Bataclan terror attack last year. Today, as if to mirror O'Neill's increased anxiety, there is not one overstuffed briefcase but three.

Sitting next to me in the back of the car, he tosses a small box from hand to hand. He opens it to reveal a Fabergé egg containing a microfilm edition of fifty pages of the original King James Bible that was sent up in the Apollo 14 space mission. He says that he lets kids hold it, so they can feel history in their hands. It's not clear which kids he means.

We enter his property. I hear sighing and turn to find O'Neill splayed against a wall, throwing the five-point handle of a vault's combination lock from left to right as if wrestling with the wheel of a mighty ship. In the close confines of a walk-in safe, he pulls items from the shelves: first editions of proceedings from the trial of Thomas Paine from 1793, and Churchill's two-volume biography of his father, signed. He shows me signed first editions of

Dickens' *Christmas Books* and two original anonymous prints of *The Ballad of Reading Gaol* by Oscar Wilde, after whom O'Neill's daughter, Ireland Wilde, is named. (Wilde means as much to him as Churchill.) Then he gets out a picture book that Joan Jett gave him. A note says: 'Dear Paul. I hope you enjoy this reflection into the past and thanks for being a big part of mine.'

'Here's Louis XV borrowing a tonne of money in 1732,' he says, presenting me with a piece of parchment, 'and Benjamin Franklin building some forts.' There's a letter from Nelson from before the Battle of Trafalgar ('I wrote a rock opera about him') and a handwritten fragment of a speech by Reagan ('I *love* Ronald Reagan'). There are dozens of letters from Thomas Edison to his engineer, detailing every stage of the invention of the phonograph. He has the whole set, apart from one he gave to Steven Tyler.

He shifts a painting out of the way – a colourful scene of some rabbits, painted by Jon Anderson for his daughter – and pulls out the *pièce de résistance*: a gorgeous first edition of *Leaves from the Journal of Our Life in the Highlands*, signed 'To Lord Kitchener of Khartoum' by Queen Victoria. 'Can you *get* any more historic?' he asks. 'Kitchener went to Khartoum two days too late and saw Chinese Gordon's head on a spear.'

Finally, with embarrassment, he shows me a letter from George Washington to Thomas Jefferson, dated 1779. It has been badly crumpled in storage. 'Maybe one of these big heavy books will help?' He reaches for a giant edition of Livy and flattens the letter under it. 'Mister Livy, can you please help out poor George?'

He drifts out of the room. 'There's other stuff I want but I've got to stop because I'm losing track of it,' he says. 'My daughter says, "Dad, don't die and leave me with all this stuff. It's like King Tut's tomb."'

He wanders out on to the patio, where the sun beats down so strongly that he must be melting in his leathers. He pulls himself up to perch on a little stucco balcony, legs swinging, and for a moment he epitomises the contradiction at the heart of rock 'n' roll wealth: the baby boomers who bought the lifestyles of the landed aristocracy but insist on looking like pickled versions of the boys they were when they first picked up a guitar.

I ask him whether he's glad that his days with Aerosmith are over. His liver shut down in the '70s; he broke one of his vertebrae wrestling with bouncers. On the one hand, these stories are badges of honour; on the other, there is relief in his voice.

'Cocaine is Russian roulette,' he says. 'One person can walk away from it and another can't. I never thought I would live this long. My mother told me I wouldn't live past thirty. I was always falling through roofs. I still feel like I'm nineteen. I'm sixty. How did this happen?'

I ask him if he is happy. He says, 'Solon said to Croesus, "Don't judge your life a success or a failure until the very end."'

*   *   *

Despite O'Neill's obsession with the British empire ('Churchill understood India better than Gandhi did'), his band is cagey about plans to play in the UK. TSO first performed in London at the Hammersmith Apollo in 2011, to an audience of about 2,000, with just six trucks of gear. The boiler was broken, the auditorium was freezing and everyone kept their coat on. Ask O'Neill if he is coming back any time soon and he gives a small sigh.

'I think he'd settle for nothing smaller than the O2 Arena,' says Anna Phoebe, 'but, for a start, they'd have to get rid of all the narration in the show because British people do not like being told what to think.'

O'Neill's characters are simplified figures – Tiny Tims or Little Match Girls, or the brazier-hugging idiots savants of '80s Christmas movies. At the age of sixteen, working as a busboy in Hell's Kitchen, he received a hundred-dollar bill as a tip from a stranger and never looked back.

'They're selling the American Dream and yet "the American Dream" no longer exists,' says Phoebe. 'Even Barack Obama said it: what your father earns is more of an indicator of your future wealth than anything else. TSO sell the romanticised version – you can be poor, you can work hard, you can get yourself out of where you came from – and we don't relate to that. But he enjoys a challenge. His brain will probably work overtime to overcome this problem.'

'I don't necessarily think it will work over here,' Greg Lake says. 'I don't necessarily think they'd be doing themselves any favours. What is it, the money? They're not going to sell 100,000 tickets!'

I ask Lake whether he can see a future in which young stage-school kids play the hits of long-dead bands, giving them eternal life. 'I've seen a Japanese "version" of Emerson, Lake & Palmer, believe it or not,' he says. 'I felt quite ill. Fact is, who *is* going to interpret the classical music of today – which is rock music – when the original players are gone?

'It's hard to imagine what sort of currency rock music will have in a hundred years' time. I've played some biblical shows – 600,000 people in one go – and that era won't be easily forgotten. I've never seen that many people in one place. You wouldn't. Other than in a war.'

Two days after we spoke, Lake's bandmate Keith Emerson committed suicide after a period of depression connected with a degenerative disease that was affecting his playing. Before he hung up, Lake had told me about the last time he saw O'Neill: he presented Lake with a gift, one volume of the multi-volume memoirs of Winston Churchill, and told him he had put a bookmark in it.

'I opened it up and it's a thousand-dollar bill,' Lake said. 'Tell him he can "whack" me whenever he wants.'

* * *

The sun goes down on Tampa as we barrel along Interstate 4. O'Neill takes his shades off in the evening light. He says he wears them because he is afraid of going blind. His father has lost his sight, and blindness has affected nine members of his family. He is tired, and when he is tired, he speaks in military history.

Is the age of the rock 'n' roll hero over?

'It's all about the idea and real heroes grasp that. Washington didn't want to be king. He had an idea, which was America.'

Who will he hand his project on to?

'Some kid who hasn't been born yet. Abraham Lincoln came out of nowhere. He had ten days of schooling in his whole life. I had the ultimate gift in life, which was low expectations. I just feel lucky that it's happened and I just hope that no one catches on that I'm getting away with murder.'

He is fed up with talking about the band, but is too polite to say so. 'Thank God for Britain,' he says instead. Congress is a mess. Obamacare? Please. Trump is a moron.

He sings a couple of bars of 'Rule, Britannia!' soft and high.

'Seriously, it's like the last days of Rome here,' he says. 'But I think it will pull together. I believe in happy endings.'

8
BULLETPROOF TENTS AND MATING RITUALS

Kiss

Like Paul O'Neill, Greg Lake died shortly after talking to me for the Trans-Siberian Orchestra piece. I often think of his summation of the crowd at an ELP gig: 'I'd never seen so many people together, except perhaps in a war.' The minds of certain men of rock operate on a militaristic scale. Though there are character traits shared by many – conceit, ego, self-delusion – there are a few remaining who see themselves as quasi-political figures, ambassadors of Western might. Their songs knock down borders, providing those borders are belief systems other than their own.

When I suggested I meet Kiss in Moscow in May 2017, President Putin was well into his late period. At the May Day parade – a vast military display which closed down the centre of town – LGBTQ+ activists, protesting against the treatment of gay men in Chechnya, were being bundled into police vans. Gene Simmons was at the time frequently making the news for his anti-Islamic comments, a brief period of press-waywardness before he decided to shut up, or someone advised him to. I wasn't allowed to ask him about Putin.

Against the tightening grip of the real dictator, Kiss − well into their senescence − played to an audience too young to have lived through the Cold War, whose parents probably had pirate Kiss records pressed onto innocuous-looking vinyl in the '80s. Their make-up, their arresting image, took them to countries who would never hear their music on the radio, and once Simmons had established the black-and-white brand, he was a slave to it for life.

They were forty-four years into their career when I met them, and they retired for good five years later. Like Trans-Siberian Orchestra, their wealth, their pomposity and their endless concern with legacy manifested in a press trip more like 1977 than 2017: days and days with the band, no expense spared. Private dressing room interviews, a ride in a cherry picker at soundcheck and the view of Paul Stanley's pants from the pit as he flew over the crowd on a wire. I'm still picking the plectrums out of my eyes.

What happened when Kiss went to Moscow
New Statesman, 2017

When Gene Simmons decided he wanted to be a rock star, he made a deal with his mother: be in a band but show me how you're going to pay the rent. He had a variety of marketable skills at his disposal. At Newtown High School in Queens, Chaim Witz, only son of Flóra, who'd brought him to New York from

Israel, took stenography and typing classes. By thirteen he could out-type his teacher. By eighteen he was a 'tele-girl' (a temp) and found himself in demand with powerful female executives in Manhattan. With his feet, he worked a Dictaphone machine to take their letters – one pedal for go, one for stop and one for rewind. The then managing editor of *Vogue*, Kate Rand Lloyd, heard about the only male temp on the floor at *Glamour*. He became her Man Friday and fixed her hectograph, rexograph and mimeograph machines.

On 29 April 1974, he made his first television appearance on *The Mike Douglas Show* as Gene Simmons, 'The Demon', of the rock band Kiss. He picked his way across the studio floor on 30lb silver platforms, his abnormally long, seven-inch tongue thrashing about in his mouth like a skinned snake. In a whisper, he declared himself 'evil incarnate'. On the sofa next to him was the comedian Totie Fields. 'Is your mother watching?' she asked. 'Wouldn't it be funny if under all the make-up he's just a nice Jewish boy?' Eighteen months later, Simmons got a cheque from his record company for $1.5 million. He showed it to his mother and she said, 'Now what are you going to do?'

Up on the roof garden of the Park Hyatt hotel in Moscow sits Simmons today, his wiry hair, like black loft insulation, pulled into a ponytail. I've been taken to see him briefly, before an interview scheduled for two days later. Despite looking, in his own words, 'at best like a baby dog at birth', Simmons claims to have slept with 4,600 women, taking a record of each with a Polaroid camera. At sixty-seven, his latest conquest is Siri, whom he has programmed to call him 'My Lord and Redeemer' on a cellphone with a special Kiss case.

Simmons stands when a woman arrives; he analyses the size of your bag, wondering how you fit your make-up in it. He thumbs through photos of Kiss products on his phone: Kiss guitars, Kiss car wraps – and a Kiss Kasket, a limited-edition coffin, part of his funeral range. The murdered Pantera guitarist Dimebag Darrell was buried in one: affection runs deep for the cartoonish glam-metal compound, now in its forty-fourth year of music and merchandising. Among the expressions Simmons claims to have trademarked are 'rich and famous' and the Chinese word *xi*, meaning 'the West'.

Rehearsals for Russia's May Day celebrations float up from Red Square, operatic folk songs and the chug-chug of army boots being put through their paces. Over in the Kremlin, Vladimir Putin prepares a phone call to Donald Trump to talk about Syria. US–Russian relations have hit a new low. In recent months, Simmons has generated a steady flow of headlines from views that wouldn't seem out of place in a hard-line administration. Drug addicts should be sent to gulags, he said; paedophiles put to death. Islam is a 'vile culture', and don't even get him started on immigration. On the night of the national festivities, Kiss will play the Moscow Olympic Stadium to 15,000 people who'd rather hear 'Crazy Crazy Nights' than 'The Song of the Volga Boatmen'.

Will Putin be at the gig?

'If he is, he will not make himself known to me,' he says, drifting off to his room.

Gene Simmons' hoist, which enables him to float 30 foot above the stage, puts a great strain on his body because his costume gives him an extra 50lb in weight. He recently fell over on to his back and couldn't get up again, like a turtle. At the show, he will be spitting fake blood. But today's soundcheck is a sedate affair: a three-hour dissection of stage manoeuvres, the testing of winches and timing of feet. In plain clothes, the band's frontmen, Simmons and Paul Stanley, step on hydraulic arms and sweep out over the empty arena like two tree surgeons. Simmons noodles on his bass – snatches of *Peter and the Wolf* and 'The Pink Panther Theme' – but seems less interested in playing the well-oiled anthems of Kiss.

It's like watching a group of men congregate around a car they're refitting, or a hole they're digging in the ground. They seem completely absorbed – but every so often, with a sting, a guitar pick hits my face, 30 feet away at the side of the stage. Throwing their personalised, painted guitar picks at people is part of Kiss's mating ritual. Stanley greeted me remotely earlier by despatching a fistful of them via the tour manager, the way a man might order a drink for a lady across a hotel bar. Another pick hits my forehead. 'Hey, *Statesman.*' And another. 'Can someone lift her on to the stage?'

There are no women in the Kiss entourage, apart from one who carries the costumes and another who manoeuvres the large wheelie bins containing the make-up and cosmetic products the men administer themselves. Both employees are on the younger side. It was a different story in Moscow thirty years ago, as Jon Bon Jovi told me, when, at the first Western rock gigs in Russia, babushkas swept the stadiums with brooms made of twigs.

At the centre of the Kiss team is a man who will confirm this: Doc McGhee, the music mogul sacked by Jon Bon Jovi after McGhee was convicted for drug smuggling. In 1989, partly to get around his jail sentence in the US, McGhee collaborated with the Russian musician Stas Namin to bring Western bands to the country. Namin's grandfather was a Bolshevik statesman who served under Lenin, Stalin and Khrushchev. The Moscow Music Peace Festival happened on Gorbachev's watch. McGhee spent three days with the president at the Kremlin, offering him $10 million for the rights to a book and film of his life. You can't blame him for trying.

It was different putting on gigs in those days. You had to allow twelve hours for an eight-hour drive to account for the number of times you'd have to stop and bribe border guards with records, or wake Alice Cooper up from the tour bus and get him to do an autograph in order to be allowed on your way. McGhee brought his own ice from Scandinavia. You couldn't buy records in Russia but there was a feverish black-market trade on street corners in albums pressed on to old X-rays. A young interpreter joins the band one night and talks about her parents' time with bright eyes. 'It's different now that you have access to everything,' she says. 'It doesn't matter so much any more.'

Outside the hotel, the teenage boys keeping a three-day vigil for Simmons and Stanley might disagree. Kirill and Daniel have flown four hours from Tomsk, Siberia, for the concert. They are fourteen and first saw the band's white faces in a magazine. Dmitri, in his thirties, knew of Kiss only from some famous graffiti in Red Square: their double 'lightning S', banned in some countries for its proximity to Nazi insignia, appealed to his teenage brain. I bring Stanley's guitar picks out of my pocket. Twenty boys scrum violently like pigeons on a loaf of bread.

Back at the soundcheck, Kiss leave the stage in strict formation, 20 feet apart, each flanked by a member of staff as though surrounded by great crowds. It's a small hint of the invisible rules, the secret rivalries, covenants and compromises that allow opposing characters to exist side by side for decades in the classic rock bands. Simmons is the face of Kiss, but Stanley's limousine always arrives first – 'because he's the boss,' someone mutters. Stanley applies his make-up – a soft-faced, effeminate character known as The Starchild – in a private room, while Simmons packs into one dressing room with the rest of the band, playing the Kinks at loud volume.

Gene takes more than two hours to complete the process 'because he is talking all the time,' Stanley says. 'It's very hard to do it when your mouth is moving. Me, I can do it in half an hour.'

Stanley drifts down the corridor and, taking my chances, I slip into his dressing room behind him. It's a triumph of interior decorating, the Soviet-style lime-green walls and strip lighting obscured by satin drapes like a black-and-white version of the purple 'foo foo room' that Prince used to set up backstage. There is a black satin bed should he need a lie-down for any reason. There are weights of various sizes and a medicine ball – and in the corner, lit with old-fashioned make-up lights, his own cosmetics area.

'Here is my clown white,' he says softly, picking up a pot of the thick, sweat-resistant foundation they discovered in the '70s. 'And here are my puffs.' Why do they do their own make-up?

'Because it's a ritual,' he says. 'It's a rite of passage. I can't imagine sitting in a chair like a dummy and having somebody painting my face. It is putting on my uniform. It's my colours. And it's better for me in here than the chaos in the other room.'

Stanley takes a seat on a leather sofa, one leg crossed over the other, eyes on the floor. On his mirror, there is a photo of him playing the burned and disfigured lead in *Phantom of the Opera*, a Toronto production, in 1999. Above it is written 'Star of the Show'.

He was born Stanley Eisen, 'a little fat kid', deaf in one ear as a result of microtia, a deformity of the ear canal. He was raised on opera and Broadway. As a young man, he drove a taxi. He speaks in careful but lyrical sentences, and gets straight down to business.

'I always found it interesting that a lot of the critics were *venomous* in their dislike of us,' he says. 'It's something that perhaps they should work out on the psychiatrist's couch. Because the dislike for the band was so out of whack, so out of proportion, you almost have to look at someone and go, "Who beat you as a child?!"'

In 1978, the *NME* ran an interview with Simmons under a headline it had also used for Freddie Mercury: 'Is this man a prat?'

'The fact is that what we do has endured,' Stanley says. 'What we are doing has no expiration date. Some of the critics who embraced us when we were struggling spurned us when we became successful. Once you gain acceptance, you have "sold out". Well, sold out means the place is full. I never felt the need to counter the vitriol because I was too busy succeeding.'

Stanley Eisen is the son of Austrian and Polish Jews who escaped to New York via Amsterdam. Simmons' mother was born in

Hungary and spent many months in a Nazi concentration camp in Austria, where she saw most of her family put to death. She fled to the new state of Israel, where her only son was born, and moved to New York in 1957 after her husband deserted the family. Stanley and Simmons have survived many line-up changes in their band: they once had a member called Vince Cusano, whom Simmons renamed Vinnie Vincent, because the old name sounded 'like a fruit vendor'. Their tour manager, Steev Toth, has Hungarian and Jewish ancestry. The guitarist Tommy Thayer is the son of Brigadier General James Thayer, who liberated 15,000 Hungarian Jews from a concentration camp in Austria which, Simmons thinks, may have been his mother's.

'We are children of immigrants,' Stanley says. 'We are children of the post-Holocaust. We have a certain mentality, and a mindset, and a work ethic. I was taught you don't take anything that isn't yours, don't take anything that you don't deserve and don't take anything you didn't work for.

'We are, more than ever, brothers. That doesn't mean we want to spend all our time together. I have said to Gene before, "I'd shoot myself if I had your life".'

Why?

'Because what is appealing to Gene in life is not my desire. And my life is boring to him.' He stretches along the whole length of the sofa, beginning to relax.

It is 4 p.m., and from behind a Superman curtain down the corridor, the muffled sound of '60s British music signals the start of the transformation. 'All right?' barks a cod London accent. I can make out Simmons' silver platforms propped up on the top of a crate, but I cannot see his face.

'He is the strangest guy,' their manager Doc McGhee told me the previous night in the hotel bar. 'I mean, the strangest *legitimate* guy I know – I know bipolar guys, guys with mental problems. He has NO friends.'

Simmons' family life played out in 2011 on a popular reality-TV show called *Gene Simmons Family Jewels*. For decades he had been 'happily unmarried' to the erotic actress Shannon Tweed, the star of films including *Meatballs III* and *Indecent Behaviour*. The couple have two children, but they did not live together.

'The show made him behave differently towards his family,' McGhee told me. 'It showed him from different angles and he didn't like what he saw.' The idea inspired McGhee to conceive another programme called *Extreme Combover*. 'You do this thing to your hair, and you think it looks good, but everyone else sees it from a different angle. My first two contestants would be Gene Simmons and Donald Trump.' Simmons appeared with Trump on *The Celebrity Apprentice* (Trump fired him), but *Extreme Combover* has yet to be made.

The Superman curtain is ajar and I can see Simmons in profile, emerging from behind a wall. The next time I look up, he has pulled himself across the room on his wheelie chair and sits facing me with legs thrown apart, groin open, presenting a silver codpiece.

'All right?'

Nothing can prepare you for the Kiss make-up transformation in the flesh, and the psychological shift it occasions in both onlooker and band. One by one, a series of giant, seven-foot space clowns, taller than anything else in the building and whiter than the moon, emerges, each with a look of surprise on its face.

KISS

High up the door frame of Stanley's dressing room peers a face like a sad mime, one eye a black star, red lips pulled into a feminine pout. He takes to the corridor with the careful elegance of a giraffe – and there is something new in his manner; glorying in eye contact now, waving his platform boots in my face. Suddenly the biggest mystery of all – how Kiss can claim to have got so much sex – is a mystery no more. The white faces are frozen as men of twenty-five. And the costumes, if you can call them that, directly facilitate inappropriate physical interplay: all rules of personal space are broken as, without thinking, you find yourself touching and poking them. A tail emerges from Paul Stanley's satin backside and my hand closes around it.

'Is it real rabbit?'

'Will you call me a fraud if it's not?'

Simmons, hair pulled into a five-inch topknot and with giant leather bat wings under his arms, is a different beast. His entire body is plated in armour – part orc, part titanium warthog – and where Stanley is charming, he bears the sense of an older, more medieval conquest; of pillage and of poor women taken by force.

He talks little, but what he wants, he gets with his body. He pulls the make-up girl in for a hug – by the hair. I am told under no circumstances to get in his line of vision after the show, because if I do so he will 'slime' me with fake blood and sweat. He pretends he hasn't seen me, then backs me into the wall with a little too much force, his spikes digging into the backs of my hands.

* * *

The next morning, up in the second-floor restaurant, Simmons has breakfast with Shannon Tweed. They finally married in 2011. Tweed, sixty, is dressed in pink and flicking through *Time* magazine. Simmons' thumbnails are short and wrecked, black with last night's make-up. Silver hair curls on his chest. In his mirrored sunglasses and military-style shirt with gold adornments, he looks like Gaddafi at leisure. He moves my Dictaphone closer.

On the way home from school, he would go to the library and read the encyclopaedias. That's where he learned that Edward VI used to torture animals. 'When you're king, who's going to tell you not to skin a frog alive?' he reasons. I ask him about his childhood heroes. 'I didn't have heroes,' he says. 'Not real people. My heroes were fantasy. My heroes didn't have flaws – Superman and Einstein and ethereal, semi-godlike figures. Because whenever you have a real-life hero, it's fucking pathetic how they wind up – like Elvis, naked and bloated on the bathroom floor.'

He picks up his phone and summons Siri to bring up a picture of the British dish of faggots in gravy. 'Explain this to me – what the hell is that?' he asks. 'The English were always a smaller people because of the food. After the war, you had beans on toast and what the fuck else did you eat? In the States, we had butter and pancakes – it was always a big supply. If Jagger got into my outfit on seven-inch heels spitting fire and flying through the air, he would be *exhausted*. Put Bono in my outfit? Good luck.'

It seems a good time to ask him how he feels on stage.

'I can glibly speak about it,' he says. 'But in real terms I am aware that there is a transformation that takes place here –' he points at his ribs. 'I am aware that my chest cavity expands, and my heart is pumping, and the only thing I can compare it to is when a boxer can be backstage toying with his little girl, then go into the ring and be oblivious to the audience, and have this *kill* thing.'

Tweed has looked up the root of the word 'faggots' and reads from her phone in her slightly anaesthetised, Beverly Hills voice: '*A bundle of pieces of iron or steel to be welded, rolled or hammered together at high temperature.*'

'It's a question of semantics,' Simmons replies. 'Though I'm not anti-semantic . . .'

I ask him about the reality show that changed his life. 'I didn't like watching myself,' he says. 'I mean, I *love* the way I look, other than these affectations [he gestures to his sunglasses]. They even filmed my facelift – I had my face thrown over my shoulder like a scarf. But in the course of the show, I realised what an asshole I was.

'When I was a little kid, my mother would smack the shit out of me as soon as I went out of line. When I went off on my own, I was my own police in certain areas. I've never knowingly got high or drunk or smoked a cigarette, because I didn't want to break my mother's heart. But other than that, I was self-entitled. I'm an only child, so I look to myself for everything. Part of that process is you get deluded with the sound of your own voice. And although I am fairly educated, that doesn't mean I have wisdom.'

In the early 2000s, Simmons launched a magazine called *Tongue*, which ran for five issues, with an emphasis on the celebration of the female form. There will be a new magazine called *Mogul* – 'high-end pop culture, entrepreneurial' – and he shows me a mock-up of the cover with him on the front. He has published several books, including *Ladies of the Night: A Historical and Personal Perspective on the Oldest Profession in the World* and the business title *Me, Inc: Build an Army of One, Unleash Your Inner Rock God, Win in Life and Business.*

'I'm a curiosity to people in high finance,' he tells me, 'because I haven't been there and done that, but I have made a decent living. They can't put a finger on how and why it has worked for me.' He adds, of music: 'What other job would give you money in advance and you never have to pay it back?'

He has read Trump's books. 'All business books are lies,' he says. 'Ten secrets of success? People want a short cut to life. You have a duty to educate yourself, and from there on it is fucking hard, back-breaking work. Forget "inherent" and "intrinsic" and other big words like "gymnasium". Nothing happens without hard work.'

In 2011, Simmons endorsed Mitt Romney, saying that America needed to be in the hands of a businessman. 'Government *is* business,' he says today. 'People don't understand that. A lot of people hate Trump, I get it. I know the man —'

'Which is not to say you like him,' Tweed mutters.

'He doesn't give a fuck what anyone thinks. You're talking about a guy who does *not* care and will go to war against all media. I want a businessman in there. Not someone to dole out favours, raise your minimum wage, meantime countries get deeper and deeper into debt. I want someone who says: "You're fat and bloated and you're going on a strict diet." The dietician is not your friend.'

'*Excuse* me,' his wife chips in.

'I'm sorry?'

'You're burping while talking.'

'I was? At least I didn't fart. To make a long story short,' Simmons says, 'I don't know why anyone gives a squat what somebody with a guitar round his neck thinks about politics. 'Cos I sure as fuck don't care what your wonderful new prime minister thinks about Kiss.'

He raises his handkerchief, mops his brow, surveys a black patch and muses: 'Hair dye.' He's not the first reactionary American rock star I've met who gets flustered talking about Donald Trump despite sharing many of his views. They're all businessmen, headline-chasers. Trump got to be president after forty years hanging around at the same galas as them.

'Rock stars are morons,' Simmons says. 'Pragmatism is much more my *milieu*.' And then: 'Let me show you a short video.' He takes his phone and fires up an interview with the American journalist Dan Rather, in which Simmons declares that immigrants in the US should learn goddam English.

'Yesterday their cousin would have wound up in a can of dog food,' he tells me. 'But today you can literally sue the president for sexual harassment and win. You want to try that here in Russia?'

'And you know what celebrities shouldn't do?' Tweed cuts in. 'Talk politics. Don't do it. Eat your food.'

As Simmons scoops the last of his porridge, I ask about his relationship with Paul Stanley. 'It's too easy to say that we're both Jewish and the other guys weren't, so they didn't survive but we did,' he says. 'With Paul and me, it's like the marriage of different alloys making titanium. Likewise with dogs. Purebreds are retarded. It's the mixture of bloods that makes them healthy.'

Surely another advert for immigration.

'Legal immigration, do you mean?' he whispers. 'Because there is a profound difference. I want to know everybody's fingerprint. I want to know everybody's social security number. Instead of just ghosts. Twenty million in America! More than most other countries have men, women and children. Know wot I mean?'

In the days after my return from Russia, I get sixteen emails from Simmons' personal account (he has no assistant), each containing a separate business venture he wishes me to know about. There's a cardboard cut-out of him advertising Dr Pepper, a reproduction of his MoneyBag clothing logo, a new Kiss sandwich toaster – and a photo of him ringing the bell at the New York Stock Exchange.

'You know why we were the number-one banned band in Russia?' he told me. '"I wanna rock 'n' roll all night", "I Was Made for Lovin' You" – the most powerful word in the English language is "I". There is no scarier word for an authoritarian regime.'

* * *

Simmons was once asked to describe the experience of performing and he put it like this:

'The only comparison I can make is with the films of Leni Riefenstahl. One word from Hitler and the masses would move in unison. It was an amazing feeling of power . . . I was King Kong, pounding his chest after chewing up some damsel in distress. Godzilla stomping through Tokyo's streets. To say I felt like God up there is not an overstatement.'

On either side of the stage at the Olympic stadium are small bulletproof tents. Paul Stanley takes a zip wire over 15,000

Russian fans and lands with force, on unforgiving platforms, on his second hip replacement. He bursts into a perfect Christ-like arc, and keeps up an energetic but slightly banal stage patter: 'Here is a song from 1988!'

Over to the left, in a pool of green light, stands a crazy lump – blank of face, rolling of eye, head jerking in time to the music with globules of viscous blood bubbling up from a black mouth. For a moment, there is something tragic about Simmons, like a mad, chained bear, a freakshow. Then he's breathing fire. Ticker tape explodes on to the crowd from two big cannons; flames leap, and then it's over.

In the hotel car park, the door of Simmons' taxi falls open to reveal him etched in light, head back, encrusted with fake blood. His minders walk him through the back of the building, but, knowing his tendency to 'slime' people, no one wants to share the lift with him.

Afterword

I was on Gene Simmons' mailing list for some months after this piece appeared, regularly receiving the intel on new merch, though nothing ever surpassed the branded coffin. They announced their retirement in 2023. Whenever I step too heavily down a stair, or jump off a tree stump in the woods, I think of Paul Stanley, the Starchild, crunching, painfully, on his third hip in foot-high platforms, night after night.

I was not a bit surprised to learn that a band so obsessed with death – and so set on defying it – would soon be making the transition to ABBA-style avatar. In April 2024, Kiss sold their master recordings, the publishing rights and even *their black and white faces* to ABBA's Björn Ulvaeus for $300 million. Their digital show will open in Las Vegas in 2027. 'Your power has made us immortal,' screams Stanley in the trailer, in that blood-curdling voice.

The first pop holograms were mawkish affairs, with the limited technology – bad lip-syncing, no 'eye contact' – compounding the sense that Tupac Shakur or Roy Orbison hadn't chosen this fate and would shimmer around the planet against their will like musical Jacob Marleys. ABBA took away the creepiness because they were still alive, modelling their avatars with their middle-aged bodies.

The ageing rock star has made increasingly sophisticated bids for immortality in the past fifteen years, from replacement front-men to franchises like TSO's, serving two coasts at the same time. But the rock hologram, as a concept, seems to have been made for Kiss, who'd been unreal since they first painted their faces in 1973. For me, this final step is rather moving. When I met the band, they were not quite ready to accept it was over. An avatar show is the biggest acknowledgement that you can't go on: a band in their late seventies, with their psychological roots in the Holocaust, handing over their bodies, newly streamlined and invincible, to the future of AI.

9

JOURNALIST DESPERATE TO CONNECT WITH MUSICIAN

Sting

In January 2018, I became heavily involved with the ideas of the Swiss psychoanalyst Carl Jung. I'd had a series of dreams featuring animals – beautiful, wounded horses, looking at me reproachfully – and the pamphlets of the British Library pointed me towards the fact that these were powerfully archetypal. Jung put names to things I'd been dimly aware of my whole life, like the animus, or 'spirit': the creative, doing part of the psyche, which sends us out into the world, writes and creates. It being the 1930s, Jung had identified this part of an individual's psychic structure as male.

Jung's wife Emma made the great man's writings more decipherable for laymen. She used the image of the legendary ghost ship, the *Flying Dutchman*, to talk about the animus; when it took hold, the effect could be almost physical, whipping you up and away. She referred to this as a kind of abduction, and, intriguingly, she drew a particular parallel with the effect of music on the psyche, describing an 'abduction by the spirit to cosmic–musical regions'. That really spoke to me. I thought about my insatiable need to travel across America alone, several times a year, with only my pink CD case; I thought about how physically altering music was, how certain guitar breaks or drum solos would change my body and make me break into a run. Something funny happened when I wrote, too – I was giddy, energised, but separated off from other people, sometimes painfully, and in a world of my own for long stretches at a time.

My Bruce Hornsby period was a prolonged example of such a state, I think. I became identified with something he had, which was thoroughly dormant in me, and while I pursued the musical obsession, I seemed to leave my ordinary life behind. Hornsby became a kind of guiding image – an animus projection. Were they all, in retrospect? These older men, these cosmic musical fathers, causing strange physical thrills and pointing me towards the numinous? God, I envy musicians. They have a direct line to the soul, and they can drop into that heightened state of being whenever they start to play.

After I got into Jung, there followed a short period when my life felt startlingly different because I suddenly started to see my insides. I saw the forces that drove me, the images that recurred in my dreams, the strange arsenal of symbolism I was compelled towards time and again. When you come into consciousness like this, your inner life pushes forcefully into your external reality and you encounter constant 'synchronicities' as your mind tries to account, in the outside world, for the new meaning inside.

It was in this heightened state that I sat in Junior's Restaurant and Cheesecake on 45th Street, Manhattan, preparing for my interview with Sting and Shaggy. I ordered a full lunch at breakfast time as I always did – probably a fried chicken breast sandwich with Russian dressing and a side of home fries – and flicked through a sheaf of old interviews from the archive Rock's Backpages. As always, I did my research reading historical features and interviews. I wanted to know what Sting had been like at my age; how he spoke to journalists back then – before the arrogant wanker/tantric sex reputation drove an enormous wedge between him and the press. I had wanted to interview him for ages, but in the end, he was only accessible to me through a two-hander with the 'It Wasn't Me' singer Shaggy, in promotion of a strange reggae album that ended up getting two-star reviews. Sting was the first concert I ever saw – my family drove to Birmingham NEC around the time he released 'If I Ever Lose My Faith in You' and dressed up like King Canute.

I leafed through the thick pile of photocopied pages laid out on the Formica diner table, dizzy with jetlag – and there it was, in the text of an *Uncut* interview from 1987. 'I don't want to be a pop star all my life,' he had said. 'I'd quite like to be a balding, rotund Jungian analyst, between forty and fifty.'

I felt an infusion of adrenaline so powerful it made my armpits itch. My mind rapidly pulled the clues together, like Jessica Fletcher at the end of an episode of *Murder, She Wrote*. The Police's seventeenth single was 'Synchronicity II'. Sting's first solo album was *The Dream of the Blue Turtles*, inspired by his own sleep-time animal archetypes. He'd worked with an analyst in New York, I discovered, who had known Jung himself. It was heart-breaking to see how sincerely he presented himself to journalists at one time: how innocently he thought that a writer from *Uncut* or *NME* would be interested to learn of the influences behind his music, or his reasons for going solo. All the complex references he shared with them in good faith were spat back at him, forming a wall of pretentious wankerness between him and the press for ever more.

Well, all that was about to change, I told myself, because I, with the synchronicity of my recent Jungian conversion and the feeling of connectedness vibrating through my bones, would single-handedly break that wall! I'd give Sting the interview he'd wanted back then, when he was my age, I said out loud to myself, marching through Central Park to his offices. I would repair three decades of hurt! Me and Carl Jung!

'Eh?' Sting asked, his eyes narrowing with suspicion at the boardroom table. He sat side-on because his hearing was failing; he cupped his hand behind his ear. 'Eh?' Shaggy stared at the floor, from under a red satin baseball cap. I'd tried to bring up Sting's plan to become a Jungian analyst and failed. It was as though I had activated a long-forgotten hurt, as though I was trying to trap him, just like journalists used to do.

It was around this time that I started to think hard about why I do this job. My route into it had been fully unconscious, a pull from the heart. But the more you come to understand about yourself, the more the stuff you do for work seems odd. There's nothing worse than desiring, and foreseeing, a genuine connection with an interviewee and being met with blankness. If you bring too much with you, it's never going to work. You have to face the fact that you *wanted* something. What? To be different, to be special? To be the one that gets through, the one they remember?

Rock journalism is unique in that it's the only place where writers are also obsessive fans, though part of the art is pretending not to be.

It's hard to accept, but there is a desire for connection that drives every moment of an interview, and with Sting, it was a connection I never got.

Sting and Shaggy: I call him the Pope of Jamaica

New Statesman, 2017

Perhaps it is not as odd as it seems. For a start, they both have 'ridiculous names', says Sting, 'which people no longer question'. Shaggy and Sting were born Orville and Gordon. Their nicknames arrived in their youth: Sting's, from a black-and-yellow striped jumper he wore in his days as bass player in a Newcastle jazz band (even his mother called him Sting). Shaggy's, from his resemblance, at the age of twelve when he was living in Jamaica, to the character from *Scooby-Doo*. His mother calls him Richard.

'*Richard?*' says Sting, looking momentarily thrown. That is Shaggy's middle name. His wife calls him Richard too. 'Don't think you can come in my house being Shaggy,' she warns him.

They sit in a boardroom overlooking Central Park. Sting wears a fashionably dishevelled pinstripe suit and traces the edge of the table with his finger. His hair is as bleached as it ever was and his expression bears decades of heavy thinking. Shaggy has a red shiny baseball jacket and a cap turned to the side, a bit like a cartoon rapper. His arms are thrown comfortably on either side of his chair. Through a mutual musical acquaintance, they met last year and jammed in a studio. The mysterious alchemy of collaboration ensued. The story is less how their new record came about, more the fact that it did at all – because, light and sunshiny as *44/876* may be (it is named after the British and Jamaican dialling codes), it is also very strange. Shaggy says this album will disrupt. Go against the status quo, and the grain.

Shaggy was delighted, visiting England around the time of his hits in the '90s, to learn the ruder significance of his name. It allowed him to flesh out his 'character' – for that is what Shaggy is to Orville R. Burrell, who speaks in a New York accent. Shaggy is a whining, grinding, priapic reggae star, composer of baby-makin' music, whom one journalist compared to a Jamaican Benny Hill. And he is developing. The mid-'90s Shaggy was Mr Boombastic ('Come lay down in me jacuzzi and get some bubble bath'). The millennial Shaggy was a wealthy Branson/ Bond-villain figure, masterminding a younger man's shagging via state-of-the-art surveillance in the video for the song 'It Wasn't Me'. Of that tuneful and explicit international hit, he tells me:

'It's about three things: either you're banging, or somebody's banging, or you wish you were banging somebody. It's something relatable in everyday life.'

And the 2018 Shaggy is more politically correct. 'I'm actually giving better advice than before,' he says. On the new album, he has a turn as moral arbiter. Sting wrote a cosmic courtroom drama called 'Crooked Tree', in which a man is sent down for a variety of sins including arson, murder, blackmail, grand larceny and human trafficking. Shaggy, Sting said, was to play the judge.

'It made me think of Jamaica,' says Shaggy. 'We have the British legal system, with the high courts – all the weight, and the wig, but with these really thick Jamaican accents.' On the song, the 'Honorable Judge Burrell' barks 'guilty as chaaaaarged!' and convicts the defendant, played by Sting, with a seismic bang of his gavel.

Says Shaggy, 'Here is this Englishman that comes to Jamaica to create a lot of felonies, and I'm just going to convict his ass!'

Sting wrote 'Every Breath You Take' in 1982 in Ian Fleming's Goldeneye estate on Jamaica's northern coastline, at the desk where Fleming had written his Bonds. He was thirty-one, already hugely successful and hiding out after a scandalous divorce. Seventy miles down the road in Kingston town, the fourteen-year-old Shaggy was already enjoying the Police, who'd had six hits in the US by then, and more in the UK, and whom he describes as 'the gateway band to a lot of reggae music'. Songs like 'Roxanne' were huge in Jamaica. Sting's voice was high and strange, Shaggy says, and he could hold long notes for a very long time – it got through to you. The Police's punk-reggae 'brought that art form to the mainstream masses'. They'd toured with Burning Spear and Aswad. The child Shaggy lived with his mother. He wore Jamaican punk garb – a tie, a collar and no shirt – to parties.

'Jamaica has influenced pop culture in such a huge way,' he says.

'Profoundly,' says Sting. 'Profoundly,' says Shaggy.

Sting's interest in reggae was both political and academic. 'Rock music is a very reactionary form,' he tells me. As Gil Evans' jazz arrangements appealed to him as a teenager, so did calypso and ska, 'in the way that the drums were played, and the bass was brought out on top. I had an understanding of Caribbean music, so for me it was always a homage, and not cultural appropriation.' You feel a bit sorry that he felt he had to bring up the phrase, but Sting is a questioning person. His first band after the Police consisted of black jazz musicians, and he asked then, 'Am I the patrician white rock star? Or am I the novice?'

Another point of similarity between these two surprising counterparts is that, in the collective consciousness at least, they are both very sexual. Shaggy and Sting are the twin poles of masculine libido – one pursuing bikinied booty on a beach like a sniffer dog; the other a paragon of psychosexual stamina, who'd mastered the practice of tantric yoga, which led to a joke boast in the early '90s (five hours) that has followed him ever since, but which pointed to a certain spirituality in Sting that few people knew what to do with.

When they interviewed him back then, male music journalists couldn't get thoughts of Sting and sex out of their heads. They all mentioned his muscle tone, his chest, chiselled bones and tantric life. I was almost afraid to be in the room with Shaggy and Sting together, thinking the sexuality might be overwhelming – but Sting looks studiously into the middle distance and Shaggy merely admires my leg warmers.

Their first single, 'Don't Make Me Wait', is a classic shagging song. Sting is thoughtful: 'I'm already sold on the idea of you and I/Just tell me where I need to sign.' Shaggy is horny: 'Come on, girl!'

'In this climate, you know, the song could be misconstrued,' muses Sting. 'As married men, you learn about compromise, you learn about . . .'

'Patience,' says Shaggy.

'Patience, as a man,' agrees Sting. 'It's not a natural thing for us! So the song needs to reflect a more balanced view. I hope we achieved it. But of course, you know, we are *keen*, we are conditioned that way. But asking a woman what she wants is one of the most important things a man can learn.'

'We're fans of women,' concludes Shaggy. A survey by his record label around the turn of the millennium revealed that women are fans of him too. Has Mr Boombastic found his feminine side?

'Have I?' he says, eyes wide. 'Embrace it all, man, and live!'

A live performance of 'Don't Make Me Wait' at the Grammys, in January, was met with some confusion, being the first that many people knew of the collaboration. It segued from Sting's 1987 hit 'Englishman in New York', which was an interesting medley: that hymn to Quentin Crisp and the exceptional richness of what Jung, whom Sting studied in the '80s, would call the hermaphroditic soul, followed by a classic banging song. Sting once said that the image of the hermaphrodite soul in art – Bowie, Boy George – was an ideal we all strive for. Crisp, 'a singular man, a very brave man', was one of the older figures he befriended in the '80s. Crisp actually said those words to him – 'I'm an alien, I'm a *legal* alien.'

Sting performed the song in Trump's New York, because of 'the ludicrous idea of calling anyone an alien'. He seems a bit reluctant to talk about hermaphrodite souls today but then says, 'I think it's important for an artist to see the world through other people's eyes. I wrote a song a couple of years ago, and I don't know why, but I started to channel a transgender prostitute. I have no experience of that, but I thought it was interesting as a

STING**177**

thought experiment. Music is an empathy machine and I take that job seriously, even though it might be odd sometimes.'

Three years ago, at the Public Theater just off Broadway, I watched a workshop of Sting's musical *The Last Ship*, which is currently wending its way around regional theatres in Britain. It is the latest sign of a prediction Sting made in 1987 to *Q* magazine: that one day, mass appeal and his personal tastes would separate. He has done symphonies, lute music, gangster movies, *Quadrophenia*, a Stravinsky adaptation with Ian McKellen and a *Threepenny Opera* among many other things. *The Last Ship* is the story of a group of men who build a ginormous tanker in Newcastle and sail it to the New World. Jimmy Nail sang at the New York performance, perched alongside Sting on a stool.

Sting grew up on Gerald Street in Wallsend, where the hulk of a 10,000-tonne ship twice as high as the houses cast a permanent shadow from the Swan Hunter slipway. Such a ship would be built every year, and everyone would watch the launch. As it blocked the space and was then released, the vessel represented a constant cycle of constraint and departure for the child Sting. His father was a milkman: the class divide between him and his Police bandmate Stewart Copeland, son of a CIA diplomat, fuelled much press interest in the early days.

'I always thought class ruled,' he says. 'I wanted not to be judged by my accent. So I developed no accent. It made it easier to be fluid and not be judged. There were no regional accents on television. Now, I only speak Geordie when I'm angry or I'm with a Geordie – and I can speak it well.'

Sting and his brother would take part in the milk round, going to the dairy at 4 a.m. He was particularly good at picking up the empties because he had big hands. He could do ten at a time, he once said. His father was hard to please – not overtly impressed by Sting's academic achievements, his passing of the 11-plus, his athletics trophies or his music career. Grammar school alienated him from his family. Sting was a bus conductor and a labourer before teaching English at St Paul's First School in Cramlington. He wasn't 'ambitious' until he discovered music.

He lost both his parents at the height of his fame, within seven months of each other. His mother, whom he credits with his musical education, was a strong character – she died of cancer, and wanted to volunteer at Chernobyl, pointing out that she was already full of radiation. He found a point of connection with his father towards the end of his life, when he sat with him and noticed how similar their hands were. He didn't write any lyrics for two years after his parents died, but his famous rainforest campaign followed instead.

At the theatre, Sting told a story about the time the Queen Mother came to their road in Wallsend. As she passed in her car and everyone lined up to wave, he told himself that he would one day be on the inside of a car like that. The wealthy donors in the theatre cheered. Sting's is a truly American tale – the very way he put his sentences together riled a UK music press that liked to see musicians hymning their roots rather than escaping them. The rainforest campaign saved an area the size of Belgium, but that too was a sign of stepping outside one's box. 'The source of pain is your motives being misunderstood,' he told *Q*. He spends most of his time in New York these days. But he votes in Britain, and by the time we talk about Brexit, he is slapping the boardroom table.

'The people who voted for it are as dispirited as the ones who voted against it, and at least we're joined in that. We're all in this fucking mess. No one knows how to fucking get out of it.'

Shaggy points out that they are both 'citizens of the world'.

'But we have the privilege of our careers, we can *do* that,' says Sting. 'Most people don't have that privilege, they're stuck. I find it depressing and dispiriting. Our society is violent and confused – and yeah, maybe all this is important for us to "figure out something about ourselves". But I see things from a different perspective than someone who lives in Sunderland and is stuck, and saying, "I just want to vote for something different, that sticks a spanner in the works." It's those people who will suffer, and that's a tragedy.'

'I know people who have never seen the ocean,' Shaggy muses. 'I was in the military with a guy, we were on the fighting roll together, and his first time he'd ever been on a plane was when they flew him over to the desert on a jet.'

Shaggy's mother, who raised him without his father, moved from Kingston to Flatbush, Brooklyn, as an illegal immigrant and worked as a medical secretary, leaving him with his grandmother and then sending for him when she'd saved enough money. She was, Shaggy says, 'the biggest dreamer'. He brings up their new song 'Dreaming in the USA', about the American Dream. Sting says, 'It's a love letter to Americans. It's about culture, and this engine that is basically fed by immigrants. America is in danger and we know why.'

Shaggy worries that Americans will take the song literally, jingoistically, like they did Bruce Springsteen's 'Born in the USA'. He is not bothered about class – 'I am motivated to better myself'

– but he's bothered about racism. 'I don't want our children to be raised with that, which is why I am raising them in Jamaica.'

His Kingston youth spanned the changeover from the People's National Party to the Jamaica Labour Party and a period of riots in the city. When he got to Brooklyn as a teenager, he enjoyed a mixed neighbourhood – Barbadians and Haitians, 'a Caribbean-American kind of life' – but was shocked by the public laundromats.

'In Jamaica, you just wash it in the backyard, you put it up on the clothes line, with a little bit of bleach on the whites and the sun dries it,' he explains. 'I'm sitting in Brooklyn and I feel embarrassed, because people were seeing my drawers. My mum would put me on folding duty: I'd sit there folding drawers. I'd say to her, "This is crazy. I'm doing this in public. There's public people looking at my drawers." She'd say, "No, man, everybody's doing it. They're clean!" That was a culture shock for me.'

Shaggy had an aptitude for pastels and won the Brooklyn Union Gas art competition more than once. He attended the Erasmus Hall High School in Flatbush, where 'all the greats' had been pupils – among them Marky Ramone and Barbra Streisand.

'You went to the same school as Barbra Streisand?' says Sting.

'Second-oldest high school in the US,' says Shaggy proudly.

Didn't Sting buy a house off Barbra Streisand?

'I did!'

After high school, Shaggy needed to get out of the house and away from his mother – 'We weren't getting along at that time, and still to this day we really don't.' He joined the Marine Corps in 1988, aged twenty, and stayed for four years. He served with the 5th Battalion, 10th Marines, and was sent to Saudi Arabia in 1991 for Operation Desert Storm, where he piloted a Humvee and worked as a cannon cocker. He became a lance corporal, but was not a committed soldier and was twice demoted in rank. His main problem was attendance; stationed at North Carolina's Camp Lejeune, he regularly drove back to Brooklyn for reggae nights.

To this day, he believes in the power of music over conflict, telling the *Military Times* in 2011 that the best way to combat Isis would be to distribute a massive bag of Jamaican weed and play them 'Shaggy music'.

'When you're listening to reggae, you only want to do two things: get high and have sex,' he observed. 'If they're listening to Shaggy music, they're not going to want to cut somebody's head off.'

Next door to Sting's management office looms the Trump International Hotel. When an *NME* journalist came to meet him in New York in 1991, he commented that Trump's buildings were the mark of a declining empire, 'a property developer's empire capsizing under the cultural meltdown at the heart of New York City'. Shaggy says he knows people who voted Trump and 'wondered if they'd been like that the whole time'. Earlier this month, he played the president in an elaborate *Late Late Show* parody, with James Corden as Special Counsel Robert Mueller ('Can we talk about the pee tape? It wasn't me'). I ask Sting about the man next door.

'I'm daunted and terrified by what is happening,' he says. 'I've been brought up with safety nets – the National Health system, my education. My further education was something I never had to dream about paying for, I could never have afforded it. So I cherish those things and they're all under threat at the moment, as is democracy. Xi Jinping and Trump saying, "I'm going to be president for life". It is medieval.'

He believes, though, that political messages in music should be 'veiled'. Agitprop is 'worse than off-putting – it is counterproductive'. And veiled they are on *44/876*. Shaggy claims to write four songs a day on average, but says he never thinks about instrumentation. Sting, who emails Shaggy in bullet points and tends to 'squirrel himself away', is all about instruments and key changes. 'Shaggy brought the vibe and I brought the structure,' he concludes.

Shaggy turns fifty this year – 'his birthday is twenty days after mine,' offers Sting. The party will happen in Jamaica and Sting is going. He is impressed with Shaggy's charity work on the island. 'I look for consistency. When celebrities take on projects, I think, *Okay, let me see you in six months and we'll see how serious you are*. I call him the Pope of Jamaica,' he says. 'He's a personage. A citizen with duties and responsibilities.'

'There is always a fear that I may be losing it,' Shaggy says. 'Am I not hip anymore?' But at the end of the day, he reasons, 'Shaggy is what Shaggy does.'

And Shaggy, after all, is an act. Is Sting an act too? 'Absolutely,' says Sting. 'Of course he is. It's been very useful for the past four decades to have a persona you can hide behind.' But it's hard to recall a time when Sting has hidden behind anything. He's been in the business for forty years now. Peers like Elton John, just a few years older, are starting to retire.

'Yeah, and he's going to do 300 gigs before he retires,' Sting says. 'That explanation didn't quite add up for me.'

10
MUSICIAN DESPERATE TO CONNECT WITH JOURNALIST

William Orbit

Some people I've interviewed were desperate to be heard. You can often tell by the communication that follows and sustains the connection, like the former Terence Trent D'Arby, improving my article with a selection of pull quotes and one-liners. While Terence wanted to get even by telling the tale of the industry that 'killed' him, others had older, more personal wounds. William Orbit is the super-producer responsible for Madonna's *Ray of Light*, the songs All Saints did for the film *The Beach*, and other key sounds that defined the country's giddy slide into the second millennium. He sent many emails after our meeting and invited me to various dinner parties. Unlike Terence, who was reclaiming a bit of the limelight, Orbit had never really been heard in the first place – but this had started a long time ago, in the back of a family car in Palmers Green.

It was the only time one of my old rockers had taken things right back to childhood of their own accord. Orbit had an unusually clear sense of where his problems had started; then, after a breakdown in his sixties, he'd gone headlong into his first self-destructive drugs binge, as though living a rock 'n' roll life backwards. When I met him, he was more peaceful, enjoying his painting, but unable to settle on one art form because he wanted to do all of them. One of his emails contained many verses of a poem he'd been working on in iambic pentameter, about the summit between Henry VIII and Francis I in 1520 known as the Field of the Cloth of Gold.

William Orbit: 'If you confound Madonna, a red mist comes down'

New Statesman, 2021

It was summer 2011 in New York and Madonna and William Orbit were hard at work on a song called 'Gang Bang'. The studio near Times Square was tucked away behind a soup kitchen. As evening drew in, Madonna announced that she had been advised to see a sunset, because she was taking a flight the next day. Orbit understood this to be an instruction from one of her many gurus. The ladders to the studio roof were rusty and vertical: as her small feet scaled them, he became convinced she was going to slip and die on his watch. They could not see the sun through the water tanks of the Manhattan skyline, so they climbed down and headed east instead. Madonna tarried near the theatres of Broadway, hiding behind tourists with her hood up and singing show-tunes.

They saw the sunset from a traffic island in the middle of Fifth Avenue, but when they returned to the studio, Orbit discovered the trip had been a ruse. In his absence, an engineer had got into 'Gang Bang' and changed his beats. 'Musicians have this skilful, passive-aggressive way of asserting themselves,' he says. 'All you had to do, Madonna, was ask me. You know, sometimes, there are looks you never forget? I still remember the look of triumph on her face.' The dynamic between megastars and super-producers is mysterious, but it is surprising to hear that Madonna would go to such lengths to avoid her own getting into a strop.

Orbit stands in socks in the headquarters of Dolby Sound, in Soho, purveyors of agonisingly loud cinema. His silver forelock gives him a certain boyishness, but his right arm is frozen from an injury caused by carrying a heavy shopping bag. His bicep does not work – he demonstrates, lifting right arm with left, as though animating the hand of a puppet.

A few months back, a walking stick arrived in the post for Orbit from Japan, a gift from a fan. In that country, he explains, this was seen as a gesture of respect. But Orbit wrote back, explaining that the crooked head of the cane reflected, to his mind, disability, whereas a Gandalf-style staff would suggest strength. The Japanese fan, a craftsman, is making him one of those.

At Dolby, in advance of a multimedia launch of his new album *The Painter*, Orbit shifts himself into his leather jacket to avoid the air conditioning. His lunch is an entire bar of Green & Black's chocolate. He has an unusual way of mirroring back what you say to him, allowing you to finish his sentences, but he is jumpy from not being allowed to smoke in the studio. He carries a notepad and writes down orders with a thick pencil: 'Get more wipes for iPads!'

Although we are here to talk about music ('my album is a grower, not a show-er!'), the room is hung with the paintings he's made in the last four years. One shows a mixing desk looking out on an intergalactic nightscape, with an oxygen tank on the floor, out of which reach the tentacles of an octopus. In the hot seat, where there should be a producer, is the silhouette of a hunched man made of white powder – 'I *was* quite powdery at that point,' he says. He applied the powder with a catapult, but he won't tell me if it's real cocaine. Is this what it feels like, sitting in his studio? 'It's exactly what it feels like,' he says. 'I didn't start to enjoy my life until two years ago. If you write this up a certain way, I'm going to come across as a really bitter saddo.'

When Orbit would DJ at the Buckingham Palace staff party, he was given his own liveried footman, who presented him with a CD of the national anthem to play at 11 p.m. (the Queen always left the party at nine). He found the experience interesting because it was one of the few times he wasn't allowed to mix the track. 'No echoes. Exactly the right speed!'

These days he is troubled by the fact that he has too many projects – 'I confuse people'. If only he was good at *one* thing, he says, he would be so happy. Yet Orbit is one of a handful of producers whose sound was so tangible, so based in melody and songwriting, that he became a star alongside Madonna, whose late '90s redesign – the warm, technicolour, cowgirl Madonna – he oversaw with 'Ray of Light', 'Beautiful Stranger' and 'American Pie'. Then there was 'Pure Shores' by All Saints, the millennium's dream pop, encapsulating that strange moment when everyone on the plane to Thailand was reading *The Beach*, and book and film and soundtrack merged, just like Leonardo DiCaprio and the French girl under the sea. Blur and Britney had Orbit too. His PR could not find a synonym for the word 'quintessential' when writing the press release for his new album, so many times did he have to describe the familiar golden sound. If only he were good at *one thing* . . .

William Orbit's rock 'n' roll life appears to have run back to front. Three years ago, at the age of sixty-one, he had his first major drugs binge. He had returned to London, where he was born, from Los Angeles, where he had lived for many years in some obscurity, and took up residence in the Leonard Hotel near Hyde Park: the Michelin-starred restaurant Locatelli was his room service. He had his own house five minutes' walk away in Connaught Square, near Tony Blair's, but he only used it as a lock-up.

'Living in hotels is the finest thing,' he says. 'You're in a womb that's going along twenty-four hours a day. You get your sheets changed whenever you want to: whoever has that? And when people come and see you, they're treated well, because it's a hotel.'

Around this period, he began, in his own words, to become a little 'over-excited' about a few projects. 'There's things you can look out for. One is delusions of grandeur. It's good to have overconfidence, I suppose. It's good to have vaulted ambitions. But there comes a point: "Wait a minute, this isn't real . . ."' He bought a large house in Ripley, Surrey, and envisioned opening a kind of retreat there. When his plan collapsed, Orbit – who, as you'll have gathered, is firmly ensconced in the establishment – moved to Chipping Norton to live on the cheese farm of his friend Alex James from Blur.

At several festivals that summer, with Chipping Norton friends, he started to take a lot of cocaine: to his surprise and delight, he discovered that it made him find other people *more interesting* ('No one ever says that about cocaine!'). Weed, ketamine and acid followed, and after entering a fugue state one night, he ended up in hospital in Banbury. Later, he had a full-blown breakdown on Praed Street in Paddington, believing he was a special agent sent to protect Prince Harry ('This was before Harry and Meghan left the royals,' he points out). He was sectioned in St Mary's Hospital for twenty-eight days. 'I was so disappointed in myself. I felt I was just nothing.' After a long recovery, and on the cusp of his twelfth album, he moved again, to Venice.

I called him there, on Zoom, after our London meeting and he was visibly more relaxed. He picked up his laptop and a tapestry with unicorns and medieval maidens flashed briefly on the screen as he angled it out of the window to show Campo San Polo, the second-largest square after St Mark's, with al fresco lunchers and a sixteenth-century church. 'There is a sonorousness to the bells in Italy,' he says. 'I've been in villages in England where they're out of tune, and it kills me.' He has recorded the bells with Pro Tools.

Why Venice? 'LA is slow, you know, and there's family in London and it got a bit complicated, whereas here . . . I just wanted to be somewhere beautiful, Kate.'

Orbit is trying to find relatives here. His Italian grandfather was a car mechanic who emigrated to England in the 1930s and worked at the Hornchurch aerodrome, fixing up planes for the Royal Air Force. His uncle served in the Special Boat Service aged eighteen 'in these bloody horrible, smelling-of-fart-and-diesel things. He was not emotionally suited to it.' His mother's other brother became a leading physicist at the Trinity College Cavendish labs in Cambridge.

His parents were teachers in Palmers Green— a headmistress and a head of English. It is a classic post-war story in one sense: leaving working-class roots to shift up the scale meant drawing a line under the past. But in talking to Orbit, I am reminded of others of his generation – writers, creatives – who could not secure their parents' approval or interest in their work, not just at the start when they were struggling artists but well into millionairedom – a frustrating, confusing lack of recognition. 'They got bang into the middle of middle class and when they got there, they fought for it. Pop music was a threat. There was a giant void between the post-war generation and the boomers, a generation gap there had never been before, and there never would be again. Imagine having parents that liked what you do . . .'

In some, it was something to kick against but in William Orbit, at sixty-five, it is an open wound, blurring the line between child and successful, adult self. In our forty-minute interview, he uses the phrase 'my fault' eight times.

'Until recently, if a door slammed somewhere, I thought someone was angry with me. I get very happy when I overhear a parent talking with their child in a respectful way. But sometimes you think, *No, no, don't talk to your children like that. It's not their fault.* I'd tell my teachers that I hated my mother, and nobody thought to look into it.'

His brother Nick is a scientist, working in the research labs at Hewlett-Packard. He has, Orbit tells me, never uttered the title of a piece of music he has written, or even said the word 'Grammy', for that matter.

'An aggressive lack of interest, a weaponised thing,' he says. 'I always think, when you're trying to gauge these very difficult family things, you have to look at the *metrics*. Let's tabulate certain things that are irrefutable. Has this person ever mentioned your children? How many times have you mentioned their children? There's a lot in this column and not a lot in that column, and that's bad. It took me fifty years to see it. You buy into it, you think it's your fault.'

Two years ago, he cut his brother out of his life. 'Oh dear, I do wish I had prepared for this interview,' he says, putting his head in his hands. 'I had this vast cloud of thoughts about it and I coalesced it down to something very simple: "William, if you can just get it down to two or three sentences that explain it – say about that thing about metrics – in a clear, simple way." Maybe I could send you an email, just to follow up . . .'

When Orbit hit upon the sound that became 'Ray of Light', he had been working with Madonna for a month, just the two of them, and had been issued with several notice periods. The moment came during a jam: him on guitar 'and a Korg MS20 with no midi', he says, getting excited. 'Record it fast because the sound will change in an hour as the oscillator heats up. It was completely analogue, patch chords, everything. Spontaneous, just with echo. It turned everything around. I knew I had a job. I was being fired every day. But her brother was nodding away.'

He recently did a DJ mix of the song in Dolby Atmos and came across old tapes with Madonna breaking out into opera after the vocal, which she achieved in just one take. Exhausted from the recording period, Orbit developed serious flu and decided to go at it, not with rest but by working with Madonna's hot-yoga teacher.

He was taken on by a new American manager as his career rocketed. 'I was almost begging him – "Please, let me have some time off" – and I don't know why I had such little self-confidence. That's what I always thought about Amy Winehouse: could she not be on a beach somewhere, getting bored? Getting a suntan, getting restless, thinking up new tunes, can't wait to get back in the studio but on her own time? Why should she rush? But the people on trickle-down never allow that to happen. They need to keep the mill turning, and when somebody says, "If you stop, you'll lose everything", we believe that.'

Orbit got his break from Miles Copeland, the music mogul who launched Jools Holland and the Police (whose drummer, Stewart Copeland, was his brother). I called Copeland in the south of France, where he spoke from his den. He remembered a 'tall nerd', one member of the electronic trio Torch Song, in the early '80s; he was blown away by what Orbit had done with their track 'Prepare to Energize', working on a little eight-track system in his squat in Westbourne Grove, Notting Hill.

'I re-recorded it on a 24-track for thousands of pounds, and the version everyone listens to, to this day, is the demo,' he says. 'He is one of the few people I've come across in my career who I'd describe as a genius. He had an awareness of playing with space and time that I've only ever heard in one act before, and that was Pink Floyd.'

Producers have a magician air about them, I suggest to Orbit: they make gold out of an ordinary song. 'I'm hard-working and diligent. I'm really good at details, and I get flashes of inspiration, that's it,' he says. 'That may account for my huge body of work. I got through it being unsettled in myself for so long.

'Luckily I'm at the stage where I can enjoy it. People say, "When's the wedding?" They assume I've got someone new, but I haven't! It's self-awareness – disconnecting from family expectations, and realising that it's not all your fault.' He prefers hearing his hits in shops because no one is paying attention. 'In Whole Foods in Kensington, they often play "Ray of Light", and I rather like it.'

Orbit was recently contacted by a production company wanting to pitch him as a kind of Grayson Perry of music, for a series on Netflix or BBC – 'drawing lines between topics that people haven't necessarily seen, fresh territory, not walking around waving my arms'. You can imagine this. Orbit is an intellectual without snobbery, and his Palmers Green accent is comforting. He had been considering their proposal when we met in London. 'But they won't know what's hit 'em!' he said.

He had reimagined the series and wanted access to a serving Navy attack submarine for an episode on subsonic sound ('it's not impossible'). The final episode would be about a 'huge pop star'. He wanted Britney. 'I don't want Madonna. There would always have to be negotiation. If you confound her, a red mist comes down and it's a battle. It needs to be someone who is part of the machine. I love working with actors. They have been trained since birth to do what they're told. I worked with Gwyneth once and she actually needed me to shout "Action!".' He is waiting to hear back on his proposal.

His PA buzzes the intercom. He'll meet her down in the café in the square, he says. 'I'll have octopus. Actually, salmon and chips.' He will give his Venice flat over to Italian relatives for the whole of October while he travels to Austria. 'Well, at this age you can choose your family, can't you?'

The album reviews were good, but he doesn't seem bothered. If he could do *three* things forever, he told me in London, he would continue his epic poem about the sixteenth-century pageant the Field of Cloth of Gold ('I can write that up in pretty decent iambic'), get a radio show and do more paintings. He showed me his cross section of a Boeing B-17 Flying Fortress American bomber ridden by an orchestra of fantastical, Boschian animals. He traced the painting with his thumb. He'd give this one to his daughter, he said, who was born when he was nineteen. 'If people told me, "I'd like to have *that* on my wall",' he added, 'I'd set about doing *only* that for a year. And I'd be so happy.'

11
'YOU HAVEN'T ASKED ME ANYTHING': HOW TO DO AN INTERVIEW

Ray Davies

I've had this feedback more than once, from the blunter interviewees; others just look relieved. When I get 'You haven't asked me anything', my soul dies, just a little. I *am* asking them things; it's just that my questions are long and rambling, and don't have a question mark at the end. This is why, when people say, 'Can we record your rock star interviews and podcast them too, as podcasts are where it's at these days?', I tell them no. No, you would not want to hear the twenty-five-second flattering, faltering train of whimsy by which I get my subjects to speak.

Nevertheless, I felt a keen connection with Ray Davies for the hour and a half that we had. His eternal sense of apartness – a certain chippiness and gloom – identified him quickly as someone comfortable to talk in observation and precise little memories. This made everything he said feel original, even when he was revisiting overtold Kinks lore. Although Ray speaks as though his own songs are the building blocks of civilisation and exaggerates his rock rivalries to cartoon proportions a little like Jeff Beck also did, he is essentially alone, and different: a documentarian of his own species and his own time. I'm not sure whether he liked me, and my lack of questions, but he seemed vaguely amused. I was a little unnerved by his final comment, as I couldn't work out whether he was trying to insult me, or simply time-travelling, as he does, and shifting about the decades with a wistful eye.

Ray Davies: 'Can hipsters change lightbulbs?'

New Statesman, 2017

On the night the Kinks finished recording 'Waterloo Sunset', in April 1967, the long-suffering wife of the twenty-two-year-old Ray Davies drove him from the studio down to the riverside spot. Ray wanted to see whether he'd got it right. He stood on the bridge, surveyed the scene, decided that he had and told her to drive him home. For the next twenty years, the women in Ray's life would be his chauffeurs. In his mid-forties, he met one he liked who couldn't drive, so he was forced to learn. He took his first test in Wood Green in north London, went up a busy side street with his foot quivering on the clutch and, he tells me, 'ran over a lady'. He got out to help, but forgot to put the handbrake on, so the car rolled over her shopping.

Five tests later, he passed – at 8 a.m. in Woking, sockless and emboldened by alcohol from the night before. Now he is 'just

another person on the road'. His instructor forgot to do rounda-
bouts with him, so he hates the North Circular. He also hates the
Dartford Tunnel. And he still gets lost in south London.

Davies lives a mile and a half from the house in Muswell Hill
where he was born, in Highgate village, a north London peak
that lies above the modern-day smog. He says he stayed here
because of the light. He sometimes does interviews on the park
bench where he broke up with his first girlfriend, but today it is
raining, so we meet at Café Rouge, in a back room, where his
whispering voice can be caught on a tape recorder. As he mate-
rialises with an umbrella, he mutters greetings to two women by
the door, saying he'll see them later in the pub. That's where
Davies conducts his social life. 'I don't have many friends,' he
says. 'I love people but when it comes to friendships, I . . . not
back off, exactly, but would rather observe than interact.'

He is a ghostly presence at seventy-two. The previous week, he
threw a party at the Kinks' studio, Konk – a sprawling Victorian
building in Hornsey, all '70s teak and brown carpet. 'You should
have been there,' he says. 'Everyone loved it. Film people, theatre people. I was late, and someone said it was like my memorial
service, because everyone had come for me but I wasn't there.
When I arrived, they looked surprised.'

I'd been at Konk a week earlier to hear a playback of his new
record, *Americana*, the first part of a double concept album about
his knotty relationship with the country. The Kinks were banned
from playing in the United States in 1965 after Davies punched
a union official; over the next four years, they missed out on the
stadium circuit that bands like the Rolling Stones were swept up
in. When Davies moved across the Atlantic years later, things

didn't go to plan, either. He was shot in the leg in New Orleans after chasing a mugger.

On *Americana*, the unique Davies formula is intact: sweet, velvet-voiced tunes laced with sarcasm and satirical observation. There are visions of a young swinger on his first trip to Los Angeles and an acerbic view of the British music 'invasion' from someone who wasn't allowed to invade.

After the record finished playing, Davies was brought in, tall, thin, with tufts of reddish hair, and he stood there on the '70s backdrop in front of journalists, like a rare animal stared at in a zoo. In the silence, he started asking the questions. For all his unwillingness to interact, it's something he does a lot. Here are sixteen of the enquiries Davies makes of the *New Statesman* during our interview in Highgate:

> *'What's the difference between a cappuccino and a latte?'*
> *'Did your mother work?'*
> *'Can hipsters change light bulbs?'*
> *'Is Diss in Norfolk?'*
> *'What does a hipster's girlfriend look like?'*
> *'Did you go to a posh school?'*
> *'Is that guy out of Depeche Mode gay?'*
> *'What would you have been if you were living in the '50s?'*
> *'What did Martin McGuinness die of?'*
> *'Is the left screwed?'*
> *'What's Pete Townshend up to?'*
> *'Does the New Statesman want to be more tabloid?'*
> *'Do you have deadlines?'*

'When is Easter?'
'Do you play an instrument?'
'Is Viz *still going? Johnny Fartpants?'*

At the end of the interview, he says, 'You haven't asked me anything.'

Davies' incessant questioning is a symptom of what he once called his 'abiding sense of apartness'. It may have led to an unhappy existence, but it served him well: he became the spokesperson for the Swinging '60s precisely because he stood outside it. He wrote 'Tired of Waiting for You' at fifteen, 'You Really Got Me' and 'All Day and All of the Night' at nineteen. And he is responsible for the first anti-hipster song, 'Dedicated Follower of Fashion', written in response to a fashion designer who owned a shop and who accused him of wearing flares.

'I said, "They're not flares, they're tapered,"' he mutters. 'He banned me. I got home and wrote the song immediately on a Remington typewriter.' According to Kinks lore, Ray kicked the designer and his girlfriend up the arse – just as he punched others during the band's tempestuous history – but today he says that it was just a spat.

Although the Kinks embraced the knockabout films and velvet trousers of the time, Davies sees the whole era as black and white. Literally. He sees decades in terms of colour. 'I think of the '60s as black and white, but the '50s as colour,' he says. 'The country had a team spirit. It wasn't all down. And the Technicolor imposed a colour sense. The '70s were black and white, too. The '80s were definitely bad colour.'

And the '90s?

'Sepia,' he says, smiling. 'Not black and white and not colour. At least, not a black and white you could trust.'

* * *

It's in keeping with his contrarian nature that the Kinks disbanded in 1996 at the very moment they could have had their biggest cash-in: when Damon Albarn was echoing 'A Well Respected Man' in Blur's 'Country House', Oasis were flapping Union Jacks and Jarvis Cocker was reflecting Davies's pipe-cleaner, deadpan class satire. *Of course* he felt alienated from the country when the country was having a party! Instead of becoming the elder statesman of Cool Britannia, he moved to the United States.

'I was in New York when it happened,' he says of Tony Blair's 1997 election win, as though talking of a natural disaster or terrorist attack. 'The Blair government set a bad tone and a bad taste. That's why I left England. It was like another world. I didn't trust it. I was a fan of John Smith. Old school. Blair was necessary, as Thatcher was necessary, as Corbyn is necessary – we need to see what it's like before we go elsewhere. I'm not saying Blair was a bad man. He was a smart man who led us down some cul-de-sacs. But I just didn't like the feel of England at the time. People in my job, we don't have an insight – we have to second-guess everything.'

In the early '70s, he wrote *Preservation Act 1*, a 'very political' concept album, he tells me, about a comedian who ends up running the country. 'Every time there's a Trump or a Boris, people say, "Revise *Preservation*",' he says. Almost every observation he makes is linked directly to music he wrote, or would like to write.

We meet the week before Article 50 is activated. He was thinking about the end of the British empire in his twenties, I point out. 'Earlier,' he corrects. 'I'm not sitting back and saying, "I told you so". I'm very concerned. But we are becoming a new country. Something will be resolved, but it will be difficult for a time. I never understood why we had the Common Market in the first place. We're not the only country that is scared. We are all going through a period of self-assessment. Except the Danish, who somehow hold it together. They're meant to be the happiest nation in the world. My brother's ex-wife was Danish.'

Was she happy?

'No!'

One of eight children, Davies had six elder sisters who seemed, he says, to be from a different generation – so far removed that he found it hard to penetrate their psyche. But through them he acquired the musical sensibility that informed his songwriting: dance hall, big band, the show tunes. His sisters were given piano lessons by a neighbourhood man called 'the Colonel', who was ex-military and 'wore one of those hats'. At primary school, his teacher Mr Lill still wore his demob suit.

'It was a time of change for me, psychologically,' he says. 'I knew something was coming. I knew society was changing. I couldn't articulate it, but I knew something was up. This was the generation that voted out Churchill after he'd led us in the war, so it was a really interesting time, mid-'50s at primary school. I had the thoughts, but I couldn't put them anywhere.'

In 1947, his younger brother, Dave – his future nemesis and creative counterpart – was born and suddenly Ray was no longer the boy baby in a house of girls. On his thirteenth birthday, his eldest sister, Rene, gave him a Spanish guitar – then died of a heart attack that same night while dancing at the Lyceum Ballroom in the West End, where *The Lion King* now plays. She was thirty-one.

Around this time, the trouble started. His uncle Frank rechristened him 'the miserable little bleeder with the long face'. He sustained a back injury by falling against some goalposts during a football match and, not long after Rene's death, his mother discovered him bashing his shins in with a hammer, hoping to strengthen his resistance in the game. A doctor sent him to therapy. He moved out of the family home to live with another sister, Rosie, a few hundred yards down the road.

'I think growing up being an isolated person in a house full of people had an impact on me,' he says. 'That's why I became . . . inside myself. For lots of kids, that's par for the course nowadays. There are names for that kind of dysfunction. I kept that dysfunction on in my adult life.'

Davies's dislocation from the '60s extended to his relationship with his peers. He claimed John Lennon once sneered, as the Kinks took to the stage, 'Don't worry . . . If you run out of songs to play, we'll lend you some of ours.' The US only wanted the Beatles and the Stones, he moaned. Jimmy Page was an 'asshole' – for some years, he was rumoured to have played the lead on 'You Really Got Me' (it was actually performed by Dave Davies using an amp he'd slashed with a razor blade).

'For all I know, Jimmy was having dinner with his mother that night,' said Ray scathingly, some years later. 'I hated my contemporaries,' he told an American journalist in 1981. 'I hated the lifestyle of Paul McCartney. I didn't want to be like Elton John or Rod Stewart' [Stewart was in the year below him at William Grimshaw Secondary Modern in Muswell Hill]. He added, 'There's only one person who's more insecure than I am, and his name is Pete Townshend.'

There is more than one parallel between Davies and Townshend, another willowy youth who stood for the '60s while looking like he wasn't enjoying it. Both had meltdowns in the '70s; both have spent the four decades since then feeding their music through increasingly complex concepts and forms, conceiving plays and stage musicals and large-scale orchestral and choral works. Townshend's long-term girlfriend, Rachel Fuller, helped him score a symphonic take on *Quadrophenia* two years ago. Davies's more experimental projects range from directing the Southbank Centre's Meltdown festival to producing the vaguely Alan Partridge-sounding film *Visions of England*, with songs set on Cromer Pier, which won a documentary of the year award for Anglia Television.

You get the sense that both are anxious to shore up a sprawling musical legacy, and that their ambitions exceed their knowledge of the formats they are working in. Davies privately took orchestration lessons in the '70s. His dream has always been to score something without an instrument, just using his head. He's tried the music software Sibelius, but is irked by how the notes flash red if they fall out of range. 'I don't like anything that slaps your hand.

'Mind you,' he reflects, 'if I'd known *too* much about music at the start, I wouldn't have written "You Really Got Me"...'

His peers – he repeats the word grandly, ironically – are 'linked by a time period but, regarding the music, we are miles apart'. What is his relationship with them like now? 'Don't have one,' he says. 'Saw the guitar player from the Faces at a function [Ronnie Wood, who has actually been in the Stones since 1976]. My girl-friend didn't know who he was. I said, "This is Ronnie Wood, the famous artist." She said, "I'd love to see your paintings."'

And Pete Townshend?

'There is a mutual telepathy,' he concedes. 'I think we listen to one another's work. When I *did* have a meaningful chat with Pete, he said, "We never talk". And I said, "Why start now?"'

The week before we met, Davies had picked up his knighthood from Prince Charles. 'All this choreography,' he says. 'Take two steps up. Wait 'til my name is mentioned. Walk four steps on. Turn. Nod your head. Kneel down. I forgot to kneel down. It was a great piece of traditional theatre.'

I ask him if his family was proud. In keeping with the genetic predisposition of the Davies family, he has four daughters and no sons. 'They don't really see me,' he mumbles. 'Or they see me, and they hear the music, but they don't really participate. My daughter Victoria changed her name to Tor. She was born when I was writing a song called "Victoria". She changed her name because she's an independent girl.' He gives a wonky smile.

In the mid-'70s, he, too, changed his name – shortly after he divorced Victoria's mother, his first wife, Rasa (she who drove him to Waterloo Bridge). He lived as Raymond Douglas for four or five years for privacy reasons. 'It was a horrible divorce,' he says. The deed poll change allowed him to marry his new love, Yvonne Gunner, a domestic science teacher from Croydon, under his new and anonymous name.

Despite the trauma of that period – a suicide attempt, from which he recovered at his brother's house – he tells me that if he could choose to live in one decade all over again, it would be the '70s. That was when the Kinks got their visas back and toured the US with experimental albums that he may not have been free to make, had mega-stardom arrived. And there was 'Lola', the ode to a Soho drag queen that prefigured Lou Reed's 'Walk on the Wild Side' by two years and filled the front rows in LA and Chicago with people who would then have been described as 'transvestites'. Davies describes Reed as 'a very nice man who passed away a few years ago'. He says there's a video somewhere of the pair at a hotel in London, in which Davies tells Reed, 'You've got to get your image together.'

'"Lola" was ahead of its time in many ways,' he tells me. 'It was more innocent than "Walk on the Wild Side". It's about a gradual disintegration into the abyss. It was banned in Australia, which is ironic because there's more drag queens in Australia than anywhere else.'

Then he says, still thinking about the '70s, 'Peter Tatchell has been going all this time. Isn't that amazing? He was a militant outsider then, and he still is!'

He tells me he has two grandchildren – *three*, he corrects himself. He says that they find him scary. 'It's not like a traditional grandparent role. I play football with them. They're warming to me as they get older, possibly. They understand I'm not a stockbroker, not a banker, I don't work at Tesco's. It's not a job you can define.'

Does he spend much time thinking about his . . . 'Legacy?' he says with luxurious sarcasm, the same way he said the word 'peers'. 'I would like to tidy up my work. I've got a lot of unfinished video, film and music on tape. I still save an old VHS player. I'm interested in retaining the so-called dead formats for archive purposes. We were talking yesterday about throwing out a load of my notes. It might be of interest to people. If I was interested in a writer, I'd like to see the detail that came to make that final piece of work. Maybe I will have a giant eBay.'

Ray saw Dave before Christmas, at the local pub in Highgate. 'We didn't know the other was going to be there,' he says. 'He had a couple of his sons with him and they were witnesses, so nothing could happen. It was a good pint of stout.'

He tells me how he put Dave up in his home a few years ago, after his brother had a stroke, for about six months. 'He only left because there was no room in the house for his pet rabbit. My cleaner saw it one day and started screaming because she thought it was a rat. I bought him a rabbit hutch.'

He recalls talking to Dave from his hospital bed in New Orleans after he got shot. 'I said, "Why don't you come across?" He was only in Florida. But he flew to LA instead.'

'What's the story?' he says suddenly, his eyes rather piercing, possibly slightly irritated. Then he makes his final observation of the day. 'I was looking at you as you looked down at your paper,' he says, 'and I suddenly saw you in fifty years' time.'

12
NO PHONERS PLEASE

Tom Jones

The whole business of interviewing has been ruined by Zoom. There was a time when it was widely acknowledged that if you couldn't sit with someone, in the flesh, you said no. The only decent phone interview I've had was with Josh Homme of Queens of the Stone Age, because it was the small hours of the morning in whatever part of the California desert he lives in, and he seemed stoned. It went on for hours, lulling me in the darkened basement of the *Word* office in Islington.

With video calls, there are obvious problems: you can't 'feel' the body, so to speak, the tics and tensions. It is harder to detect shame and embarrassment, awkwardness and irritation. But there is something else you miss too – the 'transference', or the invisible force field between two people, containing all your unconscious projections onto one another. The older man and younger woman dynamic is particularly fruitful for an interview.

The younger woman seems keen to learn at the foot of the senex, their exchange enhanced by some exciting father–daughter energy. Her challenges appear playful rather than threatening. The older man often ends up being vulnerable because he feels he is safe: *it's just a pretty lady!* This dynamic is particularly useful in rock, because the rocker brings with him – unconsciously, of course – his historical groupie associations, and because rock journalism is a traditionally male-dominated genre, populated by writers the same age as the rocker, out to prove they are on the same level, which must be both dull and unnerving.

Though I often have little physical confidence in my daily life, I have felt – and seen – the palpable relief on the face of a rocker when I show up, rather than a male writer their age: a brightening of the eyes, and a fractional loosening of the shoulders. This in turn gives me energy, and the strange transference kicks in, making for a better time had by all.

The only Zoom profile I've ever agreed to is Tom Jones, because there was a pandemic on, and I had no choice. But having been a performer for approximately sixty-three years by the time I spoke to him, Tom was a performer on Zoom, and exactly the same on laptop as he would have been in person. His entertainer energy was focused on my MacBook as though through a television, my grinning face the benign equivalent of a live studio audience. There would be no intimacy with Tom – at eighty, after a life in showbusiness, the persona and what lies beneath cannot be separated – but there was a goofy joy I'd only encountered in Shaun Ryder, a sense that he was amusing himself which, I suspect, was very slightly enhanced by my being a girl. Tom was easy to get, for a legend – he was 'in reception', as they used to say at *The Word* – which also fascinated me, as it suggested that on some level he *needs* to do interviews, to keep his energy up. I clicked the Zoom link and there Tom was, shouting, his eyes looking slightly off-screen. The show began.

Tom Jones: 'I wanted to be a man, desperately'
New Statesman 2021

Each morning, Tom Jones hangs upside down in the bathroom, ankles strapped to a board, blood rushing to his head. Inversion therapy is generally employed for backache, but Jones has used it to put an extra inch on his height. At eighty, he is back up to five foot ten and a half, the same as when he sang 'Delilah'. He is ready to tour as soon as the venues will have him back. He fastens a top button on our Zoom call.

He has had both jabs, and as for the health scare in 2018 when several shows had to be cancelled, that was just your stand-ard urinary tract infection blown out of proportion. 'I thought, *This is strange because I haven't been with anybody!*' he lilts, eyes wide. 'I used to think you got something in that area when you'd been dabbling where you shouldn't be. But the doctor said you don't have to *go* with anybody. It can develop by itself.'

His singing voice – as anyone who's seen him mentor a young hopeful on the TV talent show *The Voice* will know – is still impres-sive. He preserves it by drinking lots of water and getting lots of sleep. Yet Jones is known to go to bed at 4 a.m. 'That's right. But I don't get up 'til twelve,' he says. 'That's why they used to call me Tommy Eight Hours. Kelly from the Stereophonics – I was always Tommy Eight Hours, as far as he's concerned.'

Kelly from the Stereophonics is just one of the younger musicians Jones partnered up with in a sustained cultural reboot that stretches back over thirty years – half his career – to 1988, when he covered Prince's 'Kiss' with the synth-pop group the Art of Noise. In the '90s, when there was a nostalgic fondness for the '70s and it was fashionable to be Welsh in pop music, his popularity rocketed. There were duets with Cerys Matthews and the Cardigans, Mousse T and Wyclef Jean. And, in 2009, he took the most important decision of his career: to stop dyeing his hair, transforming him overnight from Las Vegas Casanova, recipient of flying knickers, to singer of tasteful gospel with a Jools Holland brass section.

Now, he is one of those veteran pop stars used as a lens through which to view British social history. When he speaks, the mind's eye swims with BBC archive footage of Welsh miners down the pit and children practising putting on gas masks. It is a huge achievement; the knickers nearly killed his career. Even now, people ask about them and, being an old-fashioned entertainer, he plays along. It was particularly galling, he once offered, if they were thrown in the middle of a serious song like 'Green, Green Grass of Home'. But as Jones goes into extra time on Zoom, you notice how much of his storytelling is centred not on his career but before it began, leapfrogging over the lost years as though they never happened, obscuring them behind a flaming wall of anecdote. At one point, he even mentions the Battle of Britain, which started one month after he was born.

Jones lives alone in a flat near the Houses of Parliament. He moved from Los Angeles when his wife of fifty-nine years, Linda, passed away from lung cancer in 2016. His son Mark urged him to come, and having always loved staying at the Savoy, he agreed to do so if they could find him a place on the Thames in view of 'the wheel', as he calls the London Eye. Linda always wanted to return home too. 'But she's with me, because I've got her ashes in the thing here.' He puts a thumb over his shoulder, in the direction of another room.

'She said, "Don't leave me in America. Don't put me in the ground anywhere." I said, "I won't." She's in my bedroom. In a lovely box, a beautiful box. She liked nice things, so I said, "She would like this box" when I had to go and pick something to put the ashes in. Having her ashes with me has really helped, because she's there every night, you see. In this flat, even though she's not alive to witness it, she's here.'

Jones describes the casket as 'a modern box with a modern design on it, which I'm sure she would like'. Linda was always the one interested in home furnishings, the one with the taste. 'Whatever the wife wants!' he says. In 1970, he recorded a song called 'It's Up to the Woman' and he mentions it today.

'That's the truth! I'm saying this, not as a macho person. If you're going to be married to somebody, she has to have the say, especially with the house, I think. I always wanted to live by the sea. Did I live by the sea? No. Because my wife didn't want to!'

It is hard to imagine living alone after fifty-nine years in a marriage: Tom and Linda met when they were both twelve. How has he adjusted? 'Well, I've got the remote control! You know how couples are – it's all who's got the bloody remote!'

* * *

Jones seems to love his life, and work, and all the opportunities that come his way. This attitude serves as a kind of pop carbon-dating: he is part of a generation of musicians for whom singing was a lucrative route out of manual labour. Like Glen Campbell or Johnny Cash in the Deep South, for whom country music was a workable alternative to life as a sharecropper, Jones would have been a miner like his father had he not made a career out of the family pastime, singing down the pub. He is worth a reported £170m.

When he talks, many areas of a pop star's experience – the difficulties maintaining a place in the charts, the struggle over image, the effect of it all on your sense of self – are obscured by a fearsome work ethic and almost evangelical sense of gratitude. Long ago, he admitted he'd sometimes have intrusive thoughts on stage: he'd imagine saying, 'Fuck you all' to an audience, and losing their love in a minute.

'People say showbiz is hard work,' he says. 'I say, "Look, I haven't worked since 1962, when I used to carry bricks up a ladder on a building site." Work, to me, is doing something that you don't really want to do but you've got to do it in order to make money. That's what most people have to do.'

Jones's father, Thomas, worked in the coal mines of the Rhondda Valley. He never forgave Churchill, chancellor of the exchequer at the time, for his stance on the 1926 General Strike. 'They said, "The coal miners in south Wales are starving" and Churchill supposedly said, "Tell them to tighten their belts". My father never forgot that. So, after the war, when we were kids, going to the pictures, the newsreel would come on. We were taught to boo Churchill and hurrah for Clement Attlee.'

It was more than music that kept Jones from following his father into the pits. At twelve, he caught tuberculosis and spent two years confined to his bedroom in quarantine – two years in which, he points out, his body was developing all sorts of propulsive urges, and doing things it had not done before. He used to watch his future wife from the window, climbing up the mountain with her friends. Her father had died of TB and they kept her away from him.

He was installed on the middle floor of the family home – the one with the greatest views, with the window perpetually open for his lungs. 'There was a road across the valley from us, going from Cardiff to Merthyr, and I saw the Queen come down it,' he says. 'She came there with Prince Philip when they toured – and there she was.' She would knight Jones half a century later.

His parents bought him a television in 1952, the first on the street: he breaks into a short rendition of the theme from *Muffin the Mule*. He made a promise to himself that if he made it back to play with the other children he would – a pattern is beginning to emerge – never moan about anything ever again. Did it trigger any old memories, when he was forced to isolate, during the pandemic, in the house alone? 'Yes, definitely,' he says enthusiastically, but only talks about his teenage urges.

In Jones's anecdotes, a third party often speaks up Socratically to illustrate his way of seeing the world. In 2018, a doctor said to him: 'You don't have to do this tour. You've done enough, haven't you?'

'I said, "No, I haven't done enough!"' he booms. 'There's people out there. They want me to go and do the bloody show. I've got, not an *obligation*, but I've got a *thing* . . . People have paid money to get to that show, and I'm not showing up? I don't like that. But he didn't understand because he wasn't an entertainer. Only entertainers know this: that you don't want to let the public down.'

These days, pop stars are much more likely to cancel shows for issues in their personal lives. How does he feel about that? 'Oh, that's a load of bollocks,' he says. 'I've never had trouble in that area, thank God.' In his day, there was 'no such thing as anxiety, was there? You know, I'm a Welshman. After my wife passed, I saw a grief counsellor. I saw her for one session and I said, "OK, that's that". They said, "Just a minute, it's only the beginning!" I said, "No, it's in there".' He taps his head. 'That's the way I am, you see?'

Jones is tactful about *The Voice*, whose gong this year went to Craig Eddie, a young singer from Falkirk, Stirlingshire, who suffers from anxiety and depression, and not to the smiling eighteen-year-old Grace Holden, who seemed for many weeks to be a shoo-in. Craig won, according to Jones, because he was 'different – and they look at that, because they're looking at a record contract. He writes his own songs. They're thinking, "How big can this one get?" He's different enough. I got a chance to talk to him afterwards. His mother was with him all the time.' When required to comment on Craig's final performance from his big red chair, Jones urged the Scots to vote for him. 'They're good at voting,' he added.

Jones first appeared as a judge in 2012, was replaced for a year by Boy George, about which he was livid, then returned in 2017. The gig has fostered an image of Jones as a wise lion of the music industry, something he wasn't seen as before. He doesn't

talk a whole lot on it, and watching him observe the young singers you yearn to know what he's truly thinking, as the post-*X
Factor* melismas ring out to instant applause and the stories of
personal struggle, so much a part of being a pop star these days,
are mined for each contestant. Occasionally his face tightens at a
high note, eyebrows frozen in an arch. His own mentee this season, Hannah Williams, was 'the best singer', he says. He made
a point of focusing on her lower register. 'I said to her, what I've
got to do is pull you back because you've got a lovely quality in
your lower voice. Don't go for those cash notes! You don't have
to go up there all the time. You're wonderful in the lows, which
a lot of singers fall down in.'

Then he talks about how, in his day, you knew how to perform by the time you got the record deal. *The Voice*, he says,
is 'completely reversed'. Almost anything you ask him sets him
back on the centre of his spiral, his biography. But he is entirely
happy to be interrupted. If you laugh at something he says, he
suddenly looks taller in his seat and he ramps up the story.

Jones made a career out of his masculinity at a time when male
pop stars were supposed to look like girls. Supporting the Stones
in London's Beat City club in 1964, he saw that he left Jagger's
audience cold: they looked at him 'funny' while he thrust and
gyrated in his post-Elvis way, but went mad over the gamine,
'effeminate' Mick. 'I had to do my masculine thing and hope
that it worked,' he reflected in 1991.

Almost every early interview compared him to the Texan
singer PJ Proby, deep of voice and over-tight of trouser. The
press engineered a spat that kept them both in the pop magazines. Proby dissed Jones, saying he would never be a sex

symbol – but he was. He signed three-year contracts for Las Vegas residencies and hosted prime-time American TV shows. He was so famous in the US that he was on Charles Manson's hit list, alongside Steve McQueen. Tellingly, it was reportedly thought that the easiest way of dispatching Jones was for one of Manson's female followers to seduce him and slit his throat in the act of love.

*   *   *

At the very start of Jones's career, his audience had in fact been exclusively male: he performed in the working men's clubs of Wales, earning a pound for six songs. Later, he'd get the thumbs-up from builders if he happened to pull up his sports car by a construction site. He appreciated that. He clearly still considers himself a man's man: he goes into an extended digression, complete with unrepeatable joke, about how pubs used to be the place where men could fart and be vulgar together, and women were 'protected' from that, and what a shame it is that it's all changed now. He was never into drugs – and his ideas about masculinity appear to lie behind that, too: visible intoxication would always be a sign of weakness.

'The culture that I was brought up in, you see, was drinking beer with my father and my uncles. I wanted to grow up – I wanted to be a man, *desperately*,' he says, shaking a fist. 'They used to come to get my father on a Sunday morning, my uncles and cousins – the ones that were old enough to go. I wanted to be with him. And the more beer you consumed, you know, if you started to *show* it, they'd go, "What the fuck?"'

'Cocaine, to get high fast, was going in the deep end right away. It was the reverse. Just like *The Voice* is a reverse – with people going in the deep end right away! I want to stay out of the deep end. I want to swim for a while!'

Like Elton John, Jones is rarely out of the tabloids – a steady stream of amusing revelations keep him there. He once said he used Listerine to sterilise his undercarriage before a backstage assignation. Many stories came as he hit middle age – useful, because for the first half of the '80s, he didn't scratch the UK Top 100 with a single song.

'If I'm going out with some young lady, that isn't a bad thing to say, is it?' he told Tom Hibbert in a 1991 interview. 'They're not saying that I've killed somebody or that I'm molesting children. I'm just a virile chap, so as long as the missus doesn't get pissed off, it's okay.'

There is more thought given to how Tom Jones's late wife felt about his behaviour than is given to any other pop star spouse. She stopped going to his shows very early on when she saw the level of female attention he was getting. When he'd come back off tour, he says, she'd just say, 'You got any good jokes?'. Jones still insists that had Linda explicitly been faced with his infidelities, she would have 'chinned him' – and it always gets a laugh. Instead, as one sometimes hears people say about open relationships, they didn't talk about the other women – and they didn't talk about the not talking either. Linda developed agoraphobia. Jones fathered another child with a model in the '80s but refuses to have a relationship with him.

* * *

His son with Linda, Mark Woodward, is the brains behind the act we know today. Mark took Jones's career in hand in 1987 when his previous manager died. Only with a family member, perhaps, could such things as tightness of trousers and blackness of hair be discussed.

'I do tell him to fuck off, many times, and he says it back to me many times,' says Jones. He calls Mark 'my wife reincarnated. He's taken her place. She kept my feet on the ground.'

In Jones's stories, Mark is always with him: at the clinic with the UTI, at the grief counsellor's. There are only seventeen years between them. In a 1968 interview, when Mark was eleven, Jones said he discussed all details of his career with his son and envisaged him in showbusiness one day ('He could be in an agency, or with a recording company.') At eleven, the boy could 'tell a corny song from a good one'. At sixteen, he started coming on the road. There are photos of him straightening his father's bow tie.

Less than a year after Mark became his manager, Jones had a number-two hit with 'A Boy from Nowhere' (he'd not entered the UK top ten since 1972). In pairing him up with surprising younger acts, he made a positive out of the stylistic fluidity that had dogged his father's career ('I'm just too bloody versatile!' Jones once cried). Like Johnny Cash via Rick Rubin, Jones began to tell his own story through increasingly tasteful cover versions, a habit so ingrained that he actually talks in song titles. 'One More Cup of Coffee for the Road' by Bob Dylan became all about Jones's temptations with women; 'I Won't Crumble with You if You Fall' by Bernice Johnson Reagan is a promise he made to his wife.

These tracks happen to appear on his new album, *Surrounded By Time*; Jones apologises for promoting it. But it is more than a plug. If you've never not been on stage, if you've never not been singing, there must be a dreamlike overlap between your material and your sense of what you are. He didn't care what his son did with the record's production.

'I said, "As long as it's my voice, you can do whatever the fuck you want with the sound. As long as I sound like me."'

13
IN PRAISE OF ROCK CARTOONS

Shaun Ryder and Johnny Rotten

Like Tom Jones, Shaun Ryder would be good copy on WhatsApp. He is a rock cartoon, consistent in any setting: totally transparent yet ultimately impenetrable. And though it all comes apparently without effort, he is working very, very hard. How carefully he listened, what fun he seemed to have. What these men would be like angry, or high, I hate to think . . . in the setting of an interview, they're a dream.

Like Steve Perry and Paul Stanley, Ryder had hip problems, but his body had taken unimaginable batterings besides. Like Johnny Rotten, who follows hereafter, he was a Labour boy with increasingly Tory tendencies, mainly because of tax, but also because he wished to elevate himself above the people he'd grown up with – the kind of people, he added mysteriously, who'll 'batter you' and 'take your car'.

'I look like Uncle Fester': The second life of Shaun Ryder

New Statesman, 2018

You can't help but wonder what it says about someone's psyche when they tell a stranger, within seconds of meeting them, that they currently have no pubes. A month ago, Shaun Ryder had his regular testosterone injections for his underactive thyroid, and for some reason all his hair fell out: head, eyebrows, chest and nethers. Ryder isn't happy with his appearance – a subdued moment in front of the photographer's canvas attests to that – but he is taking it on the chin. It may, after all, be temporary: his follicles are still there, he just needs injections in his head to make the hair come back.

He was sitting in the bar of the Marriott Hotel in Worsley for a long time before I knew who he was. Making anxious circles round the venue as the sky began to darken, I saw only a Russian Mafia boss in the corner, whisky in hand, arms elevated by the pressure of a thick leather jacket. When, finally, the man got up and made his way towards me, it was clear that doing so was painful: at fifty-six, Ryder has a new hip in the pipeline 'but right now it's bone on bone'. The vape in his left hand helps with the discomfort – it contains cannabidiol (CBD), the cannabis extract – 'and you can drive on it'. He looks like Uncle Fester, he points out, to the *New Statesman* photographer. Or a big toad. Or Nostrils the Vampire. 'Getting old is shit.'

For several years, Ryder's father, Derek, was involved in his band, Happy Mondays. At first, he was their manager, in the days when they hung around Phil Sachs's stall in the Arndale

Centre waiting for a record contract. Derek had never been out of the country until the Mondays went on tour. When they took off, he drove them to gigs, roadied, engineered the sound, everything. This still seems unusual. But not to Ryder. 'You had to give your dad a job,' he blinks, with nothing to add.

He was born in 1962 in Little Hulton, a difficult part of Salford. His was a Labour family; the *Sun* wasn't allowed in the house. His grandfather worked on the Manchester printing machines, on the *Mirror* and the *Guardian*. But while he appreciates Jeremy Corbyn's 'fuckoffishness', Ryder, an epic battle with the taxmen behind him, sheds light on rock stars who vote Tory. In 2012, he was enlisted as a special adviser on social class by David Cameron, after Pastygate, the unpopular decision by George Osborne to raise VAT on hot snacks. However, as he becomes gripped by one of the plosive little speeches that punctuate our interview – eyes locked with mine, cheeks pinked – it becomes clear that in defending Tory musicians, Ryder is not speaking for Phil Collins.

'I know a lot of people in the music business who came from working-class backgrounds and they vote Tory,' he says. 'The only reason is that they grew up with people they fucking despise. It's tough growing up with that – they'll rob you, they'll give you over, they'll batter you. If you're not strong enough, they'll take your car. So they grow up hating these people, and they vote Tory. The only reason I'd have to vote Tory is for the money, 'cause tax is fucking terrible.'

Ryder knows Andy Burnham and thinks he's done good things as mayor of Greater Manchester. Two years before Burnham took up his post, Ryder's life-long compadre and freaky-dancin'

Happy Mondays mascot, Bez, ran for MP of Salford and Eccles, with his Reality Party campaign ('free energy, free food and free anything'). Ryder mentions this in the same breath as the time Paul Massey, 'the kid who was assassinated', ran for mayor of Salford in 2012. Massey, who was fifty-five when he died, was the king of the criminal underworld. 'For years, Salford's gangsters have been among Europe's most committed organised criminals,' the *Manchester Evening News* wrote after the murder. You get the sense that in Ryder's Manchester fiefdom, as far as he is concerned, politicians, pop stars and fearsome hard nuts all have a shot at a piece of the pie.

For someone whose teeth fell out long ago from crack use, and who claims to remember more of the '60s than he does of the '90s, Ryder does not exhibit the blasted synapses that often suggest years of pop star self-abuse: the inability to listen, to really answer a question. He works hard, meeting my words with little metallic interjections – a straight-faced, rising grunt of satisfaction if you find something he's said particularly funny. His previous interview overran when he found out the young journalist's mother had died a week earlier. 'It is amazing what humans can put up with,' he says, of the boy's ability to turn up and talk to him. If he doesn't want to answer something – about his relationships with his three eldest children, for instance, who live with their mothers in various parts of the world – there's no getting him to: the metallic grunt just hangs in the air on its own. He paints a picture of how his apparently hapless band manipulated the press.

'I grew up reading headlines about the Rolling Stones and the Doors and Janis Joplin,' he says, 'all that 1960s shit. And then you get to a stage where that stopped, and rock 'n' roll became business, like a never-ending Brotherhood of Man song on a 1976 episode of *Top of the Pops*. Then it started again with punk – and then it went dead again. We wanted *that*. There were some miles-better bands than us. We were conscious that we weren't the best or the smartest, but we certainly knew how to work the press. *Melody Maker* or *NME* would come down and they'd be writing a piece about this big [he makes a couple of column inches with his fingers]. But slap a line out on the pool table and roll a joint, and you got a double-page spread.'

He made no money off Happy Mondays' first two albums, he claims; he continued to deal ecstasy for years. Around the time of *Pills 'n' Thrills and Bellyaches* in 1990, which included their big hit 'Step On', a cover of a 1971 hit by the South African singer John Kongos, the cash started coming in. He was ambitious. 'I wanted to go from indie to pop to keep up with Duran Duran and U2 and the other shit,' he says, which is hard to believe. Happy Mondays were set against the Stone Roses as the twin sources of Madchester music: Ryder would nod to Ian Brown in the UK's first drive-through McDonald's in Fallowfield. But with their samples and funk and comedic words, they sounded little like them.

Hits came, as did the press, but so did the slow sacrifice of the human body as the caricature took hold. In 1995 (Ryder counts from his birth year, to work out how old he was: '1962 to '72, '72 to '82, '82 to '92 – I was thirty-three'), he had Naltrexone implants – opiate blockers – inserted into his stomach to get him off heroin. The operation was preceded by standard cold-turkey, some of it sedated, which for him was particularly bad – 'five or six of them holding me down'. Like his previous attempts at rehab, it didn't work 'because I didn't want it to'. I ask him if he couldn't quit the drugs because his public image required them, and he repeats, almost word for word, the story about Happy Mondays' relationship with the press, apparently unaware that he told it to me fifteen minutes earlier. This time, the line of coke on the pool table results not just in 'a double-page spread', but 'colour photos and tales of whacky-whacky goings-on'. Perhaps the synapses are not as intact as they seemed.

No wonder the band imploded. As legend goes, Happy Mondays were on the cusp of signing a deal with EMI, after the demise of Factory Records, when Ryder went out for a KFC and never came back. Bez was never an addict, Ryder says: he is more of a human dustbin. Bez now lives in Wales, but they talk all the time. 'He is still in me life, still in me life,' says Ryder. (Both men have used reality TV to pay their tax bills.)

Despite the fact that he's fallen out with so many people – including his father and brother, for many years – he and his freaky dancer have never, he claims, had a mad, kicking-off argument. Here is his description of how their relationship works: 'We are like a married couple that don't have sex. He is like a bad dog, Bez. We lived together in a flat and if you didn't get up before him, he would get up and he would *take your clothes*. And when he did come back with them, there would be fucking joint burns all over them.

'And he would eat all the food. And because we was on giros, we got them at different times. We would get mine first and we lived off that one. Then when that was finished, and you're hustling about doing other things, the next one in was his. But he would go and get his giro and just fuck off. Then come back two days later with nothing. *But* because he's Bez, and a piss-taking bastard, he's like that dog that chews up your best Gucci slippers. The dog has hammered it, and whether you shout at it or punch it or what, two hours later the dog doesn't know what it's done. It's just a dog being a dog. Bez is a dog being a dog.'

For a time, Ryder lived in Ireland, like many other tax exiles, though he had another excuse. 'Me father-in-law at the time was Donovan, and he lived there,' he says. When he split up with Donovan's daughter Oriole, mother of his daughter Coco, he joined Bez in the Derbyshire town of Hadfield, best known as the location for the filming of *The League of Gentlemen*.

Before his Royston Vasey years, in the mid-'90s, things had gone very right for Shaun Ryder, for a time. Those of a certain age will remember, in the year that gave rise to Oasis's 'Some Might Say' and Blur's 'Country House', a different kind of band appearing on *Top of the Pops*: a shuffling, chaotic consort of rappers ('Kermit' Leveridge and 'Psycho' McCarthy), ocinara players ('Dirtycash' Dillon), guitars and beats – plus a potato-headed Ryder and lumbering Bez.

Black Grape songs, for no particular reason, all seemed to be about the church ('Reverend Black Grape', 'In the Name of the Father') or car-crash celebrities ('Kelly's Heroes') and drug crazes ('Tramazi Parti'). Ryder created the band to draw a line under Happy Mondays and – while he did end up firing all the other members, eventually – it was his musical second wind, with all the cross-pollination of his former band: the funk so at odds with the rest of Britpop, the rapping, and lyrics that probably wouldn't happen now. Song titles, such as 'Kinky Afro', that would not happen now.

Ryder grew up with eleven cousins. His musical youth, filtered through younger and older kids, encompassed Parliament and Frank Zappa, Showaddywaddy and David Bowie. He did not consider himself tribal: 'You're just you, aren't you?' He always wanted rap in the Mondays, 'but white guys didn't rap. It just didn't happen. Ten years later and it was different. In the '90s you were allowed to. That's gone now.'

He can't decide between Chuck D, Scarface, 2Pac and Eminem as the world's best rapper. He moans about Lord Jamar's dissing of the former Marshall Mathers: 'The guys that have got it − your 50 Cents − *really* talk sense. That cunt [Jamar] just don't like white people,' he alleges.

Today, his Amazon shuffle veers between Scarface and Andy Williams, 'because I'm fifty-six'. He also loves Jessie Reyez, a Colombian-Canadian singer 'like Amy Winehouse, but not'. He gets disproportionately heated when talking about brand promotion in rap: 'Gucci, Gucci, Gucci . . . where's the fucking writing? You'd think the kids would have something to say with all the shit going on in the world. All they're interested in is the dough.'

Ryder's inclination towards rap was a natural result of the way words came to him. When he started out aged twenty-four, signed to Factory with no discernible skills, he tried to force himself to write bleeding-heart love songs: 'I even wrote something about fucking Vietnam.' When that failed, he returned to his freestyling roots, remembering the words he wrote as the class clown, as a child, riffing on the teachers, 'or down the chip shop, rhyming the food on the board'.

'When I started to write like I did when I was a kid, everything came out,' he says. 'I write black comic-strip stories. I only want to send images to people. I am the walrus, that kind of thing.' On the table between us is the reason Ryder is doing interviews, a nicely packaged volume of his lyrics, called *Wrote for Luck*. It's the first time he's seen a finished copy and he turns it over in his hand, rather impressed. Some of the words look better written down than sung, he suggests. Tony Wilson of Factory once compared Ryder to W.B. Yeats – but Tony said a lot of things, 'and I was like a dog that wanted its belly scratched. Throw them on me Tony, I'll take 'em.'

So Ryder is now, officially, a Faber poet, just as T.S. Eliot was. A left-hander, at school he was forced to write with his right and his handwriting ended up in circles. He quit at thirteen: 'mad learning difficulties' – whatever it was he had, it was never diagnosed. 'I was writing in text-speak long before there was mobile phones.'

He put his two youngest children into a local Catholic primary state school a few years ago. His wife Joanne got involved with fundraising and they even went to church to secure the children a place. Now they're in prep school, and shortly they'll be off to a private Catholic secondary – 'because I don't want to put them in a fucking crowd-control jungle'.

He has known Joanne since she was seventeen, but back then, when his band was beginning, 'she was having none of it'. Around the age of forty, he says, 'she sort of wheeled me in'. He came off the heroin for good in 2002, cycling for hours a day. But the pestilence was not yet over for Shaun Ryder. And at the point at which he seemed to be able to settle into his family role, he became entangled in a legal wrangling that took up – you picture him counting it off in his head – a quarter of his life.

The exact details of the stand-off, which lasted from 1998 to 2010, will probably never be known. But the way Ryder tells it, he executed a feat of acrobatics, balancing for twelve years on a very fine line between refusing to earn any money – because any money he did earn would go to receivers – and refusing to go bankrupt, because then they'd come for his publishing rights. 'They' – he paints a picture of them hammering at his door, demanding to know how he still had electricity to light the house – were an older husband-and-wife management team, William and Gloria Nicholl: 'Real bastards, these are. *Real* arseholes.'

In 1993, the Nicholls had drawn up a contract binding Ryder to them and setting out details of the commission they'd make from his releases with Black Grape. Ryder did not bother to read those details because they 'did his nut in'. When he later realised how much money he'd lose in commission, he sacked the pair – and they sued him for £160,000. For years, every penny of his £30,000-a-year *Daily Sport* column, ghosted by John Warburton, went to the receivers, along with anything else he made. There were tax lawyers to pay, too, and 'a shit-load of child maintenance. And every time they write you a letter there is interest on the letter! Madness, it really is!' Going into the jungle – by which he means his 2010 stint on *I'm A Celebrity . . . Get Me Out Of Here!* – came at just the right time, and when he got out there was a £130,000 book deal.

As for William and Gloria Nicholl, he is pleased to say that no one will touch them now. For a time, Gloria worked as House of Commons assistant for Ann Widdecombe and then – honest to

God, he claims, eyes bulging, brief suck on the vape – she ended up at Tesco's, on the conveyors.

* * *

A few years ago, Ryder described himself as an entertainer rather than a musician. His life will always be measured in scrapes, and as he gets further from the real-life misdemeanours, the stories will only get more inflated, less tethered to place and time. In truth, the worst thing about coming off heroin was that having spent his entire adult life cocooned in a chemical bubble, he was, at forty, hit by the full onslaught of his feelings.

'It's a bit like being kicked in the bollocks and battered with a truncheon in the kidneys,' he says helpfully. 'Family members dying, carrying the coffins – nothing can get to you when you're on heroin. Then suddenly you feel it all.'

He made peace with his father, who died at Christmas from 'one of those Stephen Hawking diseases'. He says his mother is only just learning to hug, and shows me how stiff she goes when you try, arms at her sides. 'You just did not do that,' he says. 'Tell someone you loved them? What?'

He had a double whisky before our interview, the only assistance he has before he goes on stage these days. Afterwards, though he only lives five minutes away, he hangs around for another, stepping into the hotel courtyard to vape and talking on his mobile phone, looking once again like the Russian Mafia boss, calling to check that the job has been done.

I met Johnny Rotten, one of the great rock cartoons, long ago in 2014, before he supported Brexit and spoke glowingly of Nigel Farage. Because I interviewed these men for the *New Statesman*, I always asked them a bit about Westminster, and looking back, my casual questions, and their casual replies, provide something of a narrative of all those old Labour people gradually going Tory, and our slow slide into populism and political nightmare.

Rotten remained completely in character – it is impossible to think what the alternative might be. He even got a reference to butter in, since five years earlier, he'd taken a *Country Life* ad deal in order to finance the reunion of Public Image Ltd. It is not a deep piece: I took what I was given and I dug no further. But I loved Rotten's language. He is programmed to speak in strange, fresh phrases, perhaps the only way to keep yourself interested if you are always 'in character' and telling the same exhausted story – punk – over and over again.

I met him outside the *Guardian* building, where the political columnist Polly Toynbee was due to interview him for her podcast. My lasting memory of the interview is that quietly, and without making eye contact, Toynbee sat down at our table and was a third party, all the while making notes on what Johnny was saying to me, before deciding she'd got enough, standing up and heading on inside. No one said anything; not Rotten, and certainly not me. That would have been so rude.

Johnny Rotten: 'Vivienne had no concept of men's dangly bits'

New Statesman, 2014

Johnny Rotten is sitting by a brazier on the terrace at Kings Place in London, where the Regent's Canal bends round to form a little marina covered in duckweed. Wearing an oversized camel coat and gesticulating with a fag in hand, he looks like a magic tramp in a Terry Gilliam film: the only things missing are the fingerless gloves. He's talking about the problem with anarchy in the UK – not the song he wrote thirty-eight years ago, but the concept. Today, anarchy is just a 'mind game for the middle classes', he says, when asked about the activities of Russell Brand. Various writers are lining up for a one-on-one, eyeballing each other suspiciously. 'Oh, you journalists must not be *afraaayd* of one another!', Rotten wails.

The voice is part Albert Steptoe, part Uriah Heep. The hair is bleached and erect. The eyes are wild but loose; they fix on a point far over my shoulder when he talks to me, as though staring down a tiny enemy in the distance. The cartoon dimensions of the man are so inflated that it is almost impossible to imagine him being able to hold a conversation, but he can.

'In humour I find a great sense of truth,' he says, apropos of nothing. 'You find the truth by ridiculing yourself and others. The Irish side of our family were always very strong on that – you laugh at funerals and you cry at weddings. At my dad's funeral, I was quite happy to stand up and say, "That was my dad. He was a sod!" Then I bent into the coffin and gave him a big kiss and it was a very nice goodbye. And I put a few articles in there, like an Arsenal scarf. I miss him dearly. It's kind of odd, though – he died with a great smell of [dramatic bulge of the eyes] *formaldehyde* . . .'

Was that the first time Johnny Rotten had seen a dead body?

'Oh, come off it. With the lifestyles that poorer people led, coffins were being dragged in and out of the flats all the time at a fairly steady pace.'

*　*　*

He was born John Lydon in 1956 in Holloway, north London, and grew up on Benwell Road, within spitting distance of Arsenal Stadium. His father was a labourer; his parents had emigrated from Cork to a neighbourhood that was predominantly Irish and Jamaican. The eldest of four boys, Lydon was a bright but unpleasant pupil at the St William of York Catholic school in Islington, where he was taught by 'fuck-arse hateful nuns' and from which he was eventually expelled. He both loved and loathed his English teacher 'Piss Stains' Prentiss, as he knew him. 'A fantastic, amazing teacher,' he says today. 'Instilled in me a deep fascination for literature and language. He ignored me but that didn't matter. He taught me that words can empower you. Poetry was important to me. All that came from Piss Stains.'

Earlier this year, Rotten released an autobiography called *Anger is an Energy* and went up and down the country in a camper van, promoting it. His is a strange and solipsistic vision, a narrow corridor of thought in which he is right and everyone else is wrong, and as such it is one of the most entertaining accounts of the well-worn punk story. Malcolm McLaren was a phoney, Joe Strummer was 'out to grab himself a crown', Sid Vicious was a loser junkie with 'lifestyle issues'.

Much of the pre-Sex Pistols part of the book focuses on a childhood bout of spinal meningitis that put Rotten in hospital for a year. He lost his memory, which makes for a mysterious chapter in his life; it's no clearer when he describes it today. He was in 'a whole bunch of hospitals right there at the top of Archway', he says.

What were the visiting hours like?

'How would I know? I was seven and didn't know who I was.'

Was there any entertainment laid on for the children in those days? Any clowns?

'Nothing! It was complete sensory deprivation and the scary thing is you get cosy with that. There was a great fear of my being institutionalised, as far as my parents were concerned. Every now and again, strangers would sit at the end of your bed and try to touch you and you didn't know who they were. The whole thing was very, very creepy. I felt like I was up for sale.'

During his recovery months, the precocious child, who had been reading and writing since four, was often discovered by his parents in the Holloway library after school, re-teaching himself the alphabet, possibly by the light of a candle stump. Motor skills came back slowly. Using a knife and fork was hard and speech was harder.

'I thought I was conversing quite eloquently,' he recalls. 'Apparently not! My parents were told by the doctors to keep me angry, to keep the edge going. I'd be babbling and they'd say, "What? I don't understand you! Say that again!"

'I was deeply mentally frustrated,' he tells me. 'It's an amazing thing to look inside yourself and feel like two different people – one without the memory and the other one trying to kick you awake. Even today, I don't like going to sleep at night. I'm no saint. I love all kinds of chemicals that keep me awake, but I won't take *anything* that is sleep-inducing.'

A lot of rock stars have an early trauma that drives them into wanting to become entertainers, I suggest. 'A lot more don't!' he says. But surely the man who has made a career out of being – or at least looking – angry had his formative moment in that hospital? When he came out, he had thick glasses and a curvature of the spine.

'Well, you can accept that you are no one or you can fight,' he replies. 'That's a part of working-class life anyway – being told that you are no one, know your place, shut up, say nothing. I had a double-barrelled shotgun of that.'

* * *

It's nearly forty years since Malcolm McLaren's friend Bernard Rhodes spotted the nineteen-year-old Rotten on the King's Road, near McLaren's and Vivienne Westwood's boutique, Sex. He was wearing a Pink Floyd T-shirt with the words 'I hate' written across it and the band's eyes scratched out. Swiftly, after a meeting in a pub, he was enlisted to 'sing' for the McLaren-managed punk band the Strand, which included the future Sex Pistols members

Glen Matlock, Steve Jones and Paul Cook (they had already tried out Midge Ure and Kevin Rowland as frontmen).

It's easy to forget that the Sex Pistols' career spanned just two years and that they released only one album. You can't watch a rock documentary these days without the narrative suffering a seismic fracture at the moment punk emerged, sweeping away the hubristic guitar gods of previous years. It is thirty-eight years since the Sex Pistols were persuaded, by the host Bill Grundy, to swear on Thames Television's *Today* programme ('fucking rotter'), propelling them on to the cover of the *Daily Mirror*. This year, John Humphrys tried to provoke Rotten on BBC Radio 4's *Today* programme and Rotten called him a 'silly sausage'.

'What's the biggest misconception about punk?' I ask him.

'That the alleged adults who were supposedly there to look after us created it all,' he says. 'They didn't. They stole everything from us and quite happily, too. That was a nice education . . . There are thieves everywhere!'

And by 'alleged adults', he means . . .?

'Vivienne Westwood at the moment is portraying this nonsense that she conceived the idea of anarchy in the UK. Well, then, why didn't she write the song? I mean, what an audacity! Malcolm spoke this way, too – pursuing their every waking thought as an artistic statement. That is completely, *always*, the voice of the talentless.'

Earlier this year, Westwood told the *New Statesman* that she saw punk primarily as a 'marketing opportunity'. I let him know.

'That contradicts the idea of "anarchy" in the UK rather nicely then, doesn't it?!' he flashes. 'She never spoke to me. Never liked me, never wanted anything to do with me, hated me on sight. Now she's trying to move in on my territory. Nobody ever put words in my mouth, not ever. Now that Malcolm's gone – rest in pieces! – she's moved in on the territory he was trying to cover. I think it's very cheap and nasty.'

She wouldn't have admitted it was a marketing opportunity at the time, would she?

'At the time, she was nothing more than someone doing knock-off Teddy boy suits and sex toys. And that was it. She didn't invent the Teddy boy! I tell you, Vivienne's costumes were always awful – those zips! She had no concept of men's dangly bits. Safety pins had to be used to keep them together because the stitching was never finished and anything with a button or a buckle would just fly off – really, really poorly done. She was very clever at exaggerating the complexities of the concept, rather than focusing on the execution and reality.

'Well, there we differ. When I start a thing, I finish it and I make sure it's well and truly sewn up.'

* * *

Though he was expected to destroy functioning society in 1976, Rotten is a lifelong Labour voter. His childhood in Holloway appears to have instilled in him a certain respect for politicians. His local MP was Michael O'Halloran ('Never forgot him'), who was popular with the Islington Irish community and held his seat at a time when Labour was struggling in the polls.

'I would go to the Labour town hall meetings with my mum and dad and I have fond memories of it,' he says. 'When we lived on Benwell Road, it was two rooms and an outdoor toilet shared with everyone on the street. My mum and dad were desperate for a council flat because at that point there were four kids and two adults in two rooms. They got one. And there you go – I've got a fond attachment there. Labour *do* care, they *do* build housing for the poor. They *do* look out for us in a much more serious way than a Conservative government would.'

Rotten thinks that grass-roots involvement is important. 'There is nothing on television,' he says, 'and you can't afford the pub – well, go to the town hall meetings and listen to some real fun! Approach it like vaudeville!'

But where are these town hall meetings happening, I ask him? Surely the closest thing we have to vaudeville now is UKIP?

'Nah, UKIP are that bunch that will always appeal to the people that don't like to think for themselves,' he says. 'There will *always* be that sinkhole. And it's important that it's there, because by comparison other politicians shine like a beacon.

'You need that, you absolutely do. The clarity is waiting here for you, as a contrast to that *mud* going on.'

He doesn't worry about the far right?

'I'd say keep an eye on it, but at every opportunity you get, shout them down. Have they the right to be racist? Yes, they have the right. Are they right? No, they are not. Remind them of that consistently. Lest we forget, Britain is an island of immigrants, always has been. If you want to go their way, you're going to have to start thinking about removing the Romans.'

Is he concerned about the future of Labour under Ed Miliband?

'I've met the fella,' he says, 'and he seems honest enough. He dresses like a Tory, he talks like a Tory, so I'm confused. But there's a softer edge to Labour than there is to any of the others and therefore that is the right way. There really isn't an alternative. You can't be handing it back to the landed gentry because they don't give a fuck about any of us and they never will. They think it's their moral obligation to be wealthy.'

When Rotten left the Sex Pistols, he had to fight McLaren in court for the use of his name. 'The ownership of Mr Rotten was in dispute,' he recalls. 'I suppose he wanted my teeth, too.' (The name was a reference to his dental hygiene.) You can believe him when he says the character was his creation, given how little his identity has changed through later musical projects, butter ads, TV appearances and all other facets of his rich but not exactly varied career. The funny thing is that he sort of makes more sense now than he did forty years ago.

'If you want right of assembly, your local town hall is as good a place as any I know,' he says, back on the politics. 'No point trying to chisel tiles and lead off the roof. I'm not despondent about it. I can see that it can be changed. But you've got to stand up and make a noise, [his voice at its most whiney, eyes at full-capacity bulge, palm slapping the tabletop] *MAKE A NOISE!*'

'A lot of nonsenses were attached to me,' he muses, sucking on the stump of his Marlboro. 'Malcolm's idea, to give the press a free hand, would drive me crazy because I don't like things to be misinterpreted. I like things to be very precise.

'Come to me with your misconceptions and I am very happy to clarify. And that's a butter term.'

14
BUILD YOUR OWN ROCK STAR

Dave Gahan

Depeche Mode are the biggest cult band in the world: a kind of 'Radiohead with hits', and a vast standing army of fans. They didn't get on that well (I met Dave Gahan several years before the death of Andy Fletcher in 2022) and Dave said some naughty things about his bandmates in this interview, which filtered back to me in cross words from their famous PR Barbara Charone, who said I should have sat them down together.

I only ever wanted the lovely, jittery, flamboyant Dave on his own, though. In my erotic awakening three decades ago, he'd merged with Michael Hutchence, chest out, in patent leather, in those terrible '90s black-and-white videos: the feel of paramedics, and kicked-in hotel room doors, seemed to hang around them both. Leafing through decades of old features about the band, I came to understand that Gahan had put himself through a human experiment to transform himself from electropop nerd to LA rock star. Unlike the 'rock cartoons', he still wore the strain of it, in his nervous energy and explosive smile. I got obsessed with the paintings he'd produced during the band's Anton Corbijn period, when he was high: white cats, purple candles and starry skies. I tried to run them in the *New Statesman*, but the art desk weren't so keen.

Dave Gahan: 'I don't understand my own band'
New Statesman, 2017

When Neil Tennant of the Pet Shop Boys was the assistant editor of *Smash Hits*, he made the following observation:

Dave Gahan has become an accomplished bum wiggler on stage, as well as shaking his pelvis in a very suggestive way. If you think that Depeche Mode are a bunch of solemn, synthesiser-programming boffins, you'd be amazed at the waves of screaming that they arouse. A lot of the credit must be taken by Dave, whose energetic performance is one of the most sexy to be seen on a stage anywhere.

Tennant's words might not have helped the cause of a band roundly mocked by the so-called serious music press and trapped in a world of suburban, teenage, sticky-floor synthpop. But he put a finger on something about the man the critics once called Plain Dave from Basildon. He was sexy, but he hadn't always been.

Gahan sits in the windowless conference room of a Knightsbridge hotel, elbows on the table, his flexible wrists sprouting out of his leather jacket and whirling about like two little trees in a strong wind. He has silver chains and hair like a spiv, his eyes creased by years of chemical abuse and sudden, explosive smiling. Somewhere under his singlet there is a giant tattoo of angel wings which took ten hours to complete. There are piercings on him, too, not visible. One goes through his 'guiche', or perineum; he once said he had so many holes in his male apparatus that he weed like a watering can. Gahan has nearly died three times. The first was a heart attack on stage in 1993. As he was stretchered off, his bandmates finished the encore.

Two nights before we met, the accomplished bum wiggler, bathed in blue light and wearing a leather waistcoat over his naked torso, played a special gig at Glasgow Barrowlands, Depeche Mode's smallest, most exclusive crowd in thirty years. He instinctively scanned the front row for a particular fan he sees at fifty European shows a year, and eventually spotted him. 'My sight!' he mourns. 'All my sunglasses are prescription. I can see the stars at night but nothing else. We have a house way out on Long Island and, in the summer, you can lay in the garden and the stars are just – *bang*.' His fingers flash in a re-creation of astral beauty.

He speaks and thinks at the accelerated pace of an ex-addict, and his Essex accent is spiced with American R's. Across London, his bandmates Martin Gore and Andrew Fletcher do a joint interview at a different hotel. Because Depeche Mode and Dave Gahan don't get on.

No one could have known, when Tennant wrote his ode, that the band would outgrow Duran Duran, Spandau Ballet or Culture Club. Today, Gore and Gahan live on opposite sides of America. They meet only when they have to – coming together to roll out their vast electronic rock show around the world, playing to stadium crowds of 60,000 a time.

Depeche Mode fans aren't like Coldplay's. They are a race, a diaspora, a Gothic mass of supporters viewed by the band with a mixture of gratitude, obligation and fear. There are more people wanting to see Depeche Mode live now than there ever were before – and no one is quite sure why.

A successful band is a life sentence. The human animal is a different creature at eighteen, twenty-five, forty and seventy, but rock stars pass their lives together and, to a certain extent, are contractually obliged not to change. They are frozen at the age at which they began their strange journey. I ask Gahan – fifty-five years old, three times married, three times almost dead – whether going to a different school from his bandmates was part of the problem.

'They've definitely got that,' he says. 'Fletch and Martin definitely have some strange pact that I have often tried to bash my way into.' He waves to imaginary colleagues. '*Hey, I'm here, too! Just not feeling the love right now!* But I don't yearn for that any more. It's taken a long time, but I am fully aware of my place.'

Gore, chief songwriter, and Fletcher, the synth player, attended the James Hornsby School in Basildon. Alison Moyet was a classmate; she was, Fletcher once said, the best fighter in the school. They had a band with their friend Vince Clarke, who left to form Erasure and Yazoo. Fletcher and Clarke were Christians; they didn't know Gahan, who was a pupil at the Barstable School three miles away, periodically spending his weekends at an attendance centre in Romford as payback for joyriding and theft. He eventually gained a certificate from Southend Technical College that qualified him for window dressing.

Gahan was spotted by Clarke while performing David Bowie's 'Heroes' at a jam session, and joined the band 'because I had absolutely fuck all else going on'. As a child, he had done Jagger impersonations on *Top of the Pops* nights for the benefit of his aunts.

Depeche Mode were signed to one indie label – Mute Records – for three decades. Mute's founder, Daniel Miller, called them futurists, but Bananarama called them wimps. As Don Watson wrote in the *NME*: 'Describe a member of Depeche Mode? Well, one of them's got a blonde fringe, but then so have I . . .'

'Oh, they hated us!' Gahan cries. 'They *hated* us. We were a joke. But we were also misunderstood.'

* * *

In 1992, Gahan travelled to meet Gore and Fletcher at a studio session in Spain. He had not seen them for nearly two years; he'd been living in Los Angeles, where he'd moved from England, leaving behind a wife and son. He tells me his bandmates were surprised by what they saw. He had grown his hair long and was bearded and covered in piercings. He was talking about American rock music – Jane's Addiction and Alice in Chains. His weight had dropped to nine stone and he had developed a heroin habit.

'Although I was withering away,' Gahan says brightly, 'I was really empowered. I was cocksure. Our manager looked right at me and said, "*Great*. This is what we need!" I said, "Guys, everything's changing. We've got to step it up." When I think about it now, it must have been quite shocking. All of a sudden I was throwing my weight around. Sporadically, mind you.'

In America, Basildon didn't mean anything. Depeche Mode were not small-town boys. In 1988, they had played to 60,000 at the Pasadena Rose Bowl. They had a huge Goth following, and were mobbed by clubbers in Detroit.

In the sanctuary of the Spanish villa where the band and engineers would live together to work on a new album, *Songs of Faith and Devotion*, the thin, new Gahan let his dark vision percolate. The only problem was, he wouldn't come out of his room. The photographer Anton Corbijn, hired by the band to record their changing image, would go to check on him. When he wasn't in a heroin stupor, his creativity was being applied in directions other than music.

'I started oil painting!' he says. 'Mostly portrait-type things. Anton came into my room once, and I was painting this portrait of my cat at the time. The cat was just kind of floating in space. It was all purples and greens on this big canvas. [Photos remain on the internet.] Anton said: "I can't paint – that's why I take photographs." He admired my painting. He would say, "You've been up here a few days. They really want you to come down and maybe do some singing." [He giggles.] And I would come down. I think they hated me, but I really didn't care. There was something really freeing about being hated.'

Down in the studio, Gore was writing new songs – stark electronica produced with a rougher, industrial rock sound. Corbijn's intense black-and-white videos lifted Depeche Mode into the cool hierarchy of European electronic music. In Sweden and Finland today, you'd think they were the biggest band in the world. And in Gahan's bedroom, the biggest part of the transformation was taking place.

For an entire generation, the new-look Gahan was all they knew. In suburban living rooms, on *The ITV Chart Show*, a strung-out character with black pools for eyes was wringing his hands against desert backdrops or following dodgy women down darkened corridors. At the back of the adolescent mind, there was a dawning knowledge that the story was real, somehow – that the man who sang 'Personal Jesus' was undergoing his own strange process of self-flagellation. The little news bulletins on the *ITV Chart Show* flashed *Depeche Mode's lead singer was rushed to hospital last week after a suicide attempt.*

Suddenly the rock press, which loves nothing better than someone who appears to embody their art, couldn't get enough of Plain Dave. He was given lengthy features in all the titles that had mocked Depeche Mode in their early years. And, for news lines or therapy, he talked – a lot.

In 1997, he told the *NME*, in an article headlined 'Dead Man Talking', that the self-abuse had all been part of a master plan:

'I consciously thought, there's no fucking rock stars out there any more. There is no one willing to go the whole way to do this. So I created a monster . . . and I dragged my body through the mud, to show that I could do it.'

The way he describes it, it was a human experiment – a kind of rock-star Method acting. 'I *was* that guy you saw in those songs. I was living that life and it was working. I felt empowered, I really did. So it *was* cool, and suddenly I felt cool, too. I felt like I was king of the castle.'

The problem was, it was an experiment he could not control. One of the most memorable stories from the time is the rumour – during a 1993 tour that *Rolling Stone* called 'the most debauched of all time' – that Gahan had bitten the British journalist Andrew Perry on the neck, like a vampire. Depeche Mode were touring with Primal Scream, also heavily involved in heroin; their entourage included both a drug dealer and a psychiatrist. I called Perry at home in Kingston upon Thames; he told me of a backstage scene where Gahan, amid groupies and bondage folk, was brought in on a purple throne and placed in the centre of the room. The attack on the neck was 'really more of a love bite'. Months later, the two met again and Gahan said, 'You know, you were the only person that night who thought to ask me if I was okay.'

If Gahan hadn't been able to score, he would inject water. In 1994, his mother and son Jack, visiting from England, found him on the floor in the bathroom with his works round his arm. He said he was injecting steroids, for his voice. In August 1995, he called his mother and, as they talked, he slit his wrists, returned to the sofa and sat down, allowing himself to bleed. At the Sunset Marquis hotel in Los Angeles, he overdosed on a speedball – cocaine and heroin – and his heart stopped for two minutes.

I have been told before our interview that memories of those days are painful but Gahan brings them up almost immediately, in his own, strange way.

'I had a lot of fun in LA, I tell you,' he says, eyes twinkling. 'My second wife, who I married there, Teresa, we had a great time. There was nothing wrong with us – it was just me: I was really a mess. And she divorced me, rightly so. And I knew if I stayed there, I was probably going to die.'

He left LA shortly after his overdose and moved to New York, where he had one friend, the actress Jennifer Sklias, now his wife of twenty years.

'I sort of went there and latched on to her, really,' he says, almost apologetically. 'She liked Billie Holiday and John Coltrane. All of a sudden I realised I needed to be around people who couldn't care less about being around Dave Gahan.'

* * *

When Gahan was ten years old, he came home from school to find a man sitting at the kitchen table who, his mother told him, was his father. The person he thought was his father had died a year earlier. The man at the table took him and his sister out for the day – 'bought us a gift; I think he bought me a sweater' – and didn't come back.

The man, a bus driver called Len Callcott, of Malaysian ancestry, had left the family when Gahan was six months old. 'I am told I sort of *knew* about this?' he says, with an upward inflection. He later found out that Len used to call a neighbour, Mrs Clarke, one of the few people in the neighbourhood who had a phone, and ask after him. The messages were not relayed by his mother. 'I could have done with that information, probably!' he laughs. 'But everyone has these stories, don't they? My mum was raised by an aunt she thought was *her* mum. It was a generational thing. And Martin has a similar story.' Martin Gore discovered, as an adult, that his father was a black American GI.

The only other thing he and Gore have in common, Gahan says, is a love of David Bowie and peas. Recording sessions for their new album, *Spirit*, were the 'spikiest' yet, and involved a mysterious kind of intervention, organised by producer James Ford, in which Gore and Gahan sat down and had it out with each other in some way. Gore, he says, is not confrontational, 'whereas I am like *this* . . .' He raises his hands like a bear and growls.

The arguments, even after all these years, usually revolve around Gahan's desire to be taken seriously as a songwriter. 'I said, "Martin, I need to be your partner in the studio. I can no longer just be the guy who sings the songs – a very overpaid vocalist for you."'

Gahan co-wrote a song on the new record called 'Cover Me'. He becomes very intense talking about the track, which is about a man who has the opportunity to go and find another planet. When he gets to his new planet, he finds it's exactly the same – he just failed to appreciate the beauty of the old one.

'It's about that dread of realising it's not them, it's *me*,' he says. 'It's about the beauty of communication, of wanting to be understood and loved. I've spent most of my life trying to get that. But sometimes when I get it, I don't know what to do with it. When I feel that side of me that is yearning for connection, I try to get it – and then it goes away again.'

He took the song to Gore who, he says, didn't understand the metaphor.

'I'm like, "What the fuck do you know?"' he cries. '"I never question *your* songs, Martin, I just sing them!"'

* * *

Sometimes, when you're watching Gahan on stage, you think to yourself: this shouldn't work, but it does. His metrosexual moves are swollen to cartoon proportions to hit the back of huge stadiums. Traces remain of the Personal Jesus, his arms thrown out, the holes that once peppered them now healed into scars. There is a pout as big as Freddie Mercury's, an arse looser than Jagger's and a huge, deep baritone voice that always felt at odds with his compact, sinewy frame.

He may chase artistic integrity, but he is a frontman in the classic sense: in the service of something, in need of love, tricky, trapped – and fully aware of his place.

'It horrifies me to think that I might be on stage at seventy years old,' he says. 'It really horrifies me. I've got the idea of me walking on some remote beach somewhere, hopefully still with Jennifer, and a couple of dogs ['*dawgs*'], and a beard that's down to here.'

When I ask if this is just a fantasy, a little surge of energy goes through him. 'I feel like I'm getting close to the point where I will actually have to stop doing this,' he says. And then, not for the first time in our conversation, one thought seems to bring about its opposite.

'There is a sort of . . . *calling* with Depeche Mode,' he says. 'It's different. And Martin and I have this relationship that has been strange for years and years and years. The stage is the only place where I don't feel my age. We have so many songs, I see them in different blocks, for each era, and they're all different senses for me. They are all different colours and feelings. But I guess music's like that for everyone, isn't it?'

He says it took him ten years to become the singer he wanted to be – around the early '90s, then, when he ran his own human experiment. 'I wanted to get to the place where even someone else's songs would become mine if I sang them.' Gore has always enjoyed that kind of personal satisfaction, Gahan says, 'because he found himself through his songwriting'.

'I've been married three times. I'm the one that ups and leaves. And Depeche Mode is the only thing that I haven't left.'

Why is that?

'Because I haven't really understood it yet. I don't understand it, and I probably never will.'

Does Gore understand Depeche Mode?

'Yes, I think he does. I think he understands it very clearly. And he made that very clear to me.'

I ask him if there are any bands that actually get on.

'I can't imagine there are, if they're being truthful in any way,' he says. 'We all have huge egos. The trick is to work out: are those egos destroying what could be magnificent, or are they creating it?'

As our interview ends, he gets up, silver chains jangling, and beckons me in for a quick little platonic, leathery hug. On my way out, he asks for another and says, 'I'm sorry – it's what I do!'

15
DADS, GIRLS AND FRUSTRATED MUSICIANS

Jeff Beck

At the start of 2024, I was walking on Hampstead Heath – the wild bit on the hill above the swimming ponds, where you can forget that you're in a city at all – and I was listening to one of Glen Campbell's gospel albums, as I often do there. It was a cold day, but the sun cast your shadow extra-long on the ground. Glen made a few gospel records in the '90s after a down-in-the dumper '80s; he'd been baptised and born again, and you could hear it in the music. I adored the sincerity of it: 'Show me the way oh Lord, and I will give myself to thee!' Whenever I am out of sorts, I put these songs on and I connect with myself internally, like a little train slipping back onto the right track. There were a couple of killer tunes by Jimmy Webb among the number, and halfway through one – or rather, halfway through the seventh time I played it – I realised I was doing a very strange thing, and it had to do with my dad.

Some thought processes, some mental habits, are so hard-wired in us as to be invisible. You don't really know you do them at all. Then suddenly, one day, you notice yourself, and the weird things you do, and you're never quite the same.

It was a wonderfully gloomy song called 'Where I am Going', the first line of which is Glen announcing, in a crumbly voice, 'Feel like I'm comin' out of a storm . . .' I was stopping the track at the second verse and skipping back to the start in order to hear that line again and again as if for the first time. I wanted the emotional impact repeatedly − but not for myself, because the ears I was imagining hearing it were not my own. They were my father's.

Listening to music through my father's imaginary ears − for it really is that strange − has characterised my whole life. The effect is physical: the thrill of an unusual chord-change, the hair raising on your arm, is always doubled for me because I'm 'sharing' it, internally, with an imagined listener. This is not about listening to music my dad likes, I should add: some of my music he loves, and some he has no interest in at all; much of the music I imagine him hearing I will never play to him. Rather, the process is something energetic, and formative, in my psyche that I can't quite explain. My imaginary audience intensifies the experience for me. In another, less positive way, it is a slightly lonely thing. I am unable fully to enjoy the music as 'my own' because I keep stopping and starting it and handing it over to the Imagined Dad.

I think back, as I write this, to the real-life memory of sitting shotgun in the car, desperately wanting him to like the Queen songs I played him and feeling sick when a Roger Taylor track had clearly made no impact on him whatsoever. The process had, at some point, taken on a life of its own. It is there in my neural pathways, four ears not two. I may love a piece of music, but it always undergoes this imaginary splitting. Some thirty-five years after I started it, sitting on a bench in Hampstead Heath, I suddenly saw my mind from the outside.

A few years back I had this rather sad dream.

I was in a place with many rooms. There was a music class going on. I heard a thin and very pure sound which clearly came from a stringed instrument but not something I recognised, not screechy like a violin. I came round a corner and saw a little girl of about four playing the instrument that was making the sound. It was a piece of thin, pale pine wood about a foot long. It was thinner than a floorboard. The texture was dappled, like it had been roughly hewn or battered with a little hammer. It had five strings. And it was painted with beautiful medieval illumination, like a manuscript. This instrument, someone told me, was called a 'knight'. It was a medieval instrument in the same family as the psaltery. I decided to buy one. I felt really excited about buying a 'knight' and was full of plans about how I could discipline myself to learn it. I told my father about my plans and enthused to him. However, at the back of my mind, I also feared that I would not, in adulthood, be able to find the time to really apply myself to learning it. There was a feeling of the instrument being just out of my reach. I knew that a child had the ability to learn it far better than I did, and I would just give up.

People say that music is a rehearsal for adult feelings, a safe space in which to practise the unwieldy emotions of love and everything that comes with it. But I think it can go the other way too. Music is a site of regressive longing – an energy centre, deep in your core, a visit to which can rejuvenate you and bring you home again and again. It is part of an adolescent's experience to regress like this, and the process is thrilling. Love of music does indeed have all the tension and power of erotic love, but it's little wonder to me that dads and daughters so often share it – a chaste but passionate art form, a homecoming of sorts, that offers a direct line to the soul.

My sad little dream says something about a re-routing of energy, away from myself and towards a dream dad. In real life, after the song has been rewound again and again and the feeling has faded, there is a strange sense of 'what now?' I can still feel the thrill of seeing that imaginary instrument in my dream – then the little voice in my head, telling me I'm going to fail.

It's certainly the way I feel about learning an instrument these days. I took piano from the age of four to eighteen and did all my grades up to and including seven, when I had to duck out because of a complete blind spot for music theory. I adored my teacher, an anarchic woman who kept her kids out of school, breathed 'fuck' if she hit a wrong note and talked to me like I was an adult. Although it was the primary hobby of my earlier childhood, I had one problem, which was that I could not apply myself to any music that didn't give me goose pimples. The small group of composers who passed the skin test included the French Impressionists (Debussy, Ravel), Holst, who originally wrote *The Planets* suite for two pianos, and Brahms in one particular moment. While some independent schools excel at sport, mine was a centre for music, purely classical. Yet the piano is not a sociable instrument. I and a friend, another piano player, would piggyback on orchestra trips to London by getting on the percussion; I played the triangle in 'The William Tell Overture' and she played the cymbals. A large-breasted girl, she caught her boob between them in the final crash, in a concert at the Royal Festival Hall.

We had a music teacher at school called Mrs Denny who would often play Brahms's 'Intermezzo No 2 in A Major' as we walked into assembly. This particular piece of music was so devastating, so bittersweet, it sounded like a film score. I'd sit cross-legged with my eyes directed down to my beige fawn tights, as huge shivers rolled up and down my back. It was almost hard to breathe.

My anarchic piano teacher explained gently that the piece was way out of my range: it featured split chords in the left hand which would only fit the span of a big man. It was also, she hinted, emotionally beyond my reach. I ignored her advice and spent several months mastering it in my own way, equipping myself with an automatic goose-pimple machine that I could turn on any time I felt like it. I poured all my unexpressed feelings, and there were many, into the big moments of 'Intermezzo No 2 in A Major'. If you know the piece, you'll know what moments they are. I played it faster and louder than it should have been played, because fast and loud was the way I got the biggest hit.

I 'peaked' on the piano at fourteen and I still recall the shock I felt, before I left for university four years later, when my teacher said plainly, 'I think we have come as far as we can.' These days, I can barely play a note. I can smash out some nice chords, taken from the muscle memory of my Debussy days, but because I was 'classically trained', I have zero idea how to play by ear, can't improvise or compose, and can't play along with anyone else. Honestly, it is such a shame. A piano is no use at a campfire. If an instrument were a metaphor for life, better to master something stupid like the ukulele and never learn to read a note. At least that way, you will always sit at the heart of a group of players, improvising, singing and making it up as you go along.

My father is a guitarist. When my parents met, he was sixteen (she was twenty) and playing in a jazz band in a little night spot called the Birdcage in the Northumbrian college town of Alnwick, which was on the circuit for '60s jazzers heading further north. The first record he bought was Gershwin's *Rhapsody in Blue*, at ten. By the time he was fifteen, he'd done a lifesize painting of Eric Clapton on his wall. By the time Clapton was twenty-two, he had done his best work, my dad said, and when he sees Clapton now on TV, he just looks embarrassed.

My dad didn't become a professional musician. He did not want a musician's lifestyle and he has always worked from home: while I was growing up, the phone would pick up after one ring. The black and gold Les Paul sits in the corner of the living room and sometimes – very occasionally – when everyone is out, he will play twiddles of John McLaughlin through a Vox amplifier. He can't read a note and it set him in good stead. He too is a 'secret' musician: it is principally inside him rather than outside. He has a predilection for female singers – he was so into Björk that we stuck a photo of her on his shirt with Sellotape and he made it all the way to the shops and back before he realised it was there – and I'll never forget him screeching to a halt outside my school with the window down and Alanis screaming 'Are you

266

thinking of me when you fuck her?' from the Land Rover Discovery. I was so proud. He cries over music, and he sometimes cries when talking about it too.

Through my father I discovered McLaughlin and Pat Metheny, and generally grew up with a sense that music in which one heard a lot of notes was music to be excited by. But we discovered Jeff Beck together, in 2007, by fluke, when Eagle Vision released a DVD of Beck's seven-night residency at Ronnie Scott's and sent it to *The Word*. Because Beck had lived a musical life below the radar, pursuing what he wanted, my dad was not aware of what he had become. Beck became our shared musical project for a decade or so.

It was a gift that we came across the world's greatest guitarist unexpectedly, later on in life, when he was still regularly touring in all sorts of different get-ups. These concerts we would attend together, without my brother or my mum, and they held a rare thrill for me, as I walked to the venue with him puffed up by, and unable to quite release, all the things I wanted to say. My dad would get the train from Norfolk and we would meet at King's Cross and quietly make our way to the Albert Hall, or the Chelsea Hospital, where the pensioners peeped at Jeff's stage from behind their curtains – or the O2, where we once saw him doing a masterclass with a face of the '80s, his then manager Harvey Goldsmith. Presented like an athlete, he padded on stage in boxing boots. He was a type, physically, but a completely unique creature. He sounded like no one else and like six people at once, but when he spoke, it was all self-deprecating jokes and exaggerated mock-egotism – disguising, presumably, the knowledge within that he *was* the best guitarist in the world.

When I met him, I felt an instant connection that was probably only on my side (as we have established, that is a perfectly regular occurrence). But it didn't matter. What a wonderful thing, to know that accepting an offer to join the Rolling Stones, as Beck might have done in the mid-'70s, would have 'truncated his whole being', as he put it. He died, bafflingly, from a bout of bacterial meningitis in January 2023, when he was still otherwise fit to do world tours. My dad had a little cry a few times that day, and also in the following days, when I gave him a strange book that had come into my possession at *The Word* and I'd kept for years – a catalogue of Jeff Beck's vintage guitars. Perhaps Beck represented, to both of us, the secret musician, tinkering over and over with his instrument as he tinkered with his machines, and driven by emotion to play only the bits he liked. For me, sharing Jeff was about something else too. As the recent discovery of my bizarre, imaginary 'quadraphonic' listening habits suggested, I will always need my father to love any music I think is my own.

The £7m fingers: how Jeff Beck became a guitar hero by saying no

New Statesman, 2016

Michelangelo and Da Vinci loathed each other. Ingres sneered at his chief rival, Delacroix. Picasso and Matisse all but ignored each other for fifty years: a bit longer than Eric Clapton and Jeff Beck. Even now, Beck – who is one of the top three guitarists in the world and no longer needs to concern himself with Clapton – finds it hard to listen to other guitarists. His internet radio is tuned to Kurdish music. Onstage, he plays out old rivalries with high camp, welcoming other axe heroes with a touching-the-hem-of-your-garment gesture and mumbling into the microphone, 'I might as well fuck off, then.'

In 2010, Beck chopped off the tip of his left index finger while making a stew. It was hastily reattached but he took no chances, subsequently insuring his fingers and thumbs for £7 million. That his brokers felt that there was £7 million worth of music left in them is not insignificant – though for many, he will always be associated with a 1967 pop song for which he claims to have received 'forty quid' in royalties. He has likened 'Hi Ho Silver Lining' to having a pink toilet seat hung around your neck for the rest of your life.

According to rock lore, Beck's journey has been marked by strange choices, leading him away from fame and fortune. Like a musical Forrest Gump, he was present at many of music's big moments, but remains at the edge of the photograph. He replaced Clapton in the Yardbirds on the recommendation of his childhood friend Jimmy Page, but was kicked out for bad behaviour (he is thought to have been the model for Nigel Tufnel in *This Is Spinal Tap*). Pink Floyd wanted him to replace Syd Barrett, but they never got up the nerve to ask him. The Rolling Stones wanted him, but he turned down the offer at the last minute. Beck formed a band with an unknown singer called Rod Stewart, but quit just three weeks before they were scheduled to play at Woodstock.

Stewart went on to form the Faces, while Page was ascending into the stratosphere with Led Zeppelin. Stevie Wonder wrote 'Superstition' for Beck, but decided to keep it for himself. Was it bad luck or self-sabotage, or simply that the music he really wanted to play was never going to make him famous? Clapton has said that the only reason Beck was never a megastar was that he never wanted to be one. 'He deliberately carved that image,' he told *Rolling Stone* in 2010. 'He likes to be left alone. He wants to be underneath the car, working on the engines.'

Quite literally. He has restored fourteen vintage automobiles 'from the ground up' at his house in East Sussex and produced a book about them, *Beck01*, published this month. This is perhaps not as strange as it seems. Much of what Beck has done with his instrument resulted from a kind of musical mechanics, a private process of tinkering, test-driving and refinement. Years ago, while listening to Bulgarian choral music – presumably because he couldn't bear to listen to guitars – he started playing a tune with his tremolo. Pulling the whammy bar high off the body, he divined notes from an invisible scale in mid-air. The ghost voice, more like a theremin than a Strat, appears on the 1989 song 'Where Were You' ('Some people say it's not real playing but *you* try,' he says). This and other tricks punctuate his music with moments of cosmic tenderness. On message boards, men analyse his work and, he tells me, 'They say, "What string is he using? That's what *I* need, because that's what gives Jeff the sound!" *No it bloody isn't!*'

At the age of seventy-two, on the eve of his seventeenth album's release, he says that the 'guitar nerd image' has finally got to go. There's little chance of that.

A man on a galloping horse would be hard-pressed to pull Beck out of a line-up with Ronnie Wood, Mick Jagger and Keith Richards; they all have feathered hair, eternally dark, and a weather-beaten urchin face. For many years, he has worn stage outfits of an athletic style: white, nimble boxing boots laced to the calf, skinny nylon track pants. and sleeveless tops, leaving a sinewy arm free to arc down on the strings like a flesh-and-bone whammy bar. Today, at his management office in Kensington, his hair is a couple of shades lighter and his nose is comfortably bulb-like. He tells me that he might need to rethink the stage outfits. All of his clothes are designed by Hilary Wili. She did the costumes for *Downton Abbey* but, Beck says, 'she still finds time to stitch me something'. He does not have the sunken cheeks or 'keyhole face' of his Stones peers – a result, he guesses, of a teenage lust for sweets and the lack of dentistry to support it. But he is so much a specimen of that generation that he even has the middle name to prove it: Arnold.

He, Jagger, Richards and Page were born within eleven months of each other towards the end the Second World War, and baby Clapton came five weeks before VE Day. According to Google Maps, you could drive from the family homes of Mick and Keith in Dartford to Clapton's in Ripley, via Jimmy's in Epsom and Jeff's in Wallington, in an hour and fifty minutes. Suburbia, war stories, flannel trousers and a childhood conversion after hearing Bill Haley or Les Paul on the wireless: the background that gave birth to the British blues boom is well known. This was a musical ground zero for the sons of insurance clerks and factory workers. They may have heard guitars, but they couldn't see any, so they made them – Brian May (of Feltham, Middlesex) from a fireplace, Beck from cigar boxes. It was just another project alongside the boy-sized spaceship that he was constructing from the bashed-out insides of 400 Oxo tins. Hearing Les Paul for the first time or watching the Sputnik – it was all the same thing.

'Any information about guitars was so scarce. I remember getting a bus when I was fifteen and going eight miles just to *look* at this guy's catalogue of Fender,' he says. 'He wouldn't even let me in the house. He came all the way down to the garden gate and said, "Here you are, don't dog-ear it," and held it out to me.'

After botched attempts at making your own instruments came guitars on hire purchase. 'Don't talk to me about hire purchase! There was this guy – he wasn't old enough to be my dad, but he offered to be my guarantor. He said, "I'll tell them I'm your stepfather." Within a month, they'd sussed out he was nothing to do with me whatsoever and they snatched the guitar back. My dad went along and explained that we couldn't afford it, so they waived the rest of the payments and I got the guitar.'

His father walked three miles to the station every day and three miles back. 'All his life was cricket,' Beck says. His mother hoped to refine his musical tastes. 'She kept telling me how nice the boy down the road was, who plays the marvellous piano. He came in the house once and played *Moonlight Sonata* and my mum nearly collapsed with delight. I thought, *Get that bastard out of there.*'

Like many of his contemporaries, Beck went from grammar school to art college. His sister had introduced him to Jimmy Page as a teenager. Page recommended Beck to the Yardbirds because he didn't want to give up his own lucrative career as a session musician – the idea of the guitar hero as solipsistic soloing genius was still a few months away from being invented. It was two years before the 'Clapton is God' graffito appeared around London.

Clapton was a blues purist, Beck a wizard with tone and tricks. They could probably have coexisted in moody rivalry, but someone arrived in London 'with fourteen-foot hair and playing the guitar with his teeth' and ruined it for both of them. Clapton walked offstage when Hendrix played with him at Regent Street Polytechnic. 'Jimi steamrollered right through my life,' says Beck.

While Clapton was an 'ogre' in his mind – he rolls up imaginary sleeves and prepares to punch – Hendrix was direct creative competition, which was far worse. 'It wasn't the muso thing that got me recognition in the beginning. It was doing "Wild Thing",' he says. 'I had to stop that because Jimi came along. I was doing all sorts of weird things, detuning the strings, using a repeat echo, and I thought, "I can't do that any more". I had to jump out of one bus and get on another. That's what I've been doing ever since.'

The first bus he jumped – or was thrown – off was the 'converted school bus' that carried the Yardbirds around the US on the TV presenter Dick Clark's 1966 package tour. 'Lots of racial animosity,' he recalls. 'A couple of black acts on the bus that hated the sight of us, didn't like us playing the blues because it was their music. Twenty hours a time on the road. We've come 3,000 miles to play three songs a night and then it's back in the misery box. By the time I got to Amarillo, I'd thrown my towel in.

'I was in love with someone back here, too, so it didn't take me much to get back to England. But then, sitting by the pool for a day, I thought, *I wish I hadn't done this! She doesn't want me here! And I don't want to be here!* At least I got to say to Eric, "*Na-na-na-na-na* – I went to America before you."'

* * *

Beck tells his story in the way that is most amusing to him. He recently said that his temper results from a bang on the head he received when his headmaster ran him over. Yet the decisions he made were the result of serious soul-searching. In the mid-'70s, he was flown to Rotterdam to discuss the possibility of joining the Stones. 'I'd been there two days and I hadn't seen a Stone, and I thought, *Right, I'm witnessing what it's like to be a Stone – not playing, and having single malt whiskies.*'

He decided to get away under the cover of night. Down the corridor, from Keith Richards' room, Betty Wright's song 'Clean Up Woman' was emanating from a little Dansette automatic-replay record player. He entered the room and hovered over the sleeping figure of Keith and lifted the arm off the record. He left the Stones with a note slipped under someone's door.

'They were living the rock lifestyle of all rock lifestyles. I don't think anyone will ever be like that again,' he says. 'But I wouldn't have been my own master. And that would be my whole being truncated. I thought, *Now you've made your choice. You will go down that path and you will stick to it.*

'I dearly wanted to tell them how grateful I was,' he adds, of the men he has seen countless times over the past forty-five years. 'Maybe another time.'

The truth was, Beck had already had two experiences that would shape his musical life. His group had been on tour with the Mahavishnu Orchestra, the shape-shifting jazz-rock tribe fronted by John McLaughlin, Yorkshire's boy wonder who'd trained with Miles Davis. The two bands had a block booking on American Airlines, taking up the whole front of the plane, and it was joyous, he says, because they were all *Monty Python* fans.

'It was the refinement of McLaughlin that presented a way out for me,' Beck says. 'Arriving at the soundcheck and watching him and the sax player trading solos, I thought, *This is me.* He has such knowledge of scales, and he tells the story within the scale. Playing with McLaughlin, and then the Stones – *dang, dang, dang* – can you imagine?'

Although he reels off the rock 'n' roll anecdotes like Johnny Rotten or Wilko Johnson, when he talks about music, he changes. 'Mahavishnu's drummer Billy Cobham was the best I'd ever heard. Not *loud*, that's not the secret – powerful as hell when he wanted to be – but 90 per cent of the time, he was just *dancing* with the drums, you know? Just like a butterfly, all over them.'

His second revelation came when he was booked to work with George Martin, who produced *Blow by Blow*, the 1975 album that showed off the full range of Beck's jazz sensibilities and made him a tax exile into the bargain. Martin 'was a massive pair of wings. Just knowing that somebody with such sensitive ears was approving of what was going on, you were flying. I can't explain the joy. I found it almost impossible to deliver what he was looking for every day. I would feel the cut-off point, thinking, *I don't know anything else I can impress him with.* The band were looking at each other with new-found love for music, but with us playing.'

Martin encouraged Beck to play the piano, picking out skeletal melodies unhampered by style and padding. Beck finds fast playing physically upsetting. 'It sounds impressive but it doesn't mean a thing.'

Blow by Blow paid for his sixteenth-century farmhouse in Wadhurst, East Sussex, in 1976. He moved there with his girlfriend at the time, the model Celia Hammond, and Hammond's rescued stray cats had the run of the 80-acre park. They split up some years later. Her animal trust is still run from the town; he is the patron of one in Tunbridge Wells. He had been married at the age of nineteen to Patricia Brown from Crawley. The couple's first possession for their marital home was an Afghan hound; the fees from Beck's band the Nightshift scarcely covered the dog food. The future Julia Carling was another girlfriend: she left college to live with him at eighteen in the early '80s, but later said that, despite the age gap, he needed someone to mother him. He still lives in Wadhurst, with his wife since 2005, Sandra Cash, his sheepdogs Wilf and Paddy, a ewe called Bubba and a crow called Dave. He has been a vegetarian for forty-seven years.

I ask him about the old beef with Clapton. 'Eric wanted to be the underdog,' he summarises, 'the back-room boy, and I turned out to be that person, while he was like: "LAAAAAYLA!"'

Were their temperaments too similar? 'The approach to playing maybe so,' he says, 'but outside that, one of my touchstones is humour. I have to have people around who are of a certain strain of humour. I can't deal with people who have no humour. I'm not saying he doesn't . . .'

On 10 August, Beck will play the Hollywood Bowl in Los Angeles, covering fifty years of guitar music in two hours. He asked Clapton to play but he is suffering from the nerve condition peripheral neuropathy. Beck is worried about him; he says that he Googled it and sent Clapton a list of websites offering treatment.

In technique and innovation, the two haven't really been competitors for years. In 2007, Beck did a run of gigs at Ronnie Scott's in London with one of his best discoveries,

Tal Wilkenfeld, an Australian bass prodigy who turned heads because of her prodigious capabilities and possibly because she was a twenty-year-old woman in the male-dominated world of instrumental jazz. In 2010, his album *Emotion & Commotion* included a version of 'Nessun Dorma', which won him his eighth Grammy. His new one, *Loud Hailer*, features the guitar playing of Carmen Vandenberg and the voice of Rosie Bones, Bill Oddie's daughter. The women wrote the songs with him in front of a fire with a crate of Prosecco. After our interview, they're coming to the office for a meeting, with another crate of Prosecco.

'The right time to record is when you're not quite ahead of yourself,' he says. 'You're probing and you're treading carefully and it sounds that way, like you're telling a story. If you flash, people's ears clam up.'

Of the top three guitarists in the world, Beck is okay playing with John McLaughlin ('I've done John'), although he has turned down an invitation to appear with McLaughlin's 'butterfly' drummer Billy Cobham ('I'm not up to that standard'). However, he is not sure that he can go to see the third player in the Planet Earth axe triumvirate, Pat Metheny, when he appears at Ronnie Scott's the week we speak.

'They asked me if I wanted to go,' he says. 'But I don't know if I can see any other guitarists. It might just send me a curveball. Maybe I'll go. Or here's what I'll do. I'll sit in Bar Italia across the way, getting plastered, and you can tell me how it was.'

16
FROM WILDMAN TO GREYBEARD
Wilko Johnson and Nick Cave

At some point in the past decade or so, rock stars have been elevated to high culture. Two in particular, Wilko Johnson and Nick Cave, underwent cultural transformation following their personal experiences with death. Wilko faced his own death after a 2013 cancer diagnosis. He refused treatment, found unexpected resources and joy inside himself at the thought of his own mortality, and talked about this in public for months before unexpectedly returning to health – rather as John Donne preached and wrote poems about death for several years before actually dying. Julien Temple endowed Johnson with a mystic, seventeenth-century energy in his documentary *The Ecstasy of Wilko Johnson*, one of the most powerful re-brandings of a down-at-heel musician I have ever seen.

I approached Wilko's flat in Southend on a dark afternoon shortly before Christmas 2015. Inside it looked like it had been squatted; there was so little furniture, so few places to sit, just a big slippery brown couch, and several overflowing ashtrays. He talked of his girlfriend, recently returned to Japan – a 'groupie', he said, that his late wife had tolerated, who came to nurse him. After Wilko eventually passed on in 2021, the article was recirculated, and I got an angry message from this girlfriend on Facebook, accusing me of denigrating their relationship.

'I have never been a groupie,' she wrote. 'I was just a fan. I cannot believe Wilko said I was a groupie. There were groupies, but not me. I did not shout [my article includes the now questionable YOU WALK ROUND BLOCK!, an imitation of her Japanese accent]. I *persuaded* him to walk around the block, saying I would buy his favourite ice cream when he reached the half goal . . .'

Yuriko was a medical and pharmaceutical translator who had gone to live with Wilko to help him with his recovery, a true expression of the heights a fan's devotion can reach. I find that moving: God knows, I would have nursed Roger Taylor had he needed it. I tried to reply, but she had instantly blocked me. Wilko was clearly a complicated person, unable to resist a cartoonish pop at his guardian angel for the sake of a funny line, or perhaps keen to reduce her role in respect of the wife who was such a large part of his story.

Wilko's back and he's bloody annoyed
New Statesman, 2015

'Tell you what, you can take my PPI refund and *shove it up your fucking arse, you cunt!*'

WILKO JOHNSON

Wilko Johnson is well again. In spring last year, he was delivered of the three-kilogram tumour he thought would claim his life, and now he is dealing with a cosmic anti-climax: declaring in public that he was going to die, and then not doing so.

The euphoria with which Wilko was meeting his end – captured magically in Julien Temple's recent documentary *The Ecstasy of Wilko Johnson* – has evaporated, but he is better-tempered than he used to be, he says, after replacing the receiver on the unfortunate cold-caller.

Wilko may be cured, but 'well' is stretching it. He looks svelte for his age, but that's only because doctors took most of his insides out: his spleen, lower and upper intestines and, of course, the naughty pancreas that was the cause of all his troubles in the first place. He takes twenty pills a day, is diabetic, has to inject himself, and he doesn't even get a kick out of his morphine tablets. Instead, he 'doles them out like sugar cubes' to his bass player, Norman Watt-Roy who, as a 'stoner', reacts better to their effects. Wilko's own trademark psychotic stare and robotic duckwalk were the creative manifestation of vast amphetamine use.

His was a story so improbable, he tells me, it would have been rejected by publishers if it were a novel, 'then sent to a soap opera, and they wouldn't want it either'. The cancer diagnosis, the decision not to treat it, the public farewell. The full-on career revival that followed. The hit album with Roger Daltrey, the world tours and more press than he'd had since 1977. Then an amateur rock photographer, who just happens to be an oncologist, is watching you at one of your farewell gigs, gets backstage and tells you that if you *really* had what they said you have, you'd be flat on your back by now. Turns out your cancer is operable. You go into hospital flanked by your best friend (a boxer) and a Japanese lady, of whom more later. The fan who saved your life is called Charlie Chan.

Wilko's tale was bigger than a soap opera, though. It was a story about someone having faith in science – too much faith, as it turned out – and about a person's right to die as they want. It was a story about the morbid appeal of watching someone fade away in real time: once the stuff of sci-fi films, then of Jade Goody and Clive James, who has described his prolonged farewell as embarrassing. Above all, Wilko's was a story about a man's ability finally to appreciate his time on earth precisely because he knows it's going to end.

'They call it the Mercedes,' he says, lifting up his T-shirt and showing me a scar a foot long that forks out on either side, just like the logo. A few weeks back, Wilko and his Mercedes turned up at a music awards ceremony that, he tells me, had particularly naff goody bags. He was a bit of a fish out of water among the other old rockers. He barely knows Status Quo, with whom he has just done an arena tour – though he has a soft spot for their song 'Pictures of Matchstick Men' because it was big when he got married forty-seven years ago. He has shaken Pete Townshend's hand in the past, he tells me; he's supposed to be touring with the Who next year. He gets on with Van Morrison – though he must be the only person in the world who does. Wilko is the kind of figure the British rock press has always favoured above the big draw. He represents a whole world of jobbing musicians of the '70s and '80s who now live in modest terraced houses in Brighton, or Bournemouth, or Hove, still playing in bands, weathering the periods of quiet, riding the waves of interest when they come again. Folk heroes, in a way: for every Townshend, there is your Otway or John Cooper Clarke.

We talk through the serving hatch between the living room and kitchen as he makes two cups of milky filter coffee. After he got better, he went into what he likes to call a 'senior depression'. His younger son, Simon, moved in to care for him, to this pale yellow house in Westcliff-on-Sea, the one with the telescope on the roof. Simon seems to have understood that if he was going to become a carer for the most stubborn man in rock, he would have to do so with minimal fanfare. He's six foot four, but spent the first few months living in the smallest room in the house.

The living room could do, to use the old-fashioned parlance, with a woman's touch. It's one of those curiously uneven bachelor spaces where all the stuff seems to have floated down to one end. Wilko's much-loved wife, Irene, died of cancer eleven years ago: he has a plot next to hers at a green burial site near Harwich. There are pictures on the wall that Wilko painted in the early '70s, including one of his brother playing a lute. They both had long hair back then: Wilko can be seen in news footage from '73, protesting against the Occidental oil company, which was building a road through his hometown, Canvey Island. He once walked to Afghanistan with fifty quid stuffed down his Y-fronts. But he doesn't like the word 'hippie' – that was invented by the newspapers. 'We called ourselves freaks.'

Across the water, the 'Miltonic flame' of the Shell Haven refinery, which featured symbolically in Temple's film, no longer burns. It was just one piece of the Canvey landscape through which he explored the idea of Johnson – an English graduate with a love of Anglo-Saxon sagas – as a kind of rock 'n' roll psychogeographer, explaining how this strange spit of Essex land fed into the 'submarine consciousness' of Dr Feelgood, an R&B band that looked like a bunch of used-car salesmen at a time when glam rock and prog were preening their way through England. Was it their defensive toughness? Or their creative isolation ('next stop Belgium')? Or the romantic parallels they'd draw between their own ugly-beautiful surroundings and the Louisiana Delta – the same big brown rivers, the oil refineries lit up like little Meccano cities?

Feelgood had the same trajectory as every other teenage band – saw the Shadows on TV, got cheap guitars from *Exchange & Mart* – but tell the story the right way and it becomes a *Boy's Own* adventure. The singer, Lee Brilleaux, Mick to Wilko's Keith, had a little boat that he'd sail right out into the middle of the water. On Canvey, the bus shelters transformed into jewelled Arabian palaces if you took enough LSD.

In 1975, Dr Feelgood were so ordinary-looking as to be completely exotic. 'Where did they come from? They're so '63!' the American rock paper *Crawdaddy* wondered when they played a Led Zeppelin party. The Stranglers' Jean-Jacques Burnel says they were the bridge between rock 'n' roll and punk. Clem Burke of Blondie said they were gangsters. Johnny Rotten got his stare from Wilko. Paul Weller got his hair from Lee. Lady Diana Spencer came to see them during her nursery teaching days. They were the biggest band in England for a moment, in 1976. But 'Mick and Keith' couldn't keep it together.

Wilko Johnson once said that he imagined himself in old age as a venerable figure, sitting by a mullion window, imparting wisdom to the young people sitting at his feet. The vision came true: he's the only pub-rock guitarist expected to provide open discussion on matters of life and death. But a lot of his philosophies were dependent on his encroaching deadline. 'It was the most marvellous year of my life,' he says. And it's over now. Wilko had always been, by his own admission, a miserable bugger, choleric and jumpy. All contemporary rock writing focused on his doldrums and his enemies; they were as much a part of his mythology as trashed hotel rooms were to Keith Moon. 'For fame, wealth and power, I'd eat shit,' he once said. 'You see stars complaining about paparazzi. Bollocks, man, you love it.'

The band drank in hotel bars while Wilko took speed and stayed in his room. 'He was a troubled sort of person. They never knew where they were with him,' said Brilleaux's ancient mum in *Oil City Confidential*, Temple's 2009 film about the band. While Wilko casually refers to the rest of Feelgood today as a bunch of twats or bozos, his relationship with Brilleaux was more complex – built on mutual awe, and mutual murderous feeling. Some say Lee was intimidated by Wilko's university education (Newcastle, BA in English); that's why he didn't write songs. When the band imploded in 1977, one of Wilko's compositions was a trigger – 'Paradise', in which he celebrates loving two women at once: his wife, and his girlfriend in London.

'They thought it was an ego trip,' he tells me today. 'What? *That's* an ego trip? And in a few weeks' time they going to [record] a song called "Baby Jane"? Oh, *piss off!*'

The temper rises regularly today. His persona is so strong – the pleading intonation, the sideways jaw, the eyes that pop out a lot while we're first getting acquainted – that you find yourself laughing when he's being deadly serious. What irks him most is people saying he left the band, when in fact he was kicked out. Dr Feelgood soldiered on for years, but things were never quite the same without their psycho lieutenant, who always appeared to have been dropped down in the wrong band. Without him, perhaps they really did look just like used-car salesmen. Lee Brilleaux's wild energy no longer had anything to bounce off. Even his mum stopped going to see them after Wilko went.

Wilko went to ground while journalists 'picked over his corpse', as he put it at the time. Then he formed a band called the Solid Senders, who turned out to be 'useless arseholes who took all my money'. He joined the Blockheads, too, but that didn't last long. He has spent much of his life surrounded by people who are '. . . what's the modern parlance? Fucking illiterate.'

At least three times, he had a chance to patch things up with the band, and at least three times something got in the way. He recites the occasions with a Johnsonian interest in geographical location. He was in bed with a girl in West End Lane in West Hampstead, when he heard that a meeting between himself and Lee had been set up at the Ship pub on Wardour Street. 'But the girl was really pretty, and the long and short of it was, I spent the afternoon cuddling her instead.' The second time, he was in Wigmore Street with his accountant, who told him: 'Swallow your pride. Let them have their way, and in the end it will be shown that you are right. Get back together with them.' A meeting was arranged but Wilko was annoyed to find that only some of the band were present. When he pointed this out, he was told to call the other members himself. 'I said, "No, man",' he remembers, his voice pained. '"Please don't do this to me." They wanted to make me crawl.'

One of Wilko's later bands even toured with Feelgood in Japan in the mid-'80s (the promoters sensitively put them in different hotels). 'My drummer claimed that Lee was standing in the wings while we were playing, with a kind of wistful expression on his face . . .' he recalls.

Lee Brilleaux was diagnosed with cancer in 1994 and died quickly. He expressed a desire to see Wilko in his last days, but Wilko never went. 'I let it be known, that yes, I'd like to see him, but I would actually like someone to come and *get* me and take me there. I'm not going to go and knock on his fucking door, you know? And anyway, it never happened, I didn't see him. I had to have someone to take me there. But no one took me there.'

One of the things Johnson learned to do, when he was dying, was to contemplate a moment of beauty without trying to preserve it for future recollection. He also describes a strange kind of power that comes with a death sentence. 'I look on the street and think, *All these people are subject to mortality, but I'm not, because mine is established,*' he said. When he played 'Bye Bye Johnny' at a farewell show in Tokyo, all he could think was, *What a great bit of show business.* For practical reasons, his band booked shows at festivals. The thinking was, if Wilko died, it would be fairly easy to slot someone else in to the bill.

He feels no anger about his misdiagnosis, despite the complex psychological fallout it has left. He has reacted to the larger things in his life with a gentleness that seems at odds with the anger he still feels over the smaller things. He talks about his wife a lot: 'She was a good bloke, I don't know how she tolerated me.' He performs 'Paradise' nowadays, but he has written the girlfriend out of the lyric.

Until recently, there was another woman living in Wilko's house – a Japanese lady called Yuriko, who moved over to nurse him after his operation. 'She's only little,' he says, 'and she'd push me in my wheelchair right through the corridors, out of the hospital and right out to the perimeter fence. I'd be leaning on the fence, pretending I was in the country, while in fact there's all these tubes coming off me . . . I was pathetic.'

As his condition improved, Yuriko implemented a tough programme of rehabilitation, shouting, 'YOU WALK ROUND BLOCK', whether Wilko wanted to walk round block or not.

He explains that Yuriko was one of his groupies from the old days.

'There were several Japanese girls like this,' he says, 'They were what you would call girls rather than women. And they used to come and stay for Christmas. Poor Simon grew up thinking Christmas was a time when the house filled up with Japanese ladies who taught him how to count and swear in Japanese.'

And Irene was okay with catering to Wilko's groupies at Christmas? 'Oh, yeah. Irene used to love them – Kaiko, she's beautiful. They would all come down. Matthew [his elder son who now lives in Dubai] was a teenager and Simon was just a little boy.'

Yuriko is 'back in bloody Japan' now and he feels the absence. It was her birthday the other day, though he's not sure how old she is. His new management is trying to get her a partner visa, but even talking about the forms involved, and the bad grammar of the people filling them in, makes his temper rise again.

'I don't want to get married again,' he says. 'For me, it's moral. I'm in love with one woman and she's dead. There's something a little bit serious to me about marriage and it's not a dodge to get a visa!'

He is writing his memoirs for Little, Brown and should have a first draft for Christmas, though the experience is 'freaking him right out', as he's never done a book before. In other ways, he feels like he is still going through a second childhood. A few weeks ago, he realised he'd run out of one of his drugs, Creon, an essential accompaniment to every meal since the removal of his pancreas. 'So I'm hunting round the house,' he says. 'Yuriko's on the Skype, so I'm waking Simon up. In the end, we decide the best thing to do is to go up to the A&E to get some more. We're walking up there and I'm trotting behind him – I used to walk quite fast. And I see our shadows, and here's his big, long shadow, and there's my little shadow, and it looks like I'm a little kid.'

Wilko says that when his time with Feelgood ended he 'absolutely knew that the band was the greatest thing I was ever likely to do'. You can't help but wonder whether, in a strange kind of way, his death sentence replicated the fragile, heady buzz of the fame that hit him in 1975 – a few months of feverish activity laid out before you, dates set, everyone watching, and all you have to do is fly through it all like a bullet. You wonder if he responded to his approaching end in the manner he did because jobbing musicians are programmed to think, breathe, live and be happy in the short term. He may not have been able to bottle the euphoria he felt when he was dying, but I ask him whether he had ever had such feelings before: that sense of being 'vividly alive', the whole world looking suddenly different.

He thinks for a moment.

'There was a period when I realised that the band were going to make it,' he says. 'And there's one moment I'll always remember. We were returning home from London and when you get to Barking, there's a big flyover, and we were right at the top of it. I looked out and I could see the lights of Essex out before us, and I said to myself, "I wonder what is going to happen . . ."'

By the time I interviewed Nick Cave, the former Archbishop of Canterbury Rowan Williams had shown an interest in his writings on grief, following the death of Cave's son Arthur. Williams became my secondary voice in the article and, shortly afterwards, *The Times* got them together for a proper love-in, so they are now friends. It has been interesting to watch Cave's transition to public philosopher, grief counsellor and sober, non-reactionary voice of the anti-woke. I felt incredibly strange to be interviewing someone to whom the worst possible thing had happened. Cave is very polite these days (he was not always) and to be around him, one talks softly and quietly, the way one talks in a library or at a museum. Ten years ago, with handlebar moustache, he was styling himself as a deliberate porn-star parody of a musician in middle age. His real life changed the trajectory of his work, and the tragedy moved him out of the rock industry and into another world.

Nick Cave: 'Art shouldn't be in the hands of the virtuous'

New Statesman, 2022

For two decades, there have been plans for a statue of Nick Cave in his birth town of Warracknabeal, 200 miles north-west of Melbourne. Cave was to be cast in gold, riding a horse and naked to the waist, wearing a loin cloth. He cooked up the idea in the late '90s with the sculptor Corin Johnson, who also built the private, columned memorial to Princess Diana at Althorp.

This was a lifetime ago, when Cave wore a drooping moustache and a medallion, and looked like a porn star on the slide. It was a glorious era of family contentment, living with his wife Susie Bick, the model and fashion designer, and their twin sons in Brighton, enjoying the commercial and critical success of his album *Dig, Lazarus, Dig!!!*, a sleazy, humorous rock bombshell that was praised as one of many career resurrections on its release in 2008. Cave's plan was to turn up to Warracknabeal with the statue on the back of a lorry and leave it there in an act of 'extreme generosity'. If they did not want it, he'd put it in the desert. But they have hit a snag with funding, it seems. The Australians don't exactly celebrate their famous, wayward sons, he says. They're more likely to yell 'fuck off' at you out of their car.

Cave weaves his way through the tables of a family-run restaurant in Holland Park, west London, which has been opened for our purposes, a peaceful place with no other diners. Before he arrived, I asked the restaurant to put some music on, fearing it would be too quiet.

He is wearing one of his bespoke suits, of a black, satiny sheen, most likely cut by his regular tailor in Soho. His hair has been blue-black since he started dyeing it at sixteen; there is an inwardness about his posture, but every now and then he'll sweep a look up under his big eyebrows, whenever he is saying something dry. The week we meet, he had spoken to the *Church Times*. 'A whole world has opened up from a perspective that wasn't open to me before, where I basically got *Mojo*,' he says, before adding politely, 'And I can still talk to *Mojo*, too.'

What is there to say to a person who has recently experienced the worst thing that can happen to someone, not once but twice? One of Cave's sons – Arthur, fifteen – died in the summer of 2015, and his first-born – Jethro, thirty-one – in summer 2022. In the last few years, he has begun to provide a kind of public function, talking about grief with unusual clarity. 'People often say they can't imagine how it would feel to lose a child,' he said not long after Arthur's death. 'But, actually, they can – they *can* imagine what it is like.' The loss enlarged his heart in some way, he has written, and it confirmed his religious sensibility, revealing that there was energy, not failure, to be found in the ongoing struggle with faith itself.

In his new book, *Faith, Hope and Carnage*, a series of conversations with the journalist Seán O'Hagan, Cave addresses his guilt about his younger son, who fell from a cliff in Brighton after taking LSD: 'He was my responsibility and I looked away at the wrong time . . . I wasn't sufficiently vigilant.' Being forced to grieve in public saved him, he has said. But what about walking down the street today, still carrying grief like a flag? Is it not the one thing people see? Cave orders a cup of tea and asks them to turn the music down.

'That is still difficult,' he says. 'I'm quite private. I know it doesn't look that way, and people talk to me sometimes like I'm a walking agony aunt. I'm trying to learn how to be a bit more boundaried. But it's a condition of being in that state, that you're not protected, or the normal way of protecting yourself is taken away, to some extent. You're just this walking open wound and people respond to that – because most people, on some level, are.'

Cave was always distrustful of the way in which a journalist tells your story and slots your quotes into their own idea of who you are. He once described the process as 'speaking a lot of shit to some fool', adding, 'I only trust somebody when I feel they are genuinely on my side.' These days of course, most people *are* on his side, but the anxiety about being taken out of context came to a head after Arthur died. 'I decided I wouldn't do any more interviews until I'd at least worked out how to do one,' he tells me, which is something to hear from a man of sixty-five who must have done many hundreds.

On his website, the Red Hand Files, named after a song inspired by Milton's vengeful God, Cave opened the floor to questions from fans and practised figuring out what he actually thought about things, from God to free speech. Where once there was abrasiveness or mythmaking, he revealed an honesty that can at times be difficult to read.

In July this year, one fan asked him about a 'cryptic' line from a song on his 2019 album *Ghosteen*: 'The kid drops his bucket and spade and climbs into the sun.' Cave thanked the fan, started talking about a place 'potentiality adjacent to meaning', then broke off – always politely, these days – saying: 'Looking at them now, these lines are perhaps not so obscure, and without wanting to take away their power by attaching my own meaning to them, their intent seems fairly clear. They mean, the child stopped what he was doing and died.'

The former Archbishop of Canterbury, Rowan Williams, recently selected *Faith, Hope and Carnage* as his *New Statesman* book of the year. I asked him why he found it particularly moving. 'There are various familiar ways of putting together the language of faith and the experience of appalling suffering,' he told me. 'Some people simply treat faith as consolation: things look terrible but it's going to turn out fine. Others say that the experience of atrocity negates all possible reference to the sacred or the divine. Nick Cave refuses both sorts of simplicity. For him, the extremity of pain and loss *releases* something; it pushes you over the edge of whatever limits you had taken for granted and uncovers a kind of imaginative energy, not always welcome.'

Cave's book is perhaps unique in drawing connections between faith, grief and creativity. His God 'lives *here*', Williams told me, 'where the God of the Book of Job or of Elie Wiesel or Dostoevsky lives, not consoling but overwhelming and generating. Not a rationale for suffering or an excuse for looking away, but a resource for standing in the middle of it all without complete disintegration of mind and heart.'

Brighton became 'too sad' for the family after Arthur died. Cave, Bick and their son Earl moved to Los Angeles for a while, but found that too sad as well, before returning to London, where they now spend most of their time. They have put their beachfront Regency house on the market, with its purple, green and red interiors; Cave seems rueful that the *Sun* dug out the estate agents' photos and published them.

For many years, Cave's relationship with the press was uneasy. 'I didn't know how to express what I wanted to say,' he recalls. 'There was just a deep contempt for everything, and that shuts you down. I'm a naturally disagreeable character at times. I enjoyed that.'

In 1988, after a show in Hamburg, he took a swing at the head of the *NME* journalist Jack Barron and tried to boot him in the groin in an attempt to retrieve an interview tape. He called Barron a 'filthy little prick'. Barron described 'this lanky piece of literate shit' whose lyrical concerns 'rattled like skeletons in shallow graves'.

Cave's band the Birthday Party were billed by one European promoter as the most violent in the world, which Cave pointed out was an open invitation to get punched by fans. When the band first moved to the UK from Melbourne in 1980, writers on the *NME* were sick with excitement: Cave was completely feral on stage, lurching around like an early incarnation of the character he went on to play in the 1988 film *Ghosts of the Civil Dead* – an Australian backwoodsman in a maximum-security prison. The journalist Mat Snow, who attended many of those gigs, tells me that forty years ago Cave appeared 'genuinely crazed with a misanthropic rage, which over time became stylised'.

He was a heroin addict for most of the '80s and '90s. Snow rented him and his then girlfriend Anita Lane a room in his house in Brixton, and recalls their 'Terry and June' bickering, with Cave criticising Lane's addict's diet of Dairylea triangles while he himself subsisted on a tub of piccalilli. Cave was always writing at the kitchen table, Snow recalls, no matter what state he was in: 'I think his biggest addiction is his workaholism.' After their brief time as flatmates, Snow gave Cave's second single a brush-off in the *NME*, calling it a 'wan effort', and shortly afterwards found himself the subject of a song, 'Scum', which ends with Cave unloading a pistol into his eyes.

Well my un-friend, I'm the type that holds a grudge
I'm your creator
I think you fucking traitor, chronic masturbator,
Shitlicker, user, self-abuser, jigger jigger!

NICK CAVE

What rock did you crawl from?
Which, did you come?
You Judas, Brutus, Vitus, Scum!

By the mid–'80s, there was, Snow says, a feeling among certain staff on the *NME* that there was something 'almost evil' about the Birthday Party. 'What was voiced a lot, but because of the things that have happened in Nick's life is no longer a discussion, is that you don't have to be Leavis to spot a fantastic amount of violent misogyny in the work. Everything since has wiped the slate clean – and, of course, it's not a reinvention he would have ever wanted to make.'

In the murder ballad tradition that Cave adored (his band the Bad Seeds released a whole album of them), women are, of course, the recipients of most of the murdering. Cave would later split his creative persona in two with his musical alter ego Grinderman, a stoogy, sleazy id who performed the darker tasks as he himself moved into elegant middle age.

On the Red Hand Files, fans question his violent musical past. 'These days, some of my songs are feeling a little nervous,' he told one in 2020. 'They are like children that have been playing cheerfully in the schoolyard, only to be told that all along they have had some hideous physical deformity . . . But what song-writer could have predicted thirty years ago that the future would lose its sense of humour, its sense of playfulness, its sense of context, nuance and irony, and fall into the hands of a perpetually pissed-off coterie of pearl-clutchers? How were we to know?'

One of the subjects on which Cave has recently ordered his thoughts is cancel culture, and what he describes as its asphyxiating effect on creative society. 'I think the divisive nature of the cultural argument these days is religious in temperament,' he says, 'and the worst of religion is puritanical, superior, self-righteous.' I ask him about Morrissey, now considered a pariah for his nationalist sympathies. 'The hypocrisy is ridiculous,' he says. 'I don't care what Morrissey's views on things are, but I do care about his legacy. I think they're some of the most beautiful songs ever written and they meant an enormous amount to people when they came out. Those songs *saved lives*. His songs talked to these lonely, disenfranchised individuals, and certainly they had a voice.

'I think we need to be careful with these sorts of things when we're looking around for the bad actors. The music that really inspires me is almost always made by the most terrible characters. Not necessarily cancellable, but just not very nice people. I don't think art should be in the hands of the virtuous.'

Who does he listen to, when he wants to feel most moved, most in touch with the important things in life?

'I listen to Van Morrison records, which is a case in point,' he replies. 'Ha ha ha! Music is essentially good and it has the capacity to make things better. It is transcendent by nature because it moves away from who you are into something greater. It improves manners and we discard that at our peril. If we're going to insist on living in a secular world, then we need to hang on to the things that are sacred. Music is one of those things. It's religious by nature, but it's also secular and of immense value to the world.'

When he first arrived in London, Cave lived in Earl's Court – 'because I was an Aussie' – and, unlike many other struggling musicians in Thatcher's Britain, was unable to claim the dole. He worked instead, among other things picking up rubbish at

London Zoo. 'I don't know if they still do it, but if you need a bit of money, you can stand outside the zoo at six in the morning. They come out and they tend to pick young people because a lot of the other people are old or alcoholic or whatever.'

For a long time, when drugs ruled his life, he was not attached to one home or another, and lived in Berlin and São Paulo (where another son, Luke, was born). How does he get by as a globetrotting fringe artist, Q magazine asked him in 1992? 'It's a terrible, terrible situation to be in!' he deadpanned. 'I don't have any property, and I don't have a car, and all my travelling gets paid for, so the money just goes into a bank account and earns interest! So if anyone out there needs any money . . .' His sense of humour remains Australian.

Warracknabeal is a small farming town – mock Tudor post office, one church. Cave's father taught English at a technical college and his mother was a high-school librarian; at nine, Cave joined the choir of Wangaratta Cathedral. The family moved closer and closer to Melbourne over the years. In a moment more dramatic than anything he has written, he was informed of his father's sudden death in a car crash when his mother came to bail him out of jail. He was nineteen – and 'not at his best' when his father saw him for the last time.

'It was not such a good time because my life was spiralling out of control,' he says. 'So in no way did I hold any promise of anything. I was just bad news.'

What crime had he committed?

'I'd broken the window of a hotel. I'd gone into the lobby and taken a chair I thought looked good. I ran down the street to take it back to my house and I was caught by the police. I was with a mate. But he got away and I didn't because I was carrying the chair.'

He laughs. 'Sometimes, you've just got to take the chair.'

If the death of his father was Cave's original hurt, has he understood his feelings better since the death of his son?

'I'm not so sure about that. I think grief, in general, is a cumulative thing. When someone dies, all the other griefs collect around it, and I have a feeling that that's what growing older is. We are defined and joined by our sense of loss, or brought together. I can't think of the word – we are *bonded* by our sense of loss. There you go. You can fix that sentence.'

He has learned something else, too. Colin Cave, a huge presence, was the pinnacle of eloquence, a teacher who prized poetry over all other art forms, and a great raconteur who would say – Cave spreads his fingers wide – '"How was your day?" And then, when you couldn't answer' – he mumbles, head down, imitating his teenage self – 'he'd say, "Well, here's what I did with *my* day . . ." and it would all unfold.'

So, even as a teenager, there was a concern with not sounding fluent?

'Yes, I think it's because of my father. He spoke beautifully about things. I would sit at the dinner table and he would talk about his day, and he would do it in an incredibly impressive way. So I think there's a lot of my father sitting there.'

Faith, Hope and Carnage, based on some epic back-and-forths with O'Hagan over the phone during the pandemic, taught Cave how to argue and to appreciate the difference between being strident and actually being informed. 'I started to recognise this almost erotic feeling of arguing, with the wind in your sails, about something you don't know very much about,' he says. 'And I noticed that the more shrill and certain I got, it was generally about things I knew less about. I think the more volume hides a basic lack of knowledge . . .'

These days he seems content to exist in a place of uncertainty. He used to sit down to a working day of lyrics in a home office, but when Arthur died, he shut the office down and hung around the house with his wife instead, thinking up lines on the window seat in his bedroom. In fact, the whole concept of narrative no longer seemed to make much sense.

'I think that certainly *was* true,' he says today. 'But I wonder if, in time, that narrative reasserts itself. Several periods of my life, particularly around Arthur, there was a complete obliteration of the self, and that's something I get from a lot of people – they turn into something different, or they reassemble themselves into something. It feels like the idea that life is a pleasing narrative is just ludicrous.'

People who see him perform live now describe it as a semi-religious experience, whether or not they were moved by his songs in the first place. The disdain he once felt for other people extended to his audience. He had no idea what the people who came to see him were like, he said in the '80s: 'I don't know what their reasons for doing *anything* are.' At Glastonbury in 2013, years before his personal tragedies, Cave clambered aboard the crowd and communed with fans like a preacher. But he wasn't really feeling anything. 'It was like, "Here it comes" and the audience were just this *thing* that I threw myself at. It used to be exhausting to do that, just to scream in people's faces. A guy up there, and some sort of anonymous flock that they were shrieking at.

'I don't see it that way any more. It feels more like receiving something. There's this exchange that's going on with the audience and they're throwing things back in a very beautiful way. It's an outpouring, and incoming sense of love, and it's beautiful.'

Is it draining? 'Not at all. It gives me energy.'

I ask him when he last went to church. 'Er . . . last night,' he says, looking up from under his eyebrows with an almost apologetic smile. 'It was All Souls' Day and they read the list of the dead. I'm not quite sure how it works, but they mentioned my children, and it takes a long time for them to do this, and it's unbelievably moving, the music, the singing, the shape of the service. It was theatre. It was the church next door to my house.'

Cave had begun a relationship with Jethro, whose death is still being investigated, when he was seven or eight – Jethro grew up with his mother in Australia – but had not seen him for three years when he died. In talking about grief, Cave – once an assemblage of Gothic frightfulness, up to his knees in imaginary death – has gone some way to handing back his fans' projections. In another way, the events of the last few years have taken his personal myth into another dimension. Like his country music hero Johnny Cash, the family tragedies give him an awful authenticity. He no longer needs to make up stories: he just needs to express himself right.

17
ANIMUS RISING: HOW TO BREAK FREE FROM AGEING ROCK STARS

Joni Mitchell's Cary

My daughter was born in February 2020, five weeks before the pandemic. In the early months of her life, during the lockdowns, I walked up and down Euston Road with the pushchair, and through the backstreets of Bloomsbury, making big circles down to Gordon Square, the site of my old university, and across to Judd Street to the small flat we were renting at the time. In this period of my life, it was not Bruce Hornsby or Glen Campbell on repeat in my earphones, but Joni Mitchell's song 'Free Man in Paris'. I listened to it an obsessive-compulsive number of times – possibly seven or eight in one walk, and I did that walk at least twice a day. Though I was clearly immersed in several states of post-natal pandemic depression, the song made my soul soar. I loved the androgyny of it. I loved the contrast of its exhilarating 'unfetteredness' with the downbeat reality of the put-upon character at its centre, who I learned was modelled on the record mogul David Geffen. I listened to it so much, in fact, that it does next to nothing for me now. As Bruce Hornsby would say, 'you wore it out'. Maybe one day I'll get it back.

Joni Mitchell was an emotional time capsule for me, associated with Muswell Hill in the mid-'80s, and with that sweet spot in childhood where full consciousness comes without adult insecurities, where songs create feelings that are totally new, unencumbered by an understanding of romance. Mitchell's songs were a series of sense impressions and images: big frying pans, stolen cameras, cartoon coasters, Sunset pigs.

She is the only female voice in the pantheon of musical gods that lives in my psyche, but she was also frozen there many years ago. I cracked the time capsule open for the first time in three decades when I knew my daughter was on the way. It felt risky – music sends you flying back in time – but it brought only energy and wistfulness. For the first seven weeks, the baby had no name, but I'd taken to cooing over her with a sound like 'Yoni' – which basically means vag – until my boyfriend Michael and I accepted that her name was Joan and flung her in the car seat to go and register it in Islington.

A year or so after Joanie was born, I finally got Cary Raditz, Mitchell's 'mean old daddy' from 'Carey', the song named after him, to agree to an interview. I'd pestered him for years, via Facebook, but he said he was keeping his material back for a memoir. Then he changed his mind, and I felt sick because I knew I had one of those rare 'viral hits' on my hands. I loved writing this piece more than anything I'd done, apart, perhaps, from Bruce Hornsby. All those old rockers – with their deathless hits and their incredible hold over culture – and here was a man who'd been trapped in a song by a woman: a male muse. He'd had no choice about it; it happened at the age of twenty-three, and he lived it every day of his life. Cary is a walking, talking example of the fiction that is songwriting, of the gap between the reality and the images that music creates in the mind. Writing about him was a transition for me, a new way of looking at the power that music, and musicians, can have over us, and a step towards taking the projections back.

After the *New Statesman* interview, Cary wrote his memoir, *Carey: Genesis of the Song*, in just three months. In 2023, we took my daughter to stay with him on a farm in Leicestershire on one of his UK visits; being an old hippie, he is still friends with a gentleman farmer he met in the Matala caves. There is a picture of my daughter sitting on his knee: Joanie and Cary, both of their names infused with the spirit of the high priestess for ever more, when neither of them asked for it.

'I didn't want anyone to know it was me': on being Joni Mitchell's 'Carey'

New Statesman, 2021

The wall of limestone caves along the cliff in the Cretan fishing village of Matala is now a protected site. In Roman times, the caves were used as burial crypts, but when the hippies arrived in the late '60s, they became free bunkhouses. Joni Mitchell, fresh from Laurel Canyon in Los Angeles and newly separated from the singer-songwriter Graham Nash, lived in one of these caves for two months between March and May 1970. It was during this period that she wrote songs for her 1971 album *Blue*, and here that she first performed one of her best-loved songs, 'Carey', dedicated to the man with whom she shared that cave.

Mitchell's description of her muse is impressionistic, dispatched in two or three lines – 'Oh Carey get out your cane'; 'Oh, you're a mean old daddy/But I like you' – yet he remains one of the most charismatic figures ever to appear in song. And, unlike the lovers who bookended his time in Mitchell's affections (Nash and James Taylor), we know almost nothing about him.

There were casual latrines in the shrubland higher up the beach in Matala, and the hippies wove reeds together to make doors ('The wind is in from Africa/Last night I couldn't sleep'). There were stoves and lanterns and Kilim rugs, passed on to new owners each time a cave changed hands. For beds, the burial crypt itself inside the cave: a stone shelf a few feet wide. If you know that Joni Mitchell was sleeping on funerary architecture when she wrote 'Carey', it brings new meaning to the lines 'I miss my clean white linen/And my fancy French cologne'.

Today, the beach at Matala is still raked over in travel blogs by tourists smitten with the romance of the song. Like 'Woodstock', which Mitchell wrote without having been to the festival, it epitomised a hippie dream that lay out of reach for most, and which everyone thought – still thinks – sounded like paradise. Most ordinary people listening to *Blue* on its release hadn't been to Greece or Amsterdam or Paris, or anywhere much, as no one could afford the flights.

Mark Ellen, former editor of *Q, Smash Hits* and *The Word*, hitchhiked to Matala in 1974 with his girlfriend with the express purpose of recreating 'Carey'. He was one of many to do so. 'To think that here she was, gloriously rootless and drifting through Europe was intoxicating,' he told me. 'No song defined a moment like "Carey". We all tried to have as much fun, and be as original and wildly poetic and romantic as Joni Mitchell and him. He didn't just have a love affair with the woman all men would have loved to have had a love affair with: he lived the life they all dreamed of too.'

In fact, during the writing of *Blue*, Mitchell was having what she later referred to as a shamanic experience – and what others might just have called a nervous breakdown. When she'd arrived in Crete in 1970, with a female friend, she was on the cusp of fame, trying to figure out whether celebrity and art could exist side by side. In Matala, she was free, but not invulnerable. This was the moment that Cary Raditz entered her life. (The spelling mistake was hers.)

As a child – and I can't be the only one – I assumed 'Carey' was some kind of ancient lover, a sort of sugar daddy, albeit one too tight to buy the drinks. For those of us who heard Mitchell's songs via our parents in the '80s and '90s, their love story was part of an emerging sense of the sparks that occur between the sexes: 'Let's go down to the Mermaid Café/And I will buy you a bottle of wine/And we'll laugh and toast to nothing/And smash our empty glasses down.' For men of Carey's own generation, he was a handy archetype for the age of Aquarius. At the fortieth birthday of a friend a few months back, the celebrant's father – a saucy raconteur who'd done the Ibiza circuit in the '60s – told me the real Carey was a guy he'd known in Formentera. He was wrong, but wouldn't believe any other story.

In many ways the song is surprisingly literal. Yes, there was a Mermaid Café, five minutes' walk across the bay, run by Stelios Xagorarakis, who was in the cave when Mitchell played 'Carey' for the first time (it was Raditz's birthday). And, yes, Carey carried a cane: a shepherd's crook in fact, hooked at the top but smashed off half-mast. If we have an unusually strong impression of him, it's because he also appears in the other single released from *Blue* – 'California':

I met a redneck on a Grecian Isle
Who did the goat dance very well,
He gave me back my smile
But he kept my camera to sell.
Oh that rogue, that red red rogue,
He cooked good omelettes and stews
And I might have stayed on with him
But my heart cried out for you, California.

Over the years, Mitchell would introduce live versions of 'Carey' with stories to enhance the rogue she had created. She recalled their first meeting: he was working as a chef at the Delphini Taverna in Matala and she approached him with some rubbish, in an attempt to clean up. He took it from her and threw it straight on the floor.

'I latched myself on to Cary because he was fierce and kept the crowd off my back,' she told the *Wall Street Journal* in 2014. 'He was always detached and sometimes even disrespectful – either trying to belittle me or make me feel afraid. I think at the time he felt greatly superior to women, which is why I refer to him in the lyrics as "a mean old Daddy".'

JONI MITCHELL'S CARY

It's a very small club, ordinary people who have inspired immortal songs. Suzanne, Marianne, Sharona, Peggy Sue. You will spend your whole life trapped in one, but you may never get the chance to tell your side of the story. In fifty years, Cary Raditz has barely spoken about his time in Crete with Joni Mitchell, and has never told the story of what happened afterwards. Each time I tried to talk to him, he turned me down, saying he was working on a book, or promising he would travel to see friends in England when we would surely get together. Then, after *Blue* hit its fiftieth anniversary in June this year, he got in touch: he'd changed his mind.

Our meeting place, on a warm day at the end of October, was a small bistro in Paris near the Musée d'Orsay, five minutes from the Pont Royal that takes you to the Louvre. Raditz had been all over France in the previous three weeks with his wife Ann, whom he'd copied in on our email correspondence: Crestet, Provence; Avignon; Rochefort-en-Terre; and Douarnenez, Brittany – 'mostly with old friends'.

Through the plastic window of the outdoor marquee, Cary Raditz, with long grey hair and a gold loop in his left ear, looks like a gypsy or a retired pirate, poised in the corner against the burgundy fabric, nose in a book. He seems slightly self-conscious, as though wondering if he is already being watched, which he is.

'And what a small, insignificant person he turned out to be!' he announces, standing.

He is seventy-five, his voice soft and hoarse and liltingly southern. He orders lightly: a *salade de raie*, or warm skate salad, the fish shredded with a fork. Somewhere on his French trip he tried *bigorneau* for the first time, the tiny sea snails eaten with a pin.

'Have you ever tried them?' he asks. 'Well, they're *not* very good. And they're *not* very easy to get at.' Raditz got at them with a nutcracker and was told he couldn't get away with that in a restaurant. 'Think about eating langoustine!' he countered. 'What could *be* more inelegant?' He shifts quickly between amusement and a sense of mild unease.

Raditz was put out when Mitchell called him a redneck in 'California'. His mother was a southern belle from South Carolina who could prove a direct descent back to the patriot fathers. His grandfather, a bank president, died when she was young, 'leaving my grandmother with a nice portfolio which turned to mush as soon as the stock market crashed'. His mother worked as a teacher of English. 'She read to me poetry when we would take our naps in the afternoon. She was very dramatic, and certainly I received directly the most potent narcissistic genes from her.'

Raditz's father was the son of a concert pianist, Henrietta Herman, and a famous portrait painter, Lazar Raditz, who painted the Rockefellers (Lazar was the son of a rabbi from Latvia). His aunt was a famous child artist, Violetta Raditz, who had a show in the Met, New York. His father, in contrast, liked to say, 'I don't have a bone of talent in my whole body.'

'So from him I received nothing – because I don't have a bone of talent in *my* own body! Pretty funny, huh?' he laughs, taking a mouthful of skate.

This was the background from which Cary Raditz set out upon the world. After college in Chapel Hill, North Carolina, where he had moved in the same circles as James Taylor, he was writing advertising copy for an agency selling hosiery when a girlfriend over in Munich sent him a hundred-dollar bill. Ice-landair did flights to Luxembourg for $150 back then; once in Europe, he hitchhiked to Germany, where he lived with his female patron in an abandoned furniture factory, making money as an extra in a TV show (they played the part of 'hippies', with floppy hats, for DM50 a day).

As the autumn of 1969 came, they decided to head to warmer territory. 'Believe me,' Raditz says, 'if we kept going at this pace, we would be here a long time.'

At a fork on the autobahn south of Munich, they opened it to fate. If the first car to arrive was travelling to the south-east, they'd end up in Greece. If it was heading south-west, they'd go to Spain – and Cary Raditz and I would not be talking. At this point, the girlfriend seems to melt away from the story. He was twenty-three years old.

Like many romantic unions, there were two or three random collisions between Mitchell and Raditz before the one that brought them together. Having settled into a cave on Halloween, Raditz was indeed working as a chef at the Delphini Taverna: Greek omelettes were his speciality, potatoes and onions spooned into a hot frying pan and flipped with a jerk of the handle.

'She came into my taverna mid-morning,' he says. 'I don't know what I was doing, cooking, cleaning up – surrounded by four or five sycophants, fawning ex-friends of mine.' He was rattled by the buzz around Mitchell in a way that still resonates. She did bring some trash to help him with his cleaning job, and he did take it from her and throw it on the floor.

Did he know her music?

'Yeah, but I didn't give a shit. Quite frankly, I didn't know anything about her,' he says. 'I just saw that she was coming into town. And these friends of mine, who I thought were pretty good drinking buddies, were now turning into the idiots that I didn't like – the love and peace hippies, the nonsense involving all sorts of belief systems.'

Why did that bother him?

'Because it was inauthentic.'

Did he not have friends?

His demeanour, he replies, was 'don't fuck with this guy, he will bite your head off'.

Raditz wore heavy Afghan salwar kameez trousers in those days and had his red hair in a turban. Mitchell said that she saw him propelled from the door of the Delphini one day, by a propane explosion. He tells me that nursing his seared face a few days later, he got wind that she had been sighted in the Roman baths on the other side of the hill: the Romans had dug rectangular troughs that filled with seawater at high tide and warmed into 'hot tubs' in the sun. He saw Mitchell there in a yellow bathing suit. Most people were naked. She approached him with a piece of driftwood, saying, 'Look, it looks just like a mermaid!' He took it and replied, 'Looks like a piece of driftwood to me.'

'Do you know what a mystical experience is?' he says, apropos of nothing. Raditz explains that when he arrived in Crete, he was 'coming off one'. Then he just calls it a bad trip – the lingering ghost of a drug experience that occurred a year earlier in San Francisco.

Raditz's behaviour – his 'flaming red personality', as she once put it – drew Mitchell to him. 'I think this had something to do, psychologically or spiritually, with my relationship with Joni, in that we were both going through dark nights of the soul,' he says.

Did he know, at the time, that he was going through a 'dark night of the soul'?

'No, I didn't. I thought I was crazy.'

For a moment, he doesn't look comfortable.

'It's funny because there is a lot about this I don't like,' he says. 'There is something about celebrity in general – it is dangerous territory. It's addictive though, you see. It's awful. It's a facet of greed.'

Mitchell painted a picture of a wild man, a joker. How did he see himself at the time? He gives his answers as bullet points.

'I felt I might be criminally insane.

'I had a really bad temper.

'I felt I had come-and-go powers of insight and perspective.

'I felt somewhat like a chameleon. I felt tremendously passionate – a lust for things, for women, that was overpowering.'

He orders dessert – a small ball of vanilla ice cream with cassis drizzled over the top.

Their final meeting ended his hostility towards Joni Mitchell. There was an evening ritual in Matala: watching the sun go down over the tiny islands that lay beyond the bay. The sun would appear to set, and then reappear again in some trick of the light. Raditz was watching this phenomenon from the wall of Delphini's when Mitchell approached him.

'Alone without anybody trailing around her, she came and she sat down next to me.' He claims to have recited Shelley's 'To Night', which sounds entirely probable, 'and after that, the only logical thing to say was, "Do you want to go and get a drink?"'

The Mermaid Café smelled of coffee, apple pie, sautéing onions, stale beer and tobacco smoke. That night, it was full of shepherds and soldiers drinking the powerful Cretan drink, raki. One soldier went up to Mitchell with a box of Benson & Hedges cigarettes – 'a treasure in those days before the global supermarket,' Raditz says. She didn't want one because she already had a lit cigarette hanging out of her mouth, having smoked since she was nine. But she didn't know how to refuse.

'And she's going, "No, thank you! No, thank you",' he says, 'and I think, *This is getting to be hilarious*, because in Crete, when you give someone an affirmation with your head, it's like this [he tips his head forward a little], and a no is like this [a vigorous backwards]. So she's doing this mixed signal to the guy, and she says, "What can I do?"'

'I said, "Knock them out of his hand!" So she goes like that [he brings his flat palm upwards through the air], hits the box, cigarettes explode in the air and all over the place, and the taverna becomes silent. And then she just opens up with this incredible laugh from the depths of her womb or some other cavity, and I think if you ask me if I fell in love – I fell in love then, I fell in love with that laugh and where the laugh was coming from.'

Mitchell woke up in the cave after her first night with Cary Raditz with the heel of her shoe broken. She moved her things in from the small hut she was renting nearby. There wasn't room for both of them to sleep together, he recalls: they took turns in the tomb, with the other sleeping on blankets on the floor.

With him, Raditz says, people stopped following Mitchell around so much. 'No one would come into my cave uninvited.'

Mitchell remembered her Crete period in a 1979 interview with *Rolling Stone*. 'At that period of my life, I had no personal defences,' she said. 'I felt like a cellophane wrapper on a pack of cigarettes. I felt like I had absolutely no secrets from the world and I couldn't pretend in my life to be strong. Or to be happy. But the advantage of it in the music was that there were no defences there either.'

She may not have been happy, but she was open. Raditz explains that 'to her, I think I played the role of tempter, challenging her to think boldly. To bite the apple.' In the US, she was still a folk singer – Judy Collins' version of 'Both Sides Now' was better known than her own. She travelled to Europe with an Appalachian dulcimer, bought from the Big Sur Folk Festival and built by a woman called Joellen Lapidus. It was slim, like an elongated violin, with sound holes shaped like columbine flowers and a case lined in Navajo sheepskin. Lapidus tells me how, when the strings broke, Mitchell restrung the instrument with the bass string in the middle – her own idiosyncratic tuning, which also marked out her guitar playing. She would hit the instrument with a 'slap strum', using the fleshy side of her hand. You can hear it on 'Carey' and three other songs on *Blue*. *Ladies of the Canyon*, with its hit songs 'Big Yellow Taxi' and 'Woodstock', was released around the time she was in Crete. She was rapidly becoming a star.

Raditz had an entrepreneurial streak: he had noticed the fine quality leather used on the island to make the knee-high jackboots the shepherds wore – and he went into business with a fellow cave-dweller, making sandals. These sandals form a large part of our conversation because Raditz is a strange, sensual character. He thinks in fabrics, food, textures, smells, sex.

When she wasn't playing her dulcimer, he tells me, Mitchell spent a lot of time knitting: 'I want to knit you a sweater/Want to write you a love letter,' she wrote in 'All I Want'. She did knit a sweater for James Taylor a few months later – a mark of the domesticity she'd slip into, intermittently, before each bid for freedom. While she was with Raditz, she knitted one for herself. It stretched right to the knees, and he describes how she incorporated bits of beach grass, tiny shells and bleached fishbones to create textures, and spun tufts of green yarn into the tan background.

The 'ecosystem sweater of Matala', he calls it.

'How splendid!,' I thought! 'She never stops singing, laughing, making music, drawing, creating things, in praise of her friends, her surroundings, her emotions and feelings.'

They were together constantly, for two months. One day, they drove Mitchell's rented VW to Crete's capital, Iraklion, where they had boots made by a local craftsman – hers in tan and his in darker leather. She is wearing hers on the cover of *For the Roses*, the album that followed *Blue*. They also commissioned matching gold heart stud earrings, with a swoop of thin metal falling under the lobe.

Raditz recalls a trip to Athens that told him it was ending. One night at dinner, Mitchell was approached by journalists. 'I felt, I guess, a moment of jealousy. I was ready to beat them with the cane. But she invited them, gave me the bad eye, and just asked them to come and sit down and talk, and I guess that's where I realised that the world had now intruded – that there was a shift.'

A shift that she was now ready to take?

'That was the change in her whole life, you see,' he says. 'Really, after this time of weeks had gone by, this is when she really changed her whole life, from being somewhat at the effect of other people, to becoming the cause herself.'

At points, Raditz seems to have a grasp of Mitchell's inner life, then undercuts it. I ask him what he thought of her comment that he felt superior to women. He replies that she was frequently upset and recalls how she would sink into depressions, 'dark, self-deprecating spaces', to which he would respond, 'Buck up, Joan, stop whining.' (Incidentally, Mitchell told her biographer David Yaffe that her mother reacted to her depression in pretty much the same terms.)

During their short relationship, he effectively had her for himself. But on the night of his twenty-fourth birthday in April 1970, with half a dozen other people present, she played him the song that told him she was leaving him. Raditz talks about the smell of the cave and the taste of the ouzo that night, but what did he think of the song?

'I thought it was an endearing little ditty,' he says.

And what did he think of being called a 'mean old daddy'?

'I wasn't thrilled. I deserved it for my grumpiness, my unsolicited advice, talking down to her, and for my bad temper and general nastiness.'

How has it felt, being frozen in a song for his whole life?

'It is eerie,' he concedes, 'for fifty years, having this song pop up in the most unusual kind of places, in taxis, as musak in an elevator, in a bar in the Hilton hotel in Abu Dhabi, being played on stage by the band. People who didn't know it was about me would sing it at me when they realised Cary was my name.'

Was it hard to take, everyone thinking, from the song, that Joni Mitchell dumped him?

'Oh, she dumped me!' he cries. 'She dumped me and then she picked me back up! What do we call people who go into dumpsters and pull out trash and use it again?'

The relationship between Cary Raditz and Joni Mitchell did not end with 'Carey', or 'California', which she wrote in Paris shortly after leaving him. A few weeks later, around June 1970, he says he received a telex, sent to him courtesy of the Mermaid Café. It ran something to the effect of: 'Join me Hollywood. Stop. Pick up ticket American Express, Athens. Stop. Telephone. Stop. XXX Joni.'

Raditz left most of his belongings with cave neighbours and travelled to Athens, where he called Mitchell from a youth hostel, waiting the ten hours' time difference for 2 p.m., her waking hour. A ticket was waiting for him at the Athens office of Trans World Airlines, she said: she would meet him at San Francisco Airport. He took his shepherd's crook as he boarded the first-class plane.

Mitchell had returned to her place on Lookout Mountain in Laurel Canyon to write and record *Blue*. The recording sessions would feature a supergroup of David Crosby, Stephen Stills, Graham Nash and James Taylor.

Raditz pushes aside his empty ice cream bowl as though he's getting to the good stuff.

'When we were living together in Hollywood, I was totally out of place,' he says, 'bewildered and angry that I had even persuaded myself that this was a good thing to do, that I had succumbed to this weakness to follow her back to California.'

He drank so much champagne on the flight there, he says, that he arrived inarticulate, an 'idiot drunkard', barely able to speak. Mitchell met him wearing her Matala eco-sweater. Raditz was glad he had brushed his teeth.

What happened during their month together?

'It was very difficult. She was very sweet. She did what she could. We would go up to David Geffen's to swim,' he says, of the media mogul who managed Joni's label and went on to set up DreamWorks with Steven Spielberg. 'And she would introduce me to her friends, like Jackson Browne. They would come by the house to look at the gorilla she had just freed from the zoo.' He imitates her celebrity friends, aghast: '*What is she doing! Is she in her right mind? Is there something we can do to protect her? My god, he carries a knife!*'. Joni used to tell me, 'Geffen is *really* afraid of you . . .'

Why did he feel so out of place?

'All of a sudden I was this kept man,' he says. 'I don't mind being a kept man, but I want to be a kept man with some kind of mission and purpose.'

Raditz recalls Crosby, Stills and Nash coming over together one day and sitting opposite him like 'three brass monkeys'. Though he and Mitchell were a couple, he suspects he may also have been a foil.

'I protected her from unwanted attention in Matala, and now I am running interference to shield her from the unwanted attention of her ex-lover and his buddies in California,' he suggests.

Mitchell's manager Elliot Roberts, who passed away in 2019, took Raditz to Disneyland and the Hollywood Bowl. 'But it was all clearly falling apart. She was into her Joni Mitchell thing, which is a semi-trance state – for hours she would be there at the piano.' Graham Nash also spoke of this songwriting trance state. What would the gorilla do while the mystic was at work?

'Read. Watch her. Wouldn't fuck with her. She was really a different kind of being. And I didn't have anything to do. I collapsed into my own angst and spent most of the day reading philosophy and worrying.'

One person who remembers Raditz in Hollywood at that time was Joellen Lapidus, Mitchell's dulcimer maker. 'When I met him, he was a rough and tough mountain man,' she tells me. 'But when I got talking to him, I learned that he was highly educated. He was so gutsy and raw and authentic, and true to himself, like no one I had ever met.'

Raditz broke one of her dulcimers while helping to carry it. 'I can never tell whether he did it on purpose,' she says. 'He had that nasty side.'

Did Raditz leave Mitchell, or did Mitchell leave him?

'She didn't actually use her foot to kick me out of the car when she took me to the airport, but she was close to it – I'm not sure we were actually talking by that point,' Raditz says, grinning broadly. But he left the cane behind in her house.

Raditz tells me that Mitchell allowed him to cash in his first-class ticket (tellingly, she had brought him a round trip) so he could travel steerage class to wherever he went next, and save some money. He headed to England, where he contacted friends from the Crete era and ended up working on a dairy farm. A few weeks later, during a trip to London, he walked to an American Express office to cash a traveller's cheque and found a letter from Mitchell's manager at the postal window. Calling him from a phone booth, Raditz learned that Mitchell wanted his company at the Isle of Wight Festival on 29 August 1970. He can be seen fleetingly in backstage footage in the recent concert film *Joni Mitchell: Both Sides Now*, with flaming hair and stunned expression. He pulled up in the same vintage Rolls-Royce that brought Mitchell, Elliot Roberts and Neil Young onto the festival site.

The documentary captures the chaos of the festival and its crowd, notoriously on the verge of riot. Mitchell, with her 'feminine cooperative streak' (her words) agreed to go out early, at 3 p.m., to pacify them, and only got through it by appealing for their respect. Looking out of the festival crowd was like 'looking out over the armies of Caesar before the invasion', Raditz recalls. He got very drunk that night and entered Donovan's trailer demanding drugs. He says Mitchell put him in bed to sleep it off.

Was his relationship with her a *friendship* by this point?

'We don't quite know what to call it,' he says. 'I like Joan. She's good company unless she's in one of her states. Then she's not.'

And why does he think their love affair didn't work out?

'It did work out.'

Were you in love with each other?

'The way we behaved toward each other from time to time is we were very close, we cared about each other's interests, and we cared about each other's feelings, and we were, I think, mutually attracted to one another . . .'

So why did it end?

'I think that was all played out in LA,' he says. 'I mean, if you were going to ask Graham Nash, he would say he was deeply in love with her. Certainly, I *expressed* love to her. He was clingy: he was clingy to her, and that's what I think freaked her out.'

A few weeks after the Isle of Wight Festival, back working on the farm, Raditz tells me he was again summoned to London. Mitchell requested his company at the London Palladium, on 23 October, where James Taylor was playing. He arrived at the venue early and drank heavily again. She came out to meet him before the show. 'She wanted to tell me in person that she was in love with James Taylor,' he says. During their month in Laurel Canyon, Raditz had pulled the free poster that accompanied Taylor's new album, *Sweet Baby James*, out of the record sleeve and stuck it above her piano – 'though I don't know the degree of their propinquity at that point,' he says.

After watching the show, he stayed with Taylor and Mitchell at the Warner Brothers apartment in Knightsbridge. After this, in one of the strangest twists in Cary Raditz's story, a brief kind of platonic threesome appears to have occurred for several weeks in the autumn of 1970, whereby Mitchell and Taylor, newly in love, were often accompanied by Raditz – at their request, he swears. Mitchell can be heard giving a shout-out to her 'friend from Matala, London and Los Angeles and North Carolina' at the Paris Theatre on Regent Street, six days after Taylor's Palladium show.

'This was not any *Jules et Jim ménage à trois* hell,' he says. 'It wasn't like that. I don't know what it was, other than this kind of friendship. I didn't have any kind of lingering jealousy.'

Still, he is unable to explain quite why he was there. He accompanied them to the wedding of Taylor's producer Peter Asher, and to music industry dinners. He would go to late night pubs with Taylor, and drink copious amounts of the Italian liqueur Strega. He was afraid to ask why James was hanging out with him so much, he says, 'in case it stopped'.

Mitchell, Taylor and Raditz came back to the US together after the UK shows, and settled in the Albert Hotel near Washington Park, New York. 'It was all a puzzle,' Raditz says. 'I had a separate room, always. I was never interested in watching them copulate.'

One day, he went to visit his grandmother, the concert pianist, who was living over on 6th Avenue and 8th Street. Taylor and Mitchell accompanied him, bringing their guitars, and played for her. Once again, he would 'read, listen, prowl the streets', while the musicians worked.

'And then we moved up to Martha's Vineyard together, and so I had my own room in a motel. James was building his house, so it was in an early state: it had a roof on, and the walls were open inside, with table saws and carpentry equipment . . .'

Around Thanksgiving 1970, Mitchell's manager Elliot Roberts appears to have got rid of Cary Raditz. Raditz tells me Roberts said that the pair felt crowded by his constant presence, which he contested, pointing out that he had always been invited. He wonders again whether he was 'some kind of buffer' to deflect publicity about the new celebrity relationship: 'Joni has a Machiavellian streak,' he says. Roberts gave him a job – to oversee his farm in the Santa Cruz Mountains – but he was soon fired for mismanagement. He tried to connect with Mitchell and Taylor when they visited Taylor's parents in North Carolina, but they never returned his calls.

Raditz didn't talk to Mitchell for a while after that. He joined the American Peace Corps and went out to build pump stations in Mauritania. 'I wanted something that gave me the nomadic lifestyle – but with medical back-up and stuff like that.'

Mitchell called him in 1978, after she travelled to Mexico with a dying Charlie Mingus. 'She talked through that with me, and how thrilled she was to have worked with him. She's still kind of working through that, I think. I just imagine, in her instincts, that in the great hall of jazz, that there's an empty podium there that her statue should be on!' he says sarcastically. 'That's the arena of her fame, she should be *there*, not in folk singing or rock 'n' roll.'

Raditz studied development banking and went on to become an economic development consultant in Zambia. As the '80s began, he became a Park Avenue banker in New York, working for the Middle East and Africa division of Chemical Bank. In Greece, he had lived 'as though I had taken a vow of poverty'. In a few years, he went from riding camels to helicopters and limousines. Chemical Bank settled the first asset claims with Iran in 1983 – he still has the braces he bought to celebrate, printed with dollar signs.

Mitchell wrote about big-wig financiers on her 1985 album *Dog Eat Dog*, which was critical of Reagan-era economics: 'Some are treated well/In these games of buy and sell/And some like poor beasts/Are burdened down to breaking.' During this time, she would come to meet Raditz for lunch at the Chemical Bank office at 277 Park Avenue. Her 'poor and untalented ex-boyfriend' – his words – had made something of himself.

One Sunday, after dim sum in Chinatown with Mitchell and some of her photographer friends, Raditz started to come down with the flu. Mitchell took him back to her Greenwich Village loft apartment on Spring Street and Varick, where he lay sweating in blankets on the sofa for at least two days. Not for the first time, he outstayed his welcome with Joni Mitchell – and not for the first time, she eventually kicked him to the kerb.

They are still in touch. He flew to see her for his seventy-second birthday, where they had dinner with Stelios of the Mermaid Café, and he showed her pages of a draft edition of his book, for which he is trying to find a publisher. Her assistant is generally present. A 'gatekeeper', he says: Joni Mitchell has had three strokes. 'It is difficult to talk to her these days.' Mitchell's interviews, rarer than comets, take place with carefully selected writers, and I did not contact her myself. She has told the story of Carey before – her way.

You get the feeling that Raditz is not even sure quite what he is in Joni Mitchell's story. Muse? Security guard? Buffer? Lover? Hanger-on? Or was their continued connection through the years – her, the high priestess of songwriting; him, married with three 'overachieving' children – really a link back to a pivotal moment in their freewheeling past; less about love, more about some portal on to who and what they were when they met?

Having made a decision to talk at length after fifty years, Raditz remains in touch after our Paris meeting, sending me photos and extracts of poetry, his wife no longer copied into our emails. 'You get in touch and tell me you've been thinking about this guy since you were a child,' he says over lunch. 'Do you know what kind of licence that gives me?'

Mitchell gave him an identity at twenty-four: it may not have been the real one, but it was so evocative that millions of people over the world have wondered about him. He will live out that fictional identity for the rest of his life, and far beyond it. 'Songs are like tattoos,' Mitchell said on *Blue*: having one written about you is immortality and fiction rolled into one. He may find himself addicted to the interest it generates, but then again, he didn't ask for it to happen.

Did he ever wish 'Carey' had never been written?

'Yes,' he says. 'For many years. I never talked about it. I didn't want anyone to know it was me, because all they wanted to talk about was my relationship with her.'

Raditz experienced the real Joni Mitchell, too, at one point in time – in the most tumultuous, intense and fast-changing era of her life, when it's almost impossible to say who she was in love with, who she had met and what she was writing. The chronologies continue to blur with each passing year. After leaving Graham Nash, she chose the opposite of domestication on the floor of a cave in Matala, but her new protector became possessive in his way. No one could have Mitchell for long. He met her vulnerability, and he met the steeliness beneath it. Who knows why she wanted him around as her career progressed, unless he, indeed, represented some kind of audacity she wanted to keep in touch with. Maybe she kept in touch because, on some level, she felt she owed him for the songs. Maybe she really liked him.

'I was just there, you know, who knows?' he concludes. 'I can't get into this counterfactual stuff. I was there.' He is not very self-analytical.

Why is he talking to me, after fifty years?

'Well, I spent a lot of my time in Buddhist retreats,' he grins. 'And I've spent many years trying to work to free myself from the confines of my ego, and lately I've realised there isn't much beyond my ego. I've come down to: what's the amusement value? Are people amused? I would tell the story to musicians who would have an appreciation of it. But I dislike being pinned down.'

How does he feel now when he hears the song?

'I've become distanced somewhat from this character "Carey",' he says, 'and Carey can live out his variant forms in the minds of people without bothering me too much. And maybe it's a way of self-protecting, but this idea of self is really very delusional.'

Oh, and he didn't steal Joni Mitchell's camera, as you're led to believe in 'California'. She gave it to him when she left Greece. He said he'd probably have to sell it. She shrugged and said, go ahead.

EPILOGUE

My dad and I are walking along that tunnel to the Barbican Centre with the really narrow pavement, the one with the sooty air. We are going to see Pat Metheny. We haven't been to a gig together since before the pandemic. I think the last one was Jeff Beck at the Chelsea Hospital, but he's gone now; there was John McLaughlin too, many times, but he seems to have unofficially retired.

My dad is shorter than me now, though he still walks too fast and still doesn't wait for the lights to change before stepping out into roads. We've realised, on the number fifty-six bus from Angel, that it's Pat's solo tour, when we ideally wanted it to be him with his big jazz band. But as the lights go down in the Barbican, dad says, you just never know how many times you'll see them now. A few weeks earlier I'd sent him Mark Knopfler's Guitar Heroes, the astonishing tapestry of the world's most famous players woven into a ten-minute song. He had become hooked, so I'd got more hooked, knowing that he was hooked – listening again with my 'quadrophonic' ears.

I've moved beyond musicians in much of my work, as I mentioned at the start of this book; my editors at the New Statesman wanted me on the scientists and the philosophers instead. But my subjects have got older if anything: a lot of eighty-year-olds these days, and James Lovelock, the father of Gaia, who was 100 when I went to his house in Beachy Head. Each time I survey their lives, in the days before the interview, I feel like I'm standing at the foot of a mountain, and I get miserable with the expectation. But I still get that strange vibration, every so often, that we are going to get on, that I've met them before somewhere: like when I was preparing to meet the war correspondent John Simpson and read Lynn Barber's interview with him from many years ago, in which he said, 'I think I'm now like the *Flying Dutchman*, condemned to travel for ever.'

At the Barbican, Metheny – the only guitarist Jeff Beck claimed not to be able to watch – does something unheard of: he talks. He was always, to my mind, one of the technicians, one of the musical geniuses that was relatively dry in interviews. But, perhaps because he is seventy this year, Metheny has made some kind of decision to look at himself, and his instrument, with perspective. The guitar is still 'undefined', he says: every single person in the room will have a different idea of what it sounds like. He practises for between six and twelve hours a day. He talks about nylon strings and baritones; he says it started with the Beatles on *The Ed Sullivan Show*, that one of his first tunes as a child was 'House of the Rising Sun', and I can feel my dad nodding next to me in the dark, because it was the same for all of them.

Then something happened to Metheny, as it did for a handful of his generation. The recognisable became the cosmic, he entered a different sphere of music, and no one ever caught up, or will. Half an hour before the end of the show, a curtain drops and his 'orchestrionics' are revealed, a vast rig of percussion instruments, marimbas and shakers and what look like spoons, programmed to play by an army of electronic ghosts. He runs around the stage as they shake and shimmer, operating six or seven guitars that seem to be suspended in mid-air.

Pat is agile at seventy. My dad is seventy, too. Maybe seventy is young, I think; maybe this will all go on for a while yet. He finishes his set with an acoustic version of Glen Campbell's 'Wichita Lineman', the song that started my career, and I hear my dad whispering: 'For you.'

ACKNOWLEDGEMENTS

Thank you to my parents – I recently discovered my mum was responsible for bringing a lot of records into the house that I thought were my dad's – and to my brother Joe, for dreaming Queen dreams with me. Special thanks to Jason Cowley for letting me run long pieces about Bon Jovi in the country's leading politics magazine, and to Tom Gatti and Anna Leszkiewicz for editing them. I am forever grateful to my friend and mentor Mark Ellen, and I'd like to thank Caitlin Moran and Pete Paphides for early encouragement, David Hepworth and Andrew Harrison for my years at *The Word* and Jude Rogers for all her support in my career. Also my friend Fraser Lewry, who indulged each of my musical fixations with such glee.

Thank you to Pete Selby for cooking up this book with me, and for his infectious passion about music writing. To Charlie Viney, for enthusiasm and guidance; and to James Lilford at Bonnier who helped bring the book through its final stages. I could not have written it without Robert Macdonald, who has helped me see things as they really are.

IMAGE CREDITS

p. 260 © Joby Sessions/Guitarist Magazine/Future via Getty Images

p. 278 © Chris Floyd

p. 292 © Andreas Rentz/Getty Images

p. 306 © Tom Wolff

p. 332 courtesy of Cary Raditz